D1087930

an esalen book

the esalen publishing program
is edited by stuart miller

stuart miller

HOT

�֎

SPRINGS

the true �֎ *adventures*

of the ✷ *first new york*

jewish ✷ *literary*

intellectual ✷ *in the*

human- ✷ *potential movement*

NEW YORK · THE VIKING PRESS

An Esalen Book

First published in 1971 by The Viking Press, Inc.
625 Madison Avenue, New York, N.Y. 10022

Published simultaneously in Canada by
The Macmillan Company of Canada Limited

SBN 670–37962–x
Library of Congress catalog card number: 70–149271
Printed in U.S.A.

ACKNOWLEDGMENTS

National Council of the Churches of Christ: From
the Revised Standard Version of the Bible, copy-
righted 1946 and 1952, and used by permission.

for my
wife, sukie

who patted the wrung hand,
massaged the hunched shoulders,
typed, edited, and one night,
sheer desperation upon me, put
on a sheet and a sprig of pine
and appeared to me in the dark
of our bedroom as the very Muse
herself.

part one

CHAPTER ONE

✳ desengaños ✳

i had a peculiar history at Es-
alen. I was different from the others. Now, I know that some
will say—with every right—that each of us was different from
the rest. And we were: Martin was skinny and Betty was
bloated, Pamela was quiet and Marcia was loud, Joseph looked
freaky and Robert looked normal, Herbert's eyes protruded
and Sylvia's were scarcely to be seen. But there is difference
and difference.

Enter Stuart. The blast can be heard on the road above
Esalen. A high-powered engine shifts from fourth to third by
the bridge, then down to second; without braking the car skids
around the curve at the head of the driveway and plummets, at
thirty or forty miles an hour, toward Camelot/Atlantis—the
endlessly violated but seemingly serene ex-burial ground of the

ex-Esalen Indians. Who is it? Steve McQueen? A motorist gone
crazy? No. It is Stuart the Magnificent.

His hands are confidently gripping the imitation wood steer-
ing wheel of his silver Corvette; his Swiss linen tie is fluttering
casually across his Brooks Brothers shirt, from time to time
crossing his Brooks Brothers belt, grazing Brooks Brothers gab-
ardine pants. On his feet? English riding boots. Across from
him, a wooden smile of pretended pleasure on her face, sits the
most succulent looking brown olive girl, of perfect propor-
tions throughout, picked up in Berkeley for the drive down the
coast. She later turns out to be a Jew from Brooklyn. Stuffed
into the boot of the car, a properly scuffed Florentine leather
suitcase, a gray-green but charmingly ineffective Olivetti, and a
Cardin-imitation blue blazer bought at Barney's.

Do you get it? Oh, please get it, please understand me—because I know that even after all this time I do not completely
understand what was happening back then.

When I think of the beginning, the very beginning of the
first evening in the Residential Program, I think of Betty. Dear
Betty, whom I have only lately learned to appreciate. She
seemed enormous, a gigantic woman, nearly six feet tall,
weighing over two hundred and fifty pounds—hardly what I
considered to be an example of the fully developed human
potentiality. I thought her violent, dramatic even in her
moods of apparent calm. And she was loud, interrupting the
august proceedings to which I had come with a notebook
(quickly abandoned) for taking down all the presumed wis-
doms, occult and delicious, that I supposed were to come.
"Let's open a window!" she roared.

The room was hot and damp and the discussion had bogged
down. Abraham Maslow was there that first evening to greet
the new Resident Fellows. I had heard of him, read his books;
he was the father of the new humanistic psychology. I had been
excited at the prospect of meeting him, and it had been a heady

thing to me that everyone at Esalen referred to him simply as "Abe"—some hard-bitten hippies even referred to him as "Old Abe." And he was old. The elder of this hopeful tribe, President of all the American Psychologists, the investigator of ecstasy, was only an old man, tired looking, and wearing a short-sleeved shirt. There was even a whiff of the Jewish refugee about him. Not at all what I had come to California for, the rich and easy Big Sur coast replete with Technicolor and huge Hawaiian moon and water lapping the pebbled shores. I became certain that he made the room more sweaty, though I tried to pay attention.

He urged us to take ourselves seriously. He acclaimed that we were starting on a great human experiment, an important voyage of discovery. We should research our progress and keep journals and we should listen to the researcher, assigned by God knows who to the program, John Mann. As far as I could make out, this one too was a short-sleeved type.

Everything was wrong. Here we were, the chosen and adventurous of the earth, the Esalen Residential Program Fellows, and it was disappointing. The elder of the tribe, the intellectual leader of the cutting edge of mankind, seemed tired, old, and abstract. He wanted research; I was here for adventure, enlightenment, sex. And that room, crowded with badly dressed people. Bill Schutz, the program leader, was also in short sleeves—Dacron, with a little button in the back of his collar that I supposed he thought fashionable, if he even knew what he was wearing. He was built like a football player, Yul Brynner in shaved head from the neck up, but relentlessly badly dressed below. The accents—empty middle-class American accents, psychologists talking what they pretended was English. There were twenty-two in all, I counted them: short-haired men, horn-rimmed glasses, white socks, and some all-American-type lad trying to look interesting by wearing a serape with his sneakers.

But there was one beautiful couple, Robert and Martha Portman—I noticed them early. She sat between his legs, or did he sit beside hers? I remember the impression of beautiful faces, blond hair, and legs—longer legs than New York Jews like me, at least, were allowed to have. Céline says in one of his novels that you can tell the truth from the legs—the truth of real aristocracy.

That first night we disputed—I put in my two cents so that people would notice—until Betty Fuller bellowed for more air. But the air didn't help. Sylvia Dalton and Marvin Handleman argued about which of them really deserved the use of some wretched wooden shack. And I hadn't the vaguest idea who these people were except that, clearly, only two of them looked right.

It was those two I wanted. None of the others were good enough. And I knew in my belly bottom, at the floor of my being, that precisely those two would never be mine. I thought I wasn't good enough for them. I had been born wrong: I was Jewish and I was short and I had not been taught to dress right from the cradle, and my culture was not really mine simply because I had had to make it up myself.

Yet I knew what I wanted as far back as I could remember— I wanted their culture. A culture that would protect me, elevate me above things. The culture that is artifacted, culture of art, of style, of mode and manner, created by the Greeks and Romans and refined through the Italian Renaissance down to our lowly day. I wanted *that* life, that terribly pastoral life that in my mind was some weird montage of Giuliano dei Medici and the ads in *The New Yorker*, Socrates and my pipe-puffing English professors, Porfirio Rubirosa, fast cars and snapped trees, masochistic blond debutantes in garters and boots, plastic credit cards, country houses, New England ponds with pearl-green scum, *oranges glacées*, and literary criticism, and coming out of all this, above the brown and stinking smoke of life, a cool place where ladies and gentlemen lived. Only ladies and gentlemen, please. And they did not suffer except to long.

✳ first visit ✳

i had been to Esalen once, a
year before the Residential Program, and somehow I had come
to think it would offer me all I wanted. The first visit had begun like the second. A roar of engine and screech of tires, frantic braking as dust rose around me from the rutted driveway.
Hectic urban man arrives to be viewed by a row of seemingly
serene and weirdly dressed romantic still-lifes, brown men with
thick and lustrous mustaches, brown girls with white-toothed
smiles and large eyes. They lean on the porch bench looking.
That bench is destined, one cannot doubt it, to become famous
as one of the principal benches on which momentous learning
has taken place in our fading Western world. Then, I was com-
manded by George Leonard to the even more serene hot baths.
"Take a bath," he had said. There followed lit candles in

wrought-iron webs, silver surf, wood surfaces warm to the touch, the soft waitresses in long skirts floating through the dining room, rich brown home-made bread, an air of excitement, people hugging each other, smiles, a fantastic evening. I am with the celebrities, looking down from the top at all this romance and sensual splendor: George Leonard has invited me to the place; he is the Vice President, he is also an editor of *Look* magazine, we sit with Michael Murphy, the President, himself.

And then late the next morning, Saturday, and sunlight pushing away the morning fog. Sixty of us in a large room of the lodge called the "gallery." We have been talking about our dreams for the future of the world—a future full of love and pleasure, new experiences, new ecstasies. Our seminar is called "From Dream to Reality." George Leonard, whom I had met as a fellow consultant to the United States Government about "the future," tells us that new ways to joy are available. It was such rash promises that had brought me to Esalen. We will demonstrate, he says, by trying a micro-lab, a miniature encounter group. I am excited, even scared, but my confidence is high, for so far I have been a shining light at this seminar. Though not one of the official leaders, like George Leonard, I have, nonetheless, shone with brilliant speculation: the future will be wonderful, I have announced, abundance ends repression, a generation of aristocrats born in the young, the end of alienation. I smile on entering my little group of seven. We are told to stay in the here and now, to talk about feelings rather than thoughts, and to be honest. I hesitate, then dare to say openly, steadily, whom I like, what I feel, my first impressions.

Ecstasy. Sheer ecstasy: it is all right. I am still accepted. My love pours from me, I hug all, I grin, and I admire the prettiest girl—Renée is her name, a staff member, brown and serene, with pretty legs. What joy. George Leonard is right, I think, when the following afternoon I head homeward, back to New Jersey. At Esalen I can find my elusive fulfillment.

But the selective memory had blotted out the rest of that first Saturday. The micro-lab ended at noon and Renée promised me, in response to my excited invitation, my heady feeling of love for all people but especially for her, that we would meet, "After the concert, tonight." "After the concert." That phrase, after what happened, echoes in my brain with the mournful toll of "Slowly I turned, step by step . . ." from whatever old movie or comedy routine.

The time from noon until the concert began at eight o'clock passed slowly enough. I was high from the micro-lab, floating for about two hours. Then, when I came down, I thought only of my rendezvous with the sun-browned maiden (my own skin a faded New York ash color). This would be the culmination, the union of all my sensuous and also spiritual delights, tasted for the first time that wonderful weekend.

Night comes. Eight o'clock. The warm redwood lodge is packed with people in exotic dress—beads, pink eyeglasses, leather fringe, and silk. In one corner, a white-covered dais, and that white speckled with vials of flowers. The Indian musicians, handsome and swarthy, all flesh and all spirit, precariously balancing on the knife edge of intrigue and dangerous charm, begin the twang-bang-thump of the intricate rhythms. Stuart sitting on the dais, surrounded by local celebrities: the president, the editor, the various gorgeous females ages sixty-six to two possessed by the tall editor; the famous musician Ali Akbar Kahn. George Leonard has assured me of the power of this Indian music which I have never in person heard; he has spoken that it will rise upward from the base of my spine and issue through my skull like white energy. I listen, or try to listen. Of course, I am and always have been too much beaten about by the whirl of thoughts within my head to ever listen to music, so instead of bursting through my spine, it only bangs between one ear and the other. My irritation rises; George Leonard, the enthusiast, leaves; a thought crosses my mind that the exotic audience is nothing but a bunch of hopeless phonies trying to be hip.

My mind returns to Renée. "After the concert." I develop a headache. But I cannot leave the lodge because that is where we are to meet and I am not sure where to find Renée otherwise. If I went to find her, I might miss her, and my estimate of the situation is that she is not all that interested in the first place. I have to stand my ground and push nature a little bit if the total fulfillment I am seeking is to take place. No matter, look at what Michelangelo went through on his back under the Sistine Ceiling; culture takes work.

Hours drag by. "After the concert." I leave the lodge and begin circling it. Renée wasn't in the crowd, perhaps she was outside. I carefully pace my way through the dark, my eyes bulging, but trying to look as cool as all the other characters who are silently oohing and aahing about how great the music is. The pain inside my head keeps getting worse because there is no escaping the sound even outside the building: in California buildings aren't insulated.

Through the dark, stumbling on mad, acid-smashed hippies, the litany of "After the concert" becoming more acid, my fury at the music growing, my fury at Renée growing, I march.

Eleven o'clock.

Twelve.

One.

"After the concert."

Never has Ali had such an appreciative audience, he smiles with delight. The fans are wild. Everyone is in ecstasy. He will play on. I will continue to march. At two, even this audience, madmen or phonies or both, is sated and Ali's fingers are raw.

Limp, sweaty, out-of-sorts, angry, I roam around the disappearing crowd, the building, the grounds looking for the nymph, my best link to happiness. I know, Undine-like, she sleeps, mysterious "in the baths." Convinced she will not appear voluntarily, hoping that she had kept the faith but has simply missed me in the crush, I go toward the dark path leading toward the sacred waters. A knave blocks me. A sawed-off knave, Monkey by name, not animal, not man.

"Yah can't go down to da baths."

"I'm a guest."

"Not with this crowd—nobody goes to da baths."

His arms on his hips, the magic simian will not yield. I slink to bed, defeated by Mickey Rooney with bad teeth.

In the baths she was, in the massage room, where she slept, wretched water sprite, ex-psychiatric nurse, with another man from the seminar, Herbert Retter, in fact. Protected by the ape. But I would not learn. Over a year later, when I returned to be in the Residential Program, I still bore with me the disappointment and the resentment and my longing. A year in the unpoetic foothills of eastern academia (Rutgers University: street dirt frozen in water for months, like flies in amber) had brightened again the image of my California girl. Full of my mixed feelings, I searched out the elusive Renée. She was, I was told (God help me), in a trailer, living with Josephine (a neurasthenic in her late twenties who limped). I marched along the poetic coast highway with a psychologist who helped undergraduates through their miserable confrontations with reality in the counseling center of a California state college; he later killed himself. When I got near the trailer, her dog bit me. When I got in, she told me, lighting an unfiltered cigarette in spindly yellowed fingers, tan bones of digits with the covering of lizard, that she didn't want to talk about it.

I can see it all now, so clearly, how mistaken I was, wracked by enough suffering to rise from the bottom of the cell, a very Boris Karloff of an ancient inmate, scanning the wet black stones of my prison, only the stub of a candle in my hand, and with that grim and failing light I can look back and, yes, I can see it all now: my first experience of Esalen was the opposite of what I chose to remember and fantasize—it was not order but the reverse, torment of rude awakenings and contradictions, vulgarity and reality smeared over a beauteous background. Just like the rest of the world.

But my being was poisoned and I believed, somehow, that Esalen was pure. And to this purity, longed for from the cells themselves, I came, though Corvette-armored, to the Residential Program. All of me. To hear Old Abe.

CHAPTER THREE

✳ feedback begins ✳

one of the main aspirations I
had when I arrived at Esalen was to fuck. The first was Diane,
the olive-skinned maiden who rode with me from Berkeley as
part of my decoration. A senior at the university, a nearly perfect physical specimen, but disappointing in the act itself: too
young, too possessed of that athletically developed epidermis
that belongs to American girls between the ages of fourteen
and twenty-one and that guards them from softer feelings with
the healthy consistency and bounce of rubber. It is as if, despite the tans or the blushes or the blooms that their skins radiate, they had been sealed by Du Pont from dirt, dust, and feeling: better living through chemistry. They call up in me,
though I would resist it at first as being too ridiculous, the
image and simile of a tennis ball; soft and furry on the outside,
but, within, hard rubber with bounce.

History will be helpful here. When I was in full adolescence and wondering what the world was all about, and also wondering, my body pressed from within by lush and hot juices under enormous pressure, when I would lose my virginity, the person whom I most loved in the world, my adolescent chum, Fred, being more sophisticated and much more sure of things, told me, when I asked what life was all about, that I should know from visceral experience that the only important thing is sex, and, as a corollary, that means getting laid. It may seem foolish to you, it does to me, and it was appalling to Fred when I told him a dozen years later; but it is fact that this sentence of his stayed with me, and that it had more influence on the first thirty years of my life than any other single thing that happened. Of course, the sentiment was endorsed by the gross companions of my adolescent days: the youthful flower of the Lower East Side of New York City. And it was endorsed by the entire business community of American capitalism, the GNP, the labor and commerce departments, and every dollar rung up on every cash register through the agency of the American advertising industry.

Unfortunately, being a domesticated youth, a middle-class fellow, and a good sort, it was hard for me to put into practice what I felt. Accordingly, it became necessary, in order to get laid in good conscience, to convince myself that I was in love with the girl at hand and similarly to convince her. This necessity led to a large number of brief love affairs that were in themselves exciting but left nasty residues, because I would have to cut them off after several weeks or when my illusion disappeared, the super-ego satisfied along with lust; and I realized that I had not been in love, or, at any rate, it had suddenly faded, and I had an angry girl on my hands.

Clearly an unsatisfactory way of doing things. By the time I arrived at Esalen for the Residential Program I had convinced myself that I was emotionally flawed but a stupendous lover. I had further determined that here, in what I conceived to be the very honey pot of eroticism, I would pursue my satisfactions more straightforwardly.

Hence, my arrival with Diane, and my announcement to all who would listen that I was at Esalen for many reasons but chief among them was getting laid and anybody who thought about life differently was a liar. Manhood was fucking.

So it was that just a few nights after the Program began, in the cool mist of a September evening in Big Sur, I seated myself with deliberation on the moist bench, next to aristocratic Martha, Robert's wife, aforementioned, and after a few gossipy preliminaries, brushing my suède jacket against her unfortunately cheap blue nylon camping parka, I asked her if she would go to bed with me. When she shyly answered that she would, I was, of course, astonished and fearful.

Well, the Great Seducer led the way up one wooden stairway, through the first level of parked cars, and then scrambled up the dirt parapet to my room. I no longer remember the exact details. At some point we must have taken off our clothes. Her panties were college-girl white. A tall girl, with thick yellow pubic hair. She was tender, slightly distracted, half-glowing. I wanted to make her come (a matter of some importance to me in those days, otherwise I didn't feel manly). She didn't come, but it was, after all, the first time. I told her, the old romantic surfacing, that I wanted part of her marriage with Robert, or part of her. When she demurred, I began bargaining. If memory serves me right, I tried to explain myself in a way that would suit her reserve and scruples since she made clear that she wanted to be married to Robert, and I told her that I only wanted "twenty per cent." Not a hard bargain, I ask you. But she was adamant. She had to get back to Robert and she didn't know what would come of our future and it was late and she looked more and more uncomfortable. I let her go.

I can't remember what I did in the next hour or so but I wasn't able to sleep and at about one-thirty I was wandering around in the misty moonlight when whom should I meet but

Robert. Now, I don't mind telling you that I was somewhat anxious, for though I knew that Robert and Martha had agreed to experiment and to see whether they could get rid of jealousy in their relationship, well, a husband is a husband and a lover is a lover. To my relief, Robert did not seem upset. But when I told him that all I really wanted was to be a part of their marriage—in haste to get on his good side, but also to get into the security their marriage seemed to exude—when I told him that, he didn't seem interested. I realized that I had been had. The Seducer had been seduced. I was the object of their experimentation and now that the experiment had been done I was to be dismissed to the side lines while they sat together and evaluated the results.

It hurt me as I walked back to my cabin through the nighttime fog to feel how foolish they had made me. But as I thought about it I began to feel exhilarated. Here I had gone through life always assuming that at some deep level of cunning I was manipulating others. I was the crafty one, they my victims, and I would be tormented at the guilt I felt from taking advantage of the world of innocents that God had thrust me into. In an ordinary situation, I would probably not have taken a married woman to bed and then known enough from both her and her husband about what was going on in their heads to realize an important truth: I may have been manipulating experience but so were others. It was dazzling to learn that others were pursuing their ends with the same energy and, in this case, more success.

Though I was somewhat abashed, I told myself to take heart. I would learn a lot at Esalen, and, besides, there was still a chance that Robert and Martha would give me more than they already had. Though certain knowledge was seeping through my acid-proof layers of ego, I pursued my quest again, informing the group that I was still available but not mentioning the activity of the previous night. That afternoon I waited for my "dyad" with Catherine, a well-built lady of fifty-five, tall, with steel-gray hair but lively black eyes. As I waited I brooded over that horrible and unreal word, "dyad." Schutz had told us that we should have "dyads" in the afternoon and that a "dyad" was a "two-person encounter group." The incredible boobishness of them all. Social scientists they were and having discovered with suddenness the existence of real people and invented a new psychological cult called "humanistic psychology," they proceed to use language derived from the relations between things to describe human relations. So people telling you what they think about you becomes "feedback" in our encounter groups—a term from computer sciences. And a situation in which two human beings try to be as honest and as open as they can becomes "a dyad"—a term from abstract mathematics—or a "two-person encounter group." The ring of addition is there: two persons plus three persons are five persons; subtract one person (by murder or assumption into heaven, it doesn't matter) from five persons and you have two dyads or four persons. I supposed that Bill Schutz and even Robert Portman for that matter, good social engineers both, would have described the results of last night's adventures in showing me just how much I could be manipulated as an "effect of feedback coupled with the beneficial results of living in an experimental environment."

Finally, Catherine entered, and I was in no mood to mince words or indulge in Byzantine complexities or maneuvers—straightforward would I be. I began asking her why she wouldn't fuck me. She protested. She was not in the mood. She didn't feel like it, she wasn't excited. I pressed onward. I tried being charming. Finally, after fifteen minutes of insisting she said, "Well, heck, if we are going to get anywhere with each other, we'll have to get this out of the way."

I was surprised, surprised at her acquiescence but more at her implying that for her there were values equal to or greater than getting laid. What did she have in mind, I wondered. She must be kidding herself or else she is deeply repressed, or even biologically defective.

But I didn't have much time to think this through because she had begun undressing; I had to bend my thoughts now to giving a good account of myself.

Eventually I did, or so I thought, for she, unlike Martha, groaned and moaned and huffed sufficiently for me to think that she had come and that I had thereby produced evidence of my prowess.

At four o'clock, we went to the encounter-group meeting where I played it cool for about twenty minutes, hardly able to contain myself, and then announced with quiet triumph that I had vanquished two of the females in the room within the last twenty-four hours. That should show them who I am. Their absurd chattering about "breakthroughs" into God-knows-what would stop now and we would settle into some serious fucking, with me as the leader.

Dear friend, gentle reader, imagine my astonishment when my two conquests (one person plus one person equals two persons) both turned on me to tell the group how it hurt and embarrassed them that I would so coarsely announce our amorous doings. Well, if there was anything I knew I wasn't, I wasn't coarse—these clods were the coarse ones, I had seen that the first night. But I felt a little embarrassed myself as I told them that the reason they felt embarrassed at my announcement was that they really wanted to fuck, and, in fact, had.

My only intention in bringing up the incidents was to brag and *épater les bourgeois* with whom I had surrounded myself. But the ladies, in a pique, decided to discuss the events further with the group.

CATHERINE: "Well, I didn't really enjoy it, did you, Martha?"

MARTHA: "No. He was rather cold with me. He didn't make me feel that he was making love to *me*."

CATHERINE: "I know what you mean, but I was sort of expecting that. The thing that surprised me, Stuart, was that after all your talk you didn't seem to know that much. I've been around and I wasn't impressed at all. There's a lot you have to learn about touching."

MARTHA: "I agree."

What could I say? I knew I was good in bed, doesn't every red-blooded American, and didn't I make a special point of attaching myself only to girls who responded to me or I would drop them? But here were two women, not one (one I could easily have dismissed as neurotic or resentful or lying), two persons, female, each very different, and the consensus of this group of two, this dyad, was that I lacked sensitivity, "flow," and spontaneity. Mostly, I didn't know what they were talking about and wouldn't accept their estimates—but it was a blow.

CHAPTER FOUR

a series of blows

at an early session of the encounter group that formed the basis of the Residential Program, I remember telling them that I was not going "to be the first to walk the plank." We were discussing who would be the one to disclose himself to the group and trust what would happen. Who talks and thinks of walking planks? A ten-year-old who has seen Captain Kidd as portrayed by Cornel Wilde and Douglas Fairbanks, Jr., in the wombish, dark, and dangerous plush velvet, faded and smelly, of Lower-East-Side movie theaters. Alone, despite the other children and the ogre-like matron with her flashlight, single eye of fire, flashing over the unruly crowd; those gigantic images. So great is my terror at coming to Esalen this second time, despite the show of silver armor, that I revert to the images and lingo of my superstitious ten-year-old self. I find myself growing young, haunted by old presences. Do you suppose they caught it? Did they see elegant Stu slip and reveal the child?

All summer long, before I arrived in September, the fear had been building. I had come to think that were I to get from Esalen what I wanted I would have to go crazy there. A curious obsession.

The first blow—the one that had given me intuitive knowledge of other violence to come and that led me to tell the startled pirate crew that I would not walk the plank—had been given some months before in another beautiful place, a Georgian mansion, set in an English garden, bordered by yellow fields, greenhouses, and stables: Old Westbury, Long Island, an aristocratic estate now the property of The State University of New York. Stuart, Associate Professor and Member of the President's Planning Staff, is busy trying to solve the educational dilemmas of our time by designing an experimental college. His company: two other professors, a clot of former Peace Corps administrators, and half a dozen permanent student consultants who have established their ability to make educational innovations by angrily dropping out of schools that already claimed to be "experimental."

Having had such a marvelous experience in my first microlab, I had become an insistent advocate of encounter groups, affective education, and the like. I had persuaded the nonexistent college, which would be several years' planning, to send me to Esalen for nine months, and I insisted that we have an encounter group among our nascent staff first. The members of the staff were continually at one another's throats, and in principle, it was a good idea.

For an enormous fee, Bill Schutz agreed to come early in May and lead a day-long group. We sat on the new russet carpet in what had once been the ballroom (it had been built forty years before by its patrician owner for a two-week visit of the Prince of Wales). We did a long micro-lab and though it was hard for me to confront my colleagues and express feelings honestly to them, we were in this together; each of the exercises lasted only five minutes, each of us had to do them, and I got exhilarated. I remember, at morning's end, announcing to the group with a beaming face and a giggle, "I am an encounter addict."

The afternoon was another matter. Now, I was primed for this experience, I was the encounter-group advocate; I knew my colleagues were reluctant and scared. I would lead the way. But, instead of me, worse luck, they started on the President, Harris Wofford. Bill thought that since so many of us were having difficulties with this man, he should begin by going around the group and telling each person exactly how he felt about him. Harris began the circuit. By the time he got to the third person—he still had five members of the circle to encounter before he got to me—I began to cry. The sadness welled up as I foresaw what he would tell me—he would not really give to me, my boss would not approve me, give me what I wanted. I knew this already, I knew that Harris would not commit to my care one of the constituent colleges out of which the whole college would eventually be made. But I wanted that college. Status, freedom, a chance to do something original, a validation of my decision to leave literary studies to become a forward-looking college administrator, and more.

When he finally arrived, I was near to sobbing; all the while feeling a little proud of myself for suffering so openly. I would show them the road to the new education!

Harris was kind but he said he wouldn't do it: he wouldn't give me my own college. He told me he valued me; I had been his second faculty appointment. "Why not give me a school, let me try my ideas?" I insisted. He hesitated. "I don't trust you," he said. In the silence my crying began again and to my fright sobs started rippling upward from my belly. Bill called my attention. Would I do something—would I get up, walk to the center of the room with Harris, turn around, and fall backward into Harris's arms? I pulled myself toward the center; but I couldn't fall. When Bill asked me who in the room I did trust to do this exercise with, I sobbed again, down to a level of emotion and hurt I had never known before; and I confessed and learned, to my astonishment, that I trusted no one in all that company.

Well, I finally did it, after many tries, with one of them, Harry Galtzer. But as I stood there with Harris and then with others—my arms thrust outward from my sides, teetering, stiff, breath mixed with phlegm from my heaving chest, crying—I felt deep within me the knowledge that I did not trust other people, I could not call on my fellows, monsters to be careful of, to be manipulated, to be nice to, certainly, but always to be watched, never turn your back, watch carefully. Bill urged me to another game. I went around the group and asked people if they trusted me. Many said they liked me. But none of them, not even the two other professors, bluff companions of my coffee breaks, not even those smiling and hearty, hand-shaking ones, would say they trusted me.

I recovered during that day. I knew that I had been brave and I was proud of that, I was even rather happy—glad for the emotional release, the secret out. But the knowledge that I had gained ate at me. I was an outcast—not trustworthy. I could never pursue my career as long as I was what I was. For that reason alone, I would have to change everything. But how the fuck do I go about changing everything?

The fear had started then and also the anger. I passed the summer longing for the fall and my beautiful year at Big Sur, and fighting off depression and a growing desperation. It didn't help to look back on the antiheroism of that group: I discover my alienation from mankind by not being able to fall over backward, my guru is bullet-headed Bill, imitation of Yul, he and his techniques both creatures of Hollywood.

Driving across the country toward Esalen, in Indiana I urged my chariot into daring deeds: I signaled and pulled out to pass a line of five slower cars on two-lane Route 40. The sluggish, blue station wagon two cars in front of me pulled out anyway. The bastard. I slammed the accelerator and twisted the wheel to the left. At eighty, on the sloping left-hand gravel shoulder I could see the faces of only two children as the five cars glided past, the stones rattling beneath me. When the Corvette began to skid on the gravel I fought it back onto the road and slid into the right-hand lane, just in front of the pack, just in time to miss the startled red Buick coming toward me. A few minutes later, I pulled off the road, afraid of myself; I could have killed a dozen people.

How to do justice to it all, the state of mind when I came to the Residential Program? I had tried such flights before: six hundred miles from New York to college in the green plains south of Lake Erie; four thousand miles to Florence, to Rome; then to Yale, to become an English professor, tweed-equipped, to become a member of the American upper crust: with upper-crust wife, Connecticut farmhouse, my name (O God, thank you, at last) in the Boston Social Register. People used to say, when they met and talked with me, that they couldn't tell where I came from. When that last flight had crashed in divorce, a son untended, other flights followed—more tentative. I came to Esalen with hope. And I came with my armor on.

The first things to go were the little details of expectation out of which my hope had been fashioned. Starting with the girls. Renée I have spoken of. Sandra I had met with her ex-oilman husband in that first seminar a year before. She and Sidney and I had gone to the baths one night, moonlight and a candle, scent of incense, water crashing below, the cliff on the beach, warm bath floating her breasts. I had remembered the left one especially, slightly larger than the right, pink and pendant, full but with nipple pointed downward. She had a husky Southern voice that drawled over words like delights while the long fingers of her hands wafted through the warm water in idle play. A pleasant, well-bred rich lady in her thirties; mature but young—and almost available, because her husband and she were considering divorce. They lived in a big house in Palm Springs. He drove an Alfa, and she said he was becoming a painter but he didn't say much of anything, older, dull, and you could see she was going to waste—all that pleasant loving there, going to waste. We talked a little afterward, easy to talk with, educated but searching, not satisfied with being the sub- urban matron, kind of like me, only rich, slightly older, and not Jewish. My kind of woman. She became part of my dreams of Esalen and Big Sur.

The day I arrived for the Residential Program there was a wedding party in a remote part of Big Sur; outdoors there were drummers and dancing. I drove over with Diane. I wore my tie in the hot afternoon sun. Nearly a hundred hippies in exotic dress—a huge wedding cake stuffed with hash, the tom-tom of the drumming, smiles, tiny cymbals. This was the Big Sur com- munity, but I felt very uncomfortable—they seemed so differ- ent from me, so relaxed, so far-out. I felt odd in my starched shirt and tie but I just didn't have anything else to wear. I remember thinking that I would be damned if I would dress like these drugged hippies. A dancing girl caught my eye; she was wearing a long yellow and green paisley dress; two shoul- der straps scooped together, a dimple between sweet breasts. But her bare feet were splayed and dirty, her hair was slightly matted, she swayed back and forth, eyes closed, sucking a yel- low joint. It was Sandra, the matron from Palm Springs.

When she opened her eyes after her toke she saw me. We spoke. Well, it may sound silly, but I was scared. The square and gentle lady had become hip and gentle. She was stoned all of the time. She was cleaning cabins for a living.

O God, great God, look down and pity me, me with my hopes and expectations, my decorums, my yearnings for safety and clarity: the wife of a man who had recently sold twenty producing oil wells having thrown over all that money and four children, swinging and swaying with hirsute drummers, and making a living, keeping her foothold in Esalen, by cleaning cabins. Was *this* why I had come to Big Sur? To let go of everything, to lose everything, like Sandra had?

I braved it all, of course. I looked and I was quiet. I tried to puzzle things out quietly, of course. A couple of days later, Sandra came by my cabin to clean it. An aristocrat cleaning my Jewish cabin. It was too much. I would not go crazy like this. I told her she had gone too far—Sidney wasn't much fun but that didn't mean she had to desert rational middle-class living altogether. She laughed at me and told me to drop out. When we met again some hours later, she was off work. She was smoking. There was a sprinkling of fine dandruff on the shoulders of her unwashed black sweater. She looked like she had been camping out and she was strangely (I won't say "happy") enthusiastic.

Well, dandruff or no dandruff, I had come to Big Sur to fuck; and Sandra's breast had been part of my vision of erotic bliss. True, I was a bit off balance but I would assert myself. For the first time in my life I put it absolutely directly: "Sandra," said I, "let's go up to my room and fuck." When, despite my earlier haranguing her, she responded, "Why not?" I think that my disappointment was greater than my satisfaction. This was no conquest, really. This was cynical. Sandra was cynical. We went up and we fucked. No self-delusions about love in this one; no twenty per cent even dreamed of. Straight fucking. And it wasn't bad. It just wasn't much. So what was there? Another chink in the armor.

Renée, Martha, Catherine, Sandra—it was discouraging but I didn't stop trying. A day or so later I ventured forth again. Country Joe and the Fish are a rock group and in those September days there was a song of theirs, "Sweet Lorraine," at the top of the hit parade. I had heard it many times, though I had never listened to it. I listen to rock and roll no better than to Indian music. The refrain of the song, identical with the title, was particularly catchy, and I had often hummed those few bars and murmured the words—sweĕt lăw-ráyne. It was enchanting to learn upon my arrival at the putative paradise that Lorraine, the namesake of the song, was a stunningly pretty girl, who waited on tables at Esalen. Small and brown and soft, with big green eyes, she brought me my supper, Lorraine, a girl in a song.

Toward the end of the first week I got up the nerve to talk to her. It had started to rain; I knew she had no place to sleep, so I asked her to stay with me that night. It was six in the evening. She said she would meet me after cleaning up the kitchen; she would come to my room at ten o'clock. I waited for her, knowing she would not come. I wanted her, but only in a mechanical way. She was beautiful and I was testing my powers, but true physical beauty in a woman had always been frightening to me. I knew that beauty is power, beauty is mobility, and were I not to be perfectly satisfactory to this beautiful girl, she could and would go elsewhere. I knew that she had probably gone elsewhere already. As I waited, lying clothed on the bed in my room, my defenses rose, with hatred brewing, with distrust to protect me.

She came at ten o'clock.

But I was too afraid of what she could do to me. It was an even worse fuck than Sandra. And it was partly her fault. She lay there accommodating but nearly inert. Was it my fear that she felt? Was it something else, something mechanical and tight about me, something different from her hippie brothers? I let her stay with me, she was grateful for the shower; it is hard living in a sleeping bag. She had been a ski instructor—I could imagine her neat body, round bottom, dimpled cheeks in ski clothes. We smoked cigarettes. Maybe it was her fault, maybe she was the tight one? I was drastically uncomfortable.

I mustn't be too melodramatic, though. Even with Lorraine,

there were moments. All my previous years had been spent in school, as a student: I had liked it that way. When I took my Fulbright to Europe I lived with a college friend in Italy. I didn't feel comfortable with people who weren't intellectuals. My only Italian friend was a hyperintellectual who lived by his wits, grinding out highly polished articles for popular magazines about things of which he knew nothing. I thought him a daring exotic. After Italy, I returned to school as the professor.

Esalen was the first place where, since I had fled my parents to go away to college, I was compelled to associate with people who were not intellectuals, particularly literary intellectuals. This is partly the reason that all the Resident Fellows seemed dumb and uninteresting to me. They couldn't discuss interesting things like Coleridge, or original sin, or the picaresque novel.

Well, Lorraine thought that Coleridge was a place in Big Sur, like Partington Ridge, and while she disappointed me in some ways, she and others led me to new experiences, some of which were exhilarating.

Some nights after our liaison, I asked her to have a drink with me. I simply could not admit to myself that the most beautiful girl I had known could be so boring, so alien, so impossible to relate to. Somehow, I reasoned, I could find a way to touch that beauty and bring it into myself. So, we went and had a drink, and I tried to talk about skiing and what it was like in her home town, Los Angeles, as if I were interested in such things.

By this time I was learning that the unlettered of Big Sur communicated by talking a special kind of nonconversation, punctuated by much nonverbal nodding and an occasional semimaniacal laugh, a bit druggy, of mutual agreement on some unstated universal, the articulation of which would be rendered in such nonspecific phrases as "That's where it's at, Baby," or "Yeah." The method of such discourse is to be talking about people—always about people; one tells an anecdote and elicits from it, without seeming to, fragments of pathos or absurdity or sympathy. It is a bit like Hemingway dialogue, actually, except there are more snorts, laughs, and many more nods, nods (I put it so because the nods always seem to come in multiples of two). I just can't hack Hemingway dialogue. It was especially difficult in this case—with a gorgeous itinerant waitress, a road-hitching hippie with an eleventh-grade education, whose learning consisted of what she knew from drugs and half reading, once, a book on the Tarot. Let's face it, there was not much we had in common. Like, I mean, we would never have been matched by a computer-dating service. Yeah. Two nods. On the other hand, she was the prettiest around, and this brought us together, and once together, I had to confront the fact that she was a human being. I made some effort to put away the things that kept me separate from Lorraine, and from others, and I tried, now using one method, now another, to find some common ground. I even tried to learn what her ground was.

A couple of drinks had not improved things much. I took her home—she had found a cabin in the woods—and I lay beside her on the bed, beside this beautiful creature, while two voices in my head carried on a long dialogue, the gist of which was: "Go ahead, fuck her, even if it is mechanical; a lay is a lay, why go home alone?" versus "Don't fuck her unless you feel comfortable and really want to; she'll only pick up your coldness and be cold back to you; and besides, it's beneath you to be so inhuman."

Time passed; it got later; I got sleepy. I resolved my dilemma, while taking off my clothes and getting into bed, by deciding to sleep there but make no amorous move unless it really felt natural. You must understand that *I* was doing all this debating and making all the decisions. Lorraine would have been content either way. So we turned off the electric light and lit the purple-brown and arty candle Lorraine had just acquired, about which I was deceitful or well-mannered enough to compliment her. And we lay there, holding hands, eyes closed, listening to the river flow by. We were in one of those campgrounds where Esalen staff and other hip types live when there isn't room for them on the property at Esalen.

So there we were together. I finally silenced the voice of Rogerian (Carl) scruple and the other voice had sensibly just said: as long as you're here, why not make love? and I had just started to stroke my bland warm maiden, when I started at the scuff of feet climbing the two steps from the mud on to the cabin porch. Lorraine touched my shoulder and said, "It's O.K., it's Flora." The door opened, and her roommate, who worked in the Esalen office, stringy of hair and rounded of shoulder, entered. I whispered to Lorraine, "Can we still make love?" "Later," she murmured, "after Flora has gone to sleep."

Flora gave us what I suppose she thought was a discreet nod and without any fuss about modesty took off her clothes; then she got into a bed, across the room.

I can't really say that I was comfortable in all this but it was adventurous. After all, the only time I had known of a man alone in a room with girls in *beds* was in books—medieval fabliaux or those scenes at various inns in *Tom Jones*. And here it was, actually happening.

Yet I had determined to fuck, and now I had to wait for Flora to sleep. It may have been that while waiting my mind drifted back to various events of the preceding day or two, particularly to certain events; or it may not be. But a day or two before all this two sixteen-year-old boys, tall, lean, and beautiful in a kind of wicked German way, had arrived at Esalen. I had had pretentions to being a beautiful boy at their age—though I had never been quite beautiful—and I had been lovely and charming, sexy, and very popular with all the most interesting and older students at Oberlin College. I hated these two at first glance.

With no effect. Within hours of arriving, they were hired. Dressed in velvet and with rosebud lips, blond hair combed like pages, they played waiter in the dining room with much flourish of napkins over forearms, bowing and flaunting fancy manners: "A pleasure to serve you." "Let me bring you a better cut." Instead of being disgusted, people loved them.

Back in the cabin Lorraine and I still lie side by side. At last, it seems to me that enough time has passed so that even if Flora isn't asleep she can plausibly pretend to be and we can proceed. There is noise outside, however; cars arriving, motors shutting, doors opening and banging, light switches turned on in neighboring cabins. I have stretched out a hand toward Lorraine but there is a knocking at our door. A knock at such a time is always annoying but with Flora in the room too, it was doubly disagreeable: she would have to be acknowledged as officially awake now and at least another half hour would have to advance before Lorraine and I could get to the business at hand.

Lorraine, always pleasant and accommodating, called sweetly, "Who is it?"

"Sig and John."

"Who are Sig and John?" I ask with a mixture of wonderment.

"Oh those two kids who're working in the dining room; they've been staying here until they find a place."

The reader will imagine my feelings at this point.

I find it hard to recall the exact events of the next fifteen minutes. There were introductions, then discussion about the obvious dilemma: four bed spaces, five people. I got into an argument with Sig, the prettier of the two, about something else and tried to destroy his cool confidence by calling him "Sonny." Undisturbed, he told me to "Lighten up," whatever that meant. Lorraine looked on, saying nothing. The other lad was already in bed with Flora and had shut his eyes and turned to the wall. I couldn't fuck Lorraine with that creep in the same room; besides, there was this other creep, too. Was he to sleep on the floor? Or out-of-doors nearby? On the other hand, I couldn't just leave and give up my girl to a teen-ager. How would it look? And why in hell didn't Lorraine do something? It was beginning to seem absurd already, not moving from the bed either to leave or throw the guy out. He was there before me. He had no other place to sleep and I did. I couldn't turn him out into the cold night just because of his looking pretty. How would it look?

I got out of bed and began putting leg after leg into my Brooks Brothers corduroys, silently pretending to be "cool," in local phrase. By this time the loathsome Sig had slipped beneath the sheets with Lorraine (she had whispered that she didn't fuck him, hadn't she?). I think I turned out the lights on the two couples as I left.

Oh well, it was true that I hadn't wanted Lorraine very much, and it was late and I was tired. I walked the few steps to my silver car in the damp dark. I got in. That was always a pleasure. It felt so solid, the door, the seat, the grudging give of the stiff springs as my ass and back settled against the vinyl. I turned on the engine, revved it once, turned up the four head-lights, and sat while it idled, wondering if despite the charity which led me to retreat at the crucial hour I had not made an ass of myself. As if in answer, the larger lighted cabin in front of which I had parked hours before gave forth a noise. The porch light went on, and a half-dozen beatniks from the Esalen staff reeled out, beer cans in hand. They had brought Sig and John home and had been awaiting the issue of all they had anticipated when they saw my car there. When they saw me in the car, they laughed loudly, lifting their drinks and crying gaily into the night, "Tom Jones! Tom Jones!" They were singing "For he's a jolly good fellow" as I smilingly made my way toward the coast road. I was satisfied. In a way I was acquiring a reputation. I was becoming special in Big Sur and I was having experiences that before, in all those years of schooling, I had only read about.

CHAPTER FIVE

✤ the hike to tassajara ✤

new experiences, as a matter of fact, were something we were supposed to have; they were urged on us from the beginning. I remember on that first night of the Residential Program the excited talk about all the new things we could try this year. Some people spoke with gleaming eyes of the new ground we would break in human experience, the things we would try that would lift the ceiling on human potentiality. I was puzzled by this line of attack because I just assumed that everything important worth doing had already been done by somebody else. It was also urged just as strongly that each of us experience things he himself had not tried. There followed, as I remember it, much talk about experimenting with food. The food served in the dining room was scorned by Robert and Martha: ugh, too much meat, why any meat at all, ugh. They were joined by others, antimeat; and finally there were cries that we, the new Residential Fellows, take over the management of the corrupt dining room and serve only macrobiotic food. I knew that macrobiotic food had something to do with rice and I had heard that someone had died from it. But I had no idea why people ate it, and since I liked the food at the Hot Springs I put in my two cents and protested. Robert and Martha said it was good for you, particularly spiritually. Bill urged me to try it, he never had but he was going to try it. The other residents acquiesced or agreed and I began to believe that my fantasy before coming to Esalen was correct: I would have to go crazy here. Either that, or these people were already crazy. Here they were, in one breath talking about breaking through all human possibilities previously attained (my mind flashed to Shakespeare, Michelangelo) and in the next proposing that as part of the attempt to do so, we eat rice!

Bo Cahill rose to tell about his part of the program. He was the principal consultant to the program and like Bill was badly dressed. Furthermore, he seemed kind of effeminate to me. Now Schutz, at least, led encounter groups, and I already knew these were potent. But Cahill's special abilities seemed more obscure. His formula to "take this group where no one has ever been" was a lot of "work with the body," the "work program" (which meant working in the garden, a thing he insisted on), and, get this, a hike. It would get us in shape, he assured us. And it had other values which he would not specify. I could not believe what I was hearing. My leader was proposing to take me to paradise with a hike. And, besides, he was one of those who scorned the meat and potatoes of the lodge; he was a partisan of rice.

Needless to say, I was not impressed with Cahill and in the succeeding days I became less impressed. For one thing, he seemed incredibly ineffective in the encounter-group sessions. That he led the way into the garden every morning seemed to me less than an act of genius. I was disoriented but I didn't know what questions to ask and nobody bothered to take me by the hand and explain all this talk about rice and hiking. Bill told me he was going along with Bo; like me, Bill was new to Esalen, but he was just going to try things, even if he didn't understand them. That was all right for him, maybe, but he at least knew what encounter groups were about. I began to wonder about the leadership, especially Cahill's, and to ask myself and others why this eater of rice and leader of hikes was the main consultant to our group of inner-space astronauts; it didn't add up.

The hike was planned for a week after the program began. As I listened to it being discussed, I realized that hiking boots were required. I was told that they had been mentioned in the letter of instruction we Residents received before we came. I remembered no mention of it and experienced my first passing notion that these people were plotting against me; in actuality, I suppose I simply forgot the boots because I had no intention, when I sat in New York reading those instructions, of taking any hikes—who hikes in New York?

Well, out West, it seems that everybody hikes. They showed me what hiking boots were, pointing to their feet, for most of the staff and even the Residents already wore them. Hiking boots have thick rubber soles, they come up well over the ankle, and they are laced all that length to keep the ankle from turning as it scrambles over the countryside. I glanced down at the polished leather of my riding boots.

As that first week wore on, to my very great surprise, it seemed that the others were actually going to go on this hike. Sheep, I muttered, they would go over the cliff if you led them. And yet, sometime on Saturday, I decided to go on the hike too. I don't know now why I decided. Perhaps it was because everyone urged me to. Perhaps it was because I was a little bit frightened, city person that I am, of being that close to nature, and I thought my courage would be doubted if I did not come.

So, on Saturday, I went into town and bought hiking boots. I made a careful record of this investment so that I could deduct it from my income tax as an educational expense. If the Residents thought a hike was educational then an IRS agent could be expected to be that dumb, too.

The following morning, a bit late, I joined the others in front of the red pickup trucks that would take us part of the way. Bo assured us that we were being trucked over the rough part; from there the hike would be a "simple walk over level country." My costume: I was wearing what I thought would serve. Since it was cool as we left the Hot Springs, I wore casually, you understand, over my shoulders, a green wool sport jacket. It was a time when the hip young were wearing uniforms; I had picked up this little item at an Army-Navy Store in Provincetown that specialized in selling surplus to youngsters who turned them into costumes, wearing which they marched in peace parades. It was CCC forester issue, I had learned. Forester issue, eh? I thought of the solitary woodsman, L. L. Bean at home. Why not wear a tie with my blue and white Tattersall shirt? I did. Black denim trousers. On my feet, hiking boots? Wrong. I had been told that morning that hiking boots had to "be broken in." Were I to wear mine, my feet would suffer and swell. Who knows such things—crazy, I was fallen among adult campers, overgrown boy scouts in search of the ultimate, living out the last domesticated American remains of the romantic movement's love of nature. Like millions of their common counterparts, they didn't even know that romanticism had been a failure (T. S. Eliot had proved that).

Grumbling, I went back to my cabin and got my elegant boots. As I climbed into the truck, Bill Schutz surveyed me and remarked that I looked like Trevor Howard going on a movie safari. It cut, that comment, but I only replied by surveying his track shoes and sweat pants with disdain. I knew, besides, that he was skeptical of the "hike" himself.

I wore starched shirts (I forgot to mention the shirts were

starched), ties, high boots, and jackets not only because I thought them stylish, but also because they made me feel kept together. You see, and have some pity for all that I will recount in this volume, I was partly afraid that if I dressed in loose clothing or, worse, were naked, I would simply fall apart under people's gaze. Naturally, I assumed that everyone else was similarly constituted and that such sloppy-looking creatures as the Residents had already fallen apart.

The three trucks pulled out with all the Residents. We drove south, along the highway, until we came to Nacimiento Road. I silently congratulated myself on knowing enough Spanish to translate that, "birth"; on the other hand, I wasn't really sure that it meant birth, and I'm still not sure. I glanced a mini-furtive glance at the others in my truck to see whether I were one up in this respect or not.

My companions were Marcia, Bo, Susan, Bill, Joseph, Pamela, and a woman named Clarissa who was handsome, tall, and had the figure of a chorus girl, even though she was in her mid-forties. I had had my eye on her from the start of the morning; she, along with a few others who weren't members of the Program, had been allowed to come. As soon as we left the prying eye of civilization, Marcia drew from her pack a gallon jug of cheap wine. She passed it to Joseph, he passed it around. Sometimes I am very susceptible and I got very high very quickly and launched into a series of comic skits—something I tend to do when I am very happy and intoxicated. In this mood, I make Sid Caesar seem dreary. My first act was to convert the truck into an Israeli half-track prowling the Sinai in search of Arabs. When I realized how Jewish this was I dropped it. I turned the truck into a German submarine, in which I played the captain, the entire crew, the torpedoes, and the snorkel—all in German. I was gay, but a little anxious lest anyone catch the mistakes and fumbling in my German. I would prove that I had not been a professor of comparative literature for nothing. The jug kept going around and was replaced with a second one. The scene shifted to the French Resistance: cuddling my imaginary Sten gun I snuggled next to Clarissa and spoke words of love in reasonable French. Then, Italian; Ethiopia, the desert, the British are beating us back. The jug kept going around. I sang every aria I knew in every language. I hold the stage. I recite poetry, like some ancient bard, harp in hand, chanting the opening lines of Beowulf: "Hwaet! We gardena in yar dagum . . ." The jug kept circling. If they try to talk I overrule them, outentertain them. Only Pamela moves, incessantly clicking her 35mm. at me—it seemed absurd. Finally, after I had transformed the truck again, this time into flying saucer which, by means of a fictive lever, I lifted three feet off the ground to the nodded agreement of my enchanted companions, Bo, the leader, spoke solemnly to this exhibition of human talent and wit, "I had my doubts, but now I see that you are not bad; you are life-positive."

Now who could believe anybody could be that cretinous, that far removed from reality to adjudge Sid Caesar as life-positive? Clearly, he was a zombie, dead on too much rice and hiking.

We stopped for lunch and under the shade trees of the world's most remote state park I ate several sandwiches and then fought a saber duel in French, following it with a laconic but exquisitely choreographed wild west gun fight. The others looked on with admiration or occasionally tried to participate, an activity which I indulged because they soon realized their utter inferiority in the play of fancy and retired to leave me alone and busy on our rural stage. Then, we drove on to a bend in a river where there was a natural pool for swimming. So far, this wasn't bad. I was having a great time. I swam; I studied the naked girls. But the shadows were already long over the clear pool. It was time to hike. We were going to the Zen monastery up in the mountains at Tassajara, where we would learn to meditate, whatever that was.

By this time I had claimed Clarissa for my own, I would be

her cavalier servant and walk with her toward my *vita nuova*. She needed me; we were to walk on a dirt path by the boulder-strewn river and she, like me, in being told that we had only "a level walk" had worn her usual boots. They had three-inch heels. Man, I dug those black boots, but they quickly put us, me supporting and she weaving, near the end of the line. The floppy, black straw hat, which had seemed a redeeming touch of elegance in the truck, was now in constant danger of falling off and she walked with one hand on her head and the other arm swinging widely in attempt to keep her balance. Toward six o'clock we came to a point where the path simply ended. Unbelievable. Bo has made a mistake. We will have to climb and scramble up the river itself. The boulders stretched and twisted through the narrow stream and it suddenly seemed darker under the trees, especially where river and rocks turned at a bend and left us staring at the forest that rose above. What an unholy pilgrimage began there. The line lengthened gradually until most of us could not see one another. I was far toward the end with the tippy Clarissa. As I gave her one hand after another over treacherous rocks, I smiled solicitude but inwardly cursed Bo and her both. I also realized, after a while, that she could not make it without me and I was a little afraid we were both going to be stuck out there in the desolate woods, lost from the others at night. Tom and Sylvia Dalton came up as we rested for a moment. She had come equipped with those obscure rubber sandals that Americans wear in the shower in defiance of all fashion—their only merit is that they are cheap and I said to myself that they belong only on impoverished, wretched orientals who know no better and can afford no more. Tom, at that time, was in every respect a soft-voiced nonentity; the son of a Nebraskan dentist who didn't want to go into his father's business. Our leaders, before rushing onward, had chosen him to defend the slow Sylvia struggling over the rocks with the cutting edge of the human race.

I assumed the leadership of this wayward band. By this time

it was already dark, the rocks wet by the steps of those who had gone before us were slippery beyond belief; we were sliding continually into the water with our various boots and getting soaked. The overarching tree limbs covered the river and kept out the light. In answer to my Halloo's (I hallooed because that is what one does when one is lost, in books) came back no response. We were all getting scared, this was wild country. Bo had told us to stick to the river and we would arrive at the monastery, but how far was that and could one believe such an incredible bungler?

As it began to grow dark, despite my annoyance at the high-heeled Clarissa and despite my fright, I began to get a certain satisfaction at leading my little group: for I was clearly the leader; the other three were unbelievably ineffective. In the distance, I crawled forward, testing the boulders by running my hands over them to detect any wetness, signs of footprints. Natty Bumpo from the Lower East Side. Even here, I have to admit, my experience, hitherto limited to books, was being expanded. But I was a far way from forgiving the agile Cahill, whom I fancied was by now eating hot soup with the monks.

At last, night fell, and we could move no more. We had managed to catch up with another couple, Bianca Sansome and Roger Mason. They had matches and we built a fire. Roger had the matches. He was an Esalen staff member, a grizzled character whom I had met in that first micro-lab. On that account, I had still a liking for him though we had not spoken. When I grumbled derisively about the so-called leadership that had brought us around our little fire, he objected. "Everything is all right," he said, cheerfully. I was surprised: couldn't he see that we were the victims of poor planning? We might even be attacked by animals, lost forever. Disciple of Frederick "Fritz" Perls, he didn't see it that way. He had been taught by Fritz, Esalen's senior guru at the time, not to have expectations, to live in the now. This was good experience, this was the way life was, he reasoned, you can't depend on anybody. I stared at him: no one could be so stupid. I did not realize he was telling me, albeit in the inappropriate jargon and maxims of human potentialers, to relax and enjoy what there was to enjoy and cease muttering my ego-game complaints against the feckless Cahill. That I couldn't do but I did notice, to my further irritation, that though we were both lost in the woods, he was happy and I was miserable.

The six of us remained there, gathered on a brief pocket of level bank that slightly broke the river's current and was overhung by a wooded rise. We took off our clothes to dry them by the fire and waited to be rescued. I began to relax a little, now that there were six of us and one of them, Roger, whom I could think of as a native, used to rocks and stones and trees. I remember the soft orange-yellow fire light on the bodies, the black night all around, and especially the reflection of the fire in Bianca's orange hair. It was a sweet moment, really, a necessary pause in the ludicrously painful pilgrimage. I have never realized it in a rational way before, but this "hike," which we have all joked about endlessly since then, was emblematic in many ways of the journey we were all on. It was a journey on which we all got lost and on which our leaders didn't know all of the route. We were all to go our separate ways during it and to find our way together at the end. And it would be a journey with its disasters and humors, black and white.

We passed some two hours waiting there in the dark, not knowing how far from Tassajara we were or when we would be rescued or if it were to be that night. Eventually, someone came with a light. Of all people, it was Martin Capleau—the absolute nebbish of the group. A stringy young graduate student of sociology, nervous, with a high-pitched voice, not to speak of his D. H. Lawrence beard, the vague brown eyes, his long black hair, which he stroked continually, the right hand coming over his forehead and patting his hair backward in a loving way. His wife, we learned in an encounter group later,

wore his BVD's when she ran out of panties. But this was his
finest hour, old camper Marty. Having gained the monastery
with the first pack of our ragged band, he had come back with
a bright Coleman lantern. I had expected to be rescued by
Dick Price, if by anybody, the man who had founded Esalen
with Michael Murphy. Dick looked like a hero; chiseled hand-
someness, endless strength and determination; he had out-
walked all of us, and carrying the only pack. But to be rescued
by Martin! It seemed an omen of better things. Perhaps some
surprising transformations would occur on this trip. At least it
had given Martin a chance to do his thing, to be a man. He
gathered up our group and leaping from stone to stone, leading
us forward, across to one bank and then back to the other,
wherever there was a foothold, a dry place to step upon, he
brought us to the next group. And so, gradually collecting the
rest who were waiting for the laggards and on forward to the
most swift, those who had failed of Tassajara by only a mile. It
took forever, and the pleasure of my rescue was spoiled, for
instead of moving forward with the swift, as I discovered I
could do, leather-soled riding boots notwithstanding, I must
stay behind, the very model of solicitude toward the irritating
Clarissa to whom I must show attention (1) because I had before and (2) because I had determined early on going to bed
with her and I wasn't going to give that up even though I had,
once again, ceased to enjoy the prospect. So we scrambled
along and clawed and I must endure to hear myself plead with
Martin: "Please, Marty," I would call, "don't move forward so
fast. Clarissa can hardly walk in her high heels."

As we crawled and hopped, Marty carrying the light wherever it was needed with effortless leaps, I remember that my
thoughts turned to one thing: brown laundry soap. Above
everything else, I thought of the soap that people had talked of
which, if we used it in time, would keep us from getting, in
addition to what we had already suffered, poison oak. Fatigued
and exasperated, I could think only of ending the discomfort. I

had to get to the soap. And still I crawled and scratched through the night, cooing encouragement to Clarissa, pleading with Marty for more light, my mind focused on bath and safety, retirement, no sickness, please, no itch.

We struggled in at last. My starched shirt was limp from hours of sweat, Clarissa's straw hat was stuffed in my back pocket. I got my soap and slept late the next day. That night we had an encounter group where we let fly at Bo, I most of all. I was glad that Bo had failed. In fact I announced that I was glad I had come. "Not for the hike, anybody can do that, but it's shit. I'm glad I came so I could see Bo fuck up." The debacle of the hike allowed me to dismiss anything else that was offered. It had, after all, been so built up to, it was supposed to be so momentous, a Wordsworthian transformation of the ordinary into the special. Instead, it had been a superordinary failure, there were no special insights, only the most feeble fumbling on the part of the "expert."

As I gloated over Bo's absurd contretemps, I saw my chance: "I should be the leader. At least I did the decent thing." In no far out way, no trying to break through the ceiling of human potentiality, I had led three helpless people. I had not deserted them, "I didn't selfishly run ahead." I had humanely stayed behind at the potential sacrifice of myself. And in response to my claims for leadership, Ned Downing, one of the most boring of the seemingly ordinary group, remarked, tartly: "You are only leading in one thing, Stuart." He was dismissing my claims for leadership but I had no idea what he meant. Though I hated to admit missing the point, I asked him. "Fucking," he said.

I couldn't think of a reply. I couldn't imagine why he dismissed me with such a sneer. It seemed so wrong-headed. In a worldly way I was so much the most precocious of the group. Even on the hike I had become a leader of sorts. And what was so contemptible about being attractive to women? But the others seemed to understand what he was saying, or some of them did. I came to see it, but I couldn't then: I simply had no idea of what the Residential Program or Esalen was all about. For me, breaking through the human potential meant relatively simple things like further achievements along the lines which I had known before. When I thought of developing the human potential to the fullest, I thought of Leonardo: development of the intellect, of the craft of engineering, of the aesthetic sense, of the body as vehicle for performance. For me value was something that came from a human being and was bluntly externalized in the environment. I did not realize clearly until over a year later that the models that these people were proposing to imitate, insofar as they knew what they were after, were not Western artists, engineers, and scientists, but rather the mystics. Their heroes, insofar as they had them, were not Mozart or Einstein but San Juan de la Cruz and Ramakrishna. And I had never thought that accomplishments could be developments of the soul, of the heart, of the veins and arteries and the subtle messages and meanings of the blood.

I can be thankful that at some level I knew, at least, where our culture had arrived and had had the good sense to bring myself to one of the places where the new culture was being formed. But, I had no idea how different this new culture would be, how alien its values. So when Bo, the one among our teachers who was the furthest out, who most talked about strange things such as "getting into one's body" and "getting into new spaces," had shown himself incapable of succeeding in the merest task, one that the lowliest scoutmaster could perform, it was easy to dismiss him and Downing and the rest of the pack who would follow Bo rather than me. The next day, when we were supposed to sit at zazen meditation with the Tassajara monks, I scorned this endless hankering after strange gods, uncomfortable positions and walks, rice, gruel and brown bread. How could Bo know what was right? And what did these strange monks know?

And yet, even then, it could not stay this simple. No one at Tassajara walked. The monks, the students, boys and girls, they all ran through the little village-like group of buildings, up and down the main street. Even the dogs ran. How unlike Esalen with its vague sensuality. And despite the intensity with which they ran and the purposefulness with which they went about everything—eating, gardening, meditating—there was also a serenity about this place: the priests, the master, even the senior students strode toward you with the dignity and poise of Roman senators, only to break into a frantic run. Brown rice and strange rituals but it puzzled me. There was a tremendous strength and power in these people and I could never, for a moment, dismiss them as kooks. They were simply another kind of person, I decided. Religious, like the priests and rabbis that I knew: odd men, unworldly and therefore laughable, and yet, by common consent, not really failures but deserving of respect: limited but admirable. They are just different from ordinary people. All the more ludicrous that the bungling hikers and their leaders tried to settle for two days, like tourists of spiritual countries, into the habits of eating, sleeping, praying, and all the rest, of these special people. I dwelt happily with Clarissa fucking and drinking wine. I was glad to have survived the hike, glad to be in such an exotic place, glad that Bo had failed, glad that the group was being so absurd. When, at five-thirty a.m., the great ceremonial drums and gongs began sounding monks and my Residents to morning meditation, the dogs running with the boys and girls and men, I sneered as I turned over in my sleep at the pathetic attempt of worldly failures to try and imitate such serious people.

It never occurred to me that two days of meditation might be the beginning of something, maybe not a life of Zen meditation, but something. I had learned how to avoid both failure and experience. When I was fifteen the creative-writing teacher told me that my first short stories were lousy and I decided not to be a writer. No new things for me, thank you. Excellence, excellence. If you can't be excellent, don't try. Die, you incompetent mediocre son of a bitch, only test pilots in this man's air force!

CHAPTER SIX

doubts

when it was time, at last, to return to Esalen, there began again the seemingly endless rounds of encountering that we had pursued from the first day. Occasionally another Esalen guru, like Bernard Gunther, would come in to lead us in some exercise, spiritual, interpersonal, or bodily, but encountering was the heart of the Program. It was very unpleasant—continuous confrontations, eight, twelve hours a day, sniping and bickering and fighting. But Bill Schutz insisted that we keep at it—we must form a group before the Program could go on, he said, and if we had to fight in order to do it then we must fight. The tone had been set the first night by Sylvia Dalton and Marvin Handleman. Unresolved, the thing continued in the morning. She had been an Esalen staff member—when the Resident Program had started she had been turned out of her little cabin so that Marvin's young children could use it. Bill's philosophy dictated that she must explore her hostility, confront it with the hope of getting through it. By this time Handleman returned Sylvia's anger—he would protect his kids from the shame Sylvia was laying on him: someone who had turned a pretty girl out into the cold. He hadn't done it, the Esalen management had.

"Fuck you, bitch."

"I *really* hate you, now," she hissed.

Bill suggested they walk silently toward each other from opposite corners of the room, then do whatever they felt like when they met. Slowly. Slowly. Then they stand there, in the middle, glaring at each other. At last, she slaps him, he returns it, she snarls and goes for him. Grabbing her wrists in his hands, Handleman pins her to the floor. She struggles, then she gives up. She stands. Then he. He looks into her eyes and holds her at arm's length by the shoulders. And smiles.

"One hell of a broad!" he beams.

It is over but I don't believe the ending. Nothing seems accomplished. I hate violence and don't believe Bill's explanation for it: we've got to experiment with not holding anything back, if we are to live more fully. The scene seems so contrived, the confrontation so forced. People don't get to know each other this way.

I sat on my canvas-backed captain's chair, like the other spectators, watching. I sat and I observed and then I joined in. If it was brutal honesty they wanted, I could be tougher than any of them. I told them so. I told them how mediocre they were. I told Pamela how unreal she was, already Schutz's puppet. I told Betty she was a physical monster and that she would never escape being the simple-minded school teacher she had been; I told Bill that he lacked any style, Bo that he lacked everything; I dispensed large doses of advice leaning back in my captain's chair: Linda had to divorce Martin, Martin had to become a man, Joseph had to go to college, Marcia had to become more feminine, Tom had to stop pretending to be a nice guy, and so forth. And not just once, but each time something they did confirmed my intuition I straightened them out about themselves.

They were a little intimidated at first—many of them—and then the reaction began. Tom: "Don't you think it a little pretentious to wear a starched shirt and a silk tie this far out in the country?" I dismissed him with a smile. I wore my shirt and tie insistently, just for this reason, to call attention to the difference between me and the others. The dentist's son in his T shirt had fallen into the trap. The same when they attacked my English accent: I couldn't hear the accent but I knew that I had taught myself to avoid the ugly tones of Lower East Side natives, taught myself starting at age ten. I was a self-made man. No such obvious assaults could harm me—I knew myself and was proud of what I was.

It was at the beginning of the second week that they began to get to me. Nick Moskowitz, of all people, the most wooden among them, simply dismissing what I was saying about someone in the middle of my statement. He was tired of hearing the record he said. A few others nodded in disgust. I sat silently for an hour and then dispensed some other piece of advice. Again, the same reaction—this time from Tom. That afternoon when I began to speak, even buck-teethed Sylvia, she, of the Mexican serapes, rubber sandals, and Peace Corps, had learned courage: "Is it going to be the same old shit, Stuart?"

Old shit? My students had been interested in what I had to say, my professorial colleagues had been interested, even the United States Government had been interested. But these people, with whom I had been the most candid, had lost interest in a week. I was too disengaged, they said, too uninvolved, not giving enough. Somehow, I was missing the point of a lot that went on. I puzzled and puzzled and it did no good. I grew angry. How dare they not be interested in me? Fuck them, I know my own worth.

I counterattack, ignoring their ignoring my comments. Robert Portman, with exasperation as if to swat a fly: "Stuart, you always sit with one foot tucked under you. Where did you learn that?" I thought. "I don't know, Robert, I think I remember one of my first girl friends, one I loved very much, doing it. I guess I picked it up from her." What is he after, I wonder. Is he going to say I'm effeminate because I imitated an old girl friend? I feel uncomfortable. Robert is tall, a psychologist. He studies me, mouth hanging open, and his brown eyes pointing into me. Robert: "I think you do it because it makes you seem taller, it elevates you above people and you want to be above them so you can deliver your pronouncements." "Nonsense," I swat back. But this trivial remark gets me going. What if he's right? Can it be that someone sees something about me that I don't? I am a short man. Do I resort to such an obvious ploy, and so unconsciously?

And then there was that comment of Betty Fuller's when I boasted to them how, from earliest childhood, I had consciously created myself, piece by piece, and I had made myself an accomplished person. Because of these efforts, I made more money (for my age), my accent was better than theirs, my manners, my mind, my knowledge.

"Don't you have any sense of yourself as a whole?" she asked.

"No," I answered. "I wrote a book to show that people aren't whole." * She shook her head and it made me wonder, barely at the level of consciousness. Am I wrong? Is my heartfelt book about picaresque people really only about me? NO, NO. They are lying, *they* are self-deceived, it must be so, but a sense of doubt begins to come upon me.

* *The Picaresque Novel* (Cleveland, Ohio: Case Western Reserve University Press, 1967).

I ride Bo. I ride him as hard as I can. He seems meek, soft-voiced, effeminate. (Secretly, dimly: I am afraid I am effeminate but he really is effeminate.) He is incompetent. He is vague. "Come on, Bo, let's see you lead this group. Let's see you do something. You don't like encounter, so let's see something else. Come on, Bo. You know what I want to do with you, Bo? Fuck you up the ass. Up the ass!"

"How about fighting me, Stuart?" I look him over, a touch of fear in me. My chest is bigger, my muscles bulkier, better defined—one of the accomplishments, I had put on muscles. I had lifted weights as a teen-ager. I was well built. Bo seemed soft, like a peach.

"Bo, if I fight with you, I'm not going to fuck around. I'll try to kill you. I've never had a fight since I was a kid [the showy muscles were supposed to protect me from having to fight: see these muscles, don't mess with me], but I think if I fight now I won't be able to control myself." I am trembling. He doesn't back down. I would become a monster, the hurts in me would be released and I would rip him open, I would seize his jaw and rip it open.

We fight. I go for his balls, true to my anticipation of what would happen. He knocks me down, wrestles me to the ground, his elbow clips my eye, I am defeated quickly, like a child, I give up, all I have to show is my black eye given me by Bo, the crypto-faggot/incompetent.

(What the hell is happening? How could he beat me? I know I am stronger and yet he beat me. In the arm-wrestling we did, others, whom I can see are weaker, have beat me too. What the hell is wrong? Where is my strength? Why can't I call on it?) Everywhere I turn, doubt; every experience generates doubt; and then fear; and from fear and doubt I return, I have no choice, I cannot abide this much doubt, doubt about my strength, about my manhood, about the way I sit, about the worth of my remarks—all challenged. I return to my clothes, my education, my taste, my muscles, my accent, my clothes, my education, my taste . . .

Bo had told us a lot about the importance of "body work." Schutz had agreed. They both talked a lot about the body saying how important "body work" was, how we had all gotten alienated from our bodies, lost the capacity for pleasure, for self-expression. They said that it was a typical problem for modern people to perceive their bodies split off from their minds—one reason why people felt alienated from themselves. Techniques of "body work" would help us get ourselves back together.

I had no idea what they were talking about. My body was fine. Well, muscled, I fucked a lot, and despite Catherine and Martha, I assured myself that I did it well.

We had a "sensory awakening" session with Bernard Gunther. A gentle man, he asked us to do such simple things as walk casually among ourselves and simply touch hands or faces as we walked. Or he asked us to sit opposite one another and have a "conversation" with our hands alone, touching, including in the "conversation" a variety of emotions like anger and caring.

I remember the two sessions with agony. I felt scared. I didn't understand it. Other people seemed to be having a good time being playful with each other but I was baffled.

"Stop. Close your eyes and simply feel what is happening in your back right now." I didn't feel anything—what did he mean? What were these people experiencing that they would open their eyes with blissful looks? My mind raced to think my way through this thing, to no avail.

Bernie came up to me after the second session and remarked, "You find this very difficult, don't you? Maybe we could do some work privately sometime."

I was comforted, in a way, but it annoyed me, too. He had

seen my fright. Why was he so interested in me? Did he think there was something wrong?

Even the positive experiences were unsettling. One day, after long hours of quarreling in the group, Joseph said it: "I'm Jewish." There was a long sticky silence and we looked at each other and then at the floor. Then Herbert Retter: "Me, too." As if one couldn't have guessed with his hooked nose. Then Schutz, and Handleman, and me. The measure of our hesitation to come right out and *say* it was the brazen directness to which we forced ourselves: Miller-Jew, Retter-Jew, Schutz-Jew. We admitted as we identified ourselves that part of us wanted to hide the fact and then, brushing aside the voice of tolerant American reason ("so big deal, you're Jewish—you're still like the rest of us"), there we rushed, to the middle of the floor in front of the goyim who watched the pain, and also the pride. I tasted a wonderful warmth of recognition but afterward I didn't like it. It was safer to keep concealing, keep running from the past, pretending I was nothing: not Jew, not Christian. I shrunk from the seduction of comradeship we had offered to each other.

It seemed harder and harder to keep my perspective on who these people were. The focus came round to Ned Downing, the boring but handsome young man, about twenty-five. He had been a championship college wrestler and his bulky muscles showed under his tight clothes. His voice was too quiet. I sensed, lurking in that powerful body, behind the cover of nice guy quietness, a mighty engine for physical harm. Good-looking though he was, it came out that he was a virgin. I was surprised and somehow I made an intuitive leap: I announced that I sensed that he wanted to kill women. Of course the gentle lad denied it. He wanted to talk about his mother and father. Finally, Bill suggested Ned put a pillow in front of him so that he might imagine his mother seated there, in the room. "Talk to her." He began and it all came out. The father had deserted them early. The mother had turned to alcohol. The boy was frequently left alone. She came in late, drunk. She brought men to the house and they slept with her. She yelled. She beat the boy. As he told all these recollections to the pillow, he began to get angry. Bill encouraged him to hit the pillow and with a great howl the anticipated explosion came; he gnashed his teeth and spitted from between them with hurt, he pounded with iron fists, a fit of rage. "Bitch! Bitch! Bitch!" Bill asked for volunteers to play the roles of Ned's parents in a psychodrama.

I sat smirking with satisfaction about the keenness of my insight. But I wasn't going to risk myself for the putative therapy of this monster. The whole group held back. You could feel the fear of those well-developed muscles and the fury that hid behind that pleasant looking face of Downing's.

And then Catherine moved forward, that pathetic old bag. Here she was stepping forward to help this fellow and risking her person to do it.

She was very good at it. She played the mother well, showing him the other side: "Dear, your father deserted me, I was all alone with a little boy. I know I wasn't a good mother but I did my best. Remember how I used to cuddle you?" But it was too soon for Downing, he couldn't see the other side, too angry, he slapped back at Catherine. Again and again. And she stayed there, playing the mother who had suffered along with the little boy. She was brave. That old bag was brave. And I was a coward. She had given. I had held back.

Herbert Retter looked, when I first saw him, like the all-time cornball. A tall man of about forty, with bulging black eyes, a great beaked nose, and tiny feet. He was wearing cheap, city sport clothes at Esalen. Pushed back to expose his black curly hair he wore a cheap Mexican straw hat with a short brim—the kind made for American tourists who want something to take home that the boys at the bowling alley will find droll. All over it he had pinned buttons for SANE, CORE, SNCC, all the four-letter organizations, and Women's Strike for Peace. When this character told me he was writing novels, I nearly choked on the roast pork I was eating for dinner. He had heard I was an English professor and he wanted me to read one of his unpublished manuscripts.

I hated to read original works. I had spent a decade reading the greatest literary works in many languages. I had standards and they were high. It was always an embarrassment to come up against a hopeful author because the stuff was *never* any good. As one of my former Yale professors paraphrased Horace, "Pretty good poetry is like pretty fresh eggs—either poetry, literature, is first class, or it tastes bad."

Herbert kept dogging me, insisting, like one of the bad authors in the *Dunciad*. He trapped me on the second Sunday out by the back porch. It was sunny but a cool breeze was blowing. I wanted to relax and just think about the new week of encountering that would begin the next day. But he insisted. So I took the white manuscript box from his hand and began to read.

I was right in my expectation. The book was badly written; the characters were wooden, the style lacked any metaphorical or symbolic force. It was a long and tedious tale about a tuberculosis patient facing death on a desert island. It was supposed to be highly significant; all it lacked, I thought, were neon signs, erect at fifteen-page intervals and flashing: PORTENTOUS MESSAGE, PORTENTOUS MESSAGE, PORTENTOUS MESSAGE.

I read the first few chapters with care, taking notes on what I saw as the book's flaws. I never liked doing that kind of thing. Too often, on student papers, when asked for an evaluation I would have to work like mad to provide a rationale for my judgment. Students, as had Retter, would put their hearts into papers and when they came back with a "C" I felt bad for them. I had to explain. I had to justify the verdict. I owed them

that much. I didn't want to have to judge, the system made me
and I didn't want to be thought arbitrary or cruel. But I la-
bored over those first few chapters. After that I realized the
book didn't work, so I skimmed onward, turning over a hundred of those carefully typed pages in an hour, scribbling some
ten pages of notes. I searched my learning for helpful compari-
sons with Flaubert and James, the masters of fiction. I did my
duty. I had no desire to demolish.

At the end, as if getting up from a bad meal that I had been
forced to eat against my will, I found Herbert, who had been
wandering around the lodge. He had seen me reading and
skimming. As I handed the manuscript back I reluctantly gave
him the bad news: the book had many flaws, from a literary
point of view. I had read it critically and carefully and here
were my notes, which I hoped would be of some use, ten pages
—see, Herb, I'm not dismissing you, I'm a good guy, a responsible critic.

He took the manuscript with one hand, the ten pages of
notes with the other. Then he leaned over and let the slight pile
of notes slide with a thud into the empty wooden wastepaper
basket by the bench on the front porch.

I was astonished. I protested. I had worked, I had written
notes to be helpful even though I hadn't wanted to read any
book this afternoon.

He came at me from left field: "Anybody who reads a book
about death, into which has gone so much life experience and
real suffering, in two and a half hours, and still finds time to
take notes, has nothing to say. You don't know anything about
life."

"Listen, Herbert, experience or not, I can tell good writing."
"You can't if you just did what you did."
"O.K., so what's your claim to experience?"
"I'm the guy in that book. I've spent six months in a hospital
thinking I'm going to die. Want more? I marched in my first
labor union protest when I was ten. I've worked in prison as a

psychologist, with guys who murdered. I've sold aluminum siding door-to-door. Once I ran a chain of cleaning stores. How's that, boychick? I haven't spent my life in school." His anger was passing as he spoke and he put his white box under his arm and strolled away.

It had never occurred to me before that books were really versions of experience. Maybe he was right, maybe I couldn't understand a book about death, couldn't judge it at all because death hadn't entered my life: no pain, no sickness, no one close had died, even.

My parents used to tell me that book-learning isn't everything. It was beginning to occur to me at Esalen that their hated homily might be right. I had made a life out of books but the books, I was realizing, were about life. It was true what Henry James had said: experience needn't be gross like Herbert's hospital beds, cleaning stores, and prisons. Experience could be the observation of a hand flicking a fan in a way that reveals to the double-eyed opera glasses of the acute observer all the contents of a heart. But I was beginning to realize that I didn't know all that much about hearts, and besides there weren't, it turned out, all that many fans and opera glasses in my own 1960s America. There were a lot of Herbert Retters and Catherines and cooks and cabin girls, Bettys and Neds and countless others, all of whom I was meeting for the first time since childhood, I was allowing myself to meet, at Esalen. Such souls, who in other days I had considered negligible philistines, were very much here, telling me things, interfering with my prejudices, hitting hard. And when they hit, I found, I could hit back but they did not disappear; they were persistently there. I wondered how was I to get this experience that Herbert talked of? Could it be that I really knew nothing as he implied, as others seemed to imply?

The encounter group resumed the next day with a new excitement. We were breaking through barriers and taboos quickly—fighting, crying, confessing. A sense of exhilaration began to blow up—maybe we were heading toward a new intimacy and free experimentation. Even I felt something of this.

I went to the morning meeting on the fifteenth day, thinking, despite my alienation and suspicion, of doing something extraordinary: taking off my clothes. I had not really "thought" about it, it just felt like the appropriate thing to do, the next step. But I was afraid and held back.

Herbert entered, in his absurd straw hat and huge puffy pants, a tasteless black jersey with chartreuse collar and wrists. He seated himself in his chair, leaned back, held the fingertips of his hands together, staring at them with his bulging black eyes, thinking.

After a while, I noticed him, already half-undressed. He took off the rest of his clothes and sat down, utterly diverting attention from whatever else was going on. "I felt like it," he said. "I've exposed myself in other ways, and it seemed right."

I was annoyed that he had grabbed the chance instead of me but I was also a bit frightened. I had seen many of these people naked, of course, in the baths. I had even been in bed with a couple of the women. But this was different, taking off clothes in a meeting room, everybody sitting back, relaxed and intelligent, in their canvas captain's chairs. I took mine off. It felt good—kind of heady to take such a chance. Others followed our lead, standing up, taking off their clothes, sitting down again, totally naked, grinning at each other.

I looked cheerfully around the room and saw Linda hesitating. She was dressed, as usual, in cheap faded pedal pushers and a worn red T shirt, so many times washed and stretched as to have no shape. Her hair was cut like a boy's. I wanted her to stop hiding herself under that wretched costume. She was a woman, damn it, and it was time to confront the fact. Just because her husband was a weakling, she didn't have to deny her womanhood. Divorce the bastard, I thought. I put aside the irritation though, and in a kind of loving way I did a good thing for Linda. I asked her to undress. She thought about it and she did. But she stayed in her chair while she did it. With that cumbersome awkwardness, one knee raised, the other foot steadying the performance by gripping the floor, she managed to slip off her pants and panties and bra without getting out of her chair, seeking to withhold some last secret shame from us by hurriedly crossing her knees and arms and hunching forward. She looked thoughtfully, a trifle depressed, at the floor. Very slowly, I said, "Linda, now I am going to ask you to do something very, very brave," almost as if to a child, cooing the frightening request. "I want you to stand up and show us yourself." She hesitated. I was asking a lot from her. Then, she stood up, awkwardly, and I remember the surprise, the general gasp in the room: "You're beautiful!" And, indeed, she had been hiding a perfect woman's body, muscled, yet finely formed, like an ancient Greek statue.

There was, you see, kindness, too, though we were all pushing so hard for enlightenment or happiness or the human potential or whatever the hell it was we were pushing for. There was love.

CHAPTER SEVEN

⁂ rat pack and death trip ⁂

i knew there were things about myself that all agreed were bad, absurd, and trivial, but I didn't understand what they were talking about. I suspected that there was something in what they said, but in the larger group we never seemed to get to the point of clarification. There were so many of us, and we were inclined to be impatient and I would not trust myself to all of them together. I hated being labeled "impossible," whatever that meant, and not taken seriously, but I would not trust myself to Sylvia, and Tom, and Martin, and the great mass of mediocrities.

Late one afternoon, I asked for special help. I asked Bill, and Robert and Martha to make a small group for me and help me through my impasse. "Keep it in the group," Bill said, "no sub-grouping." He thought it a bad idea and refused to help. But I was getting so scared of being totally bewildered by the Residents that I insisted. Bo and Robert agreed to meet with me right then, before dinner, and to try their hands. "We've got to break through to him" said Bo, and Robert nodded. I smiled to myself—I liked the special attention.

We went to Bo's room, a dreary brown place with the mattress laid on the floor, for reasons of orthopedic hygiene no doubt. I thought that a bad omen. The mattress was in the corner opposite the door and it was on the mattress that they asked me to sit. Robert was the prime mover in the affair. Robert put it: "Bo, let's get him to take off his clothes, that way it will be easier for us to get to him." I have often wondered whether they meant to be as mean as they seemed. Their object was to get me to expose myself physically, thinking that then I could better expose myself in other ways, but no one seemed to realize that they were literally cornering me and that they were undressing only me: it seemed like it was to be a one-way confrontation. Later on, when it was getting late and there was danger that we would miss dinner, they sent Susan Kalla down for stuff but refused to feed me, the better to break down my "resistances." Robert and I discussed the affair months later and he admitted with some reserve that they had "rat-packed" me but I don't suppose I was clear about that until these moments writing this account. They were trying to help me but in their frustration, their inexperience, and for whatever other reasons, they turned on me viciously.

It went on for hours.

"I can't reach him Robert, can you?"

"I'll try again, Bo. Now, Stuart, all we want from you is an emotional response—something genuine and personal, something you really feel. Now, how do you feel about us, for example?"

"I like you, Robert."

"Now, come on, Stuart—you think that Martha and I re-

jected and humiliated you. Can you get in touch with that feeling of hurt?"

"I don't feel it now."

"You're blocking, Stuart. Can you try to feel it in your body,
the hurt?"

"Sorry, Robert, I don't feel anything."

BO: "O.K. How do you feel about the rest of us, then?"

"Well, Bo, I guess I like you, in a way. I think you're incompetent as a leader of the program, and I don't approve of . . ."

"Stuart!" he yelled at me, "can you come up with a feeling
and not an essay? We all know you can think!"

"But that's the way I feel, Bo."

He shook his head.

It went on for hours like that. I watched them eat. After
dinner, Susan, Bo's girl friend, got up, bored. She was twenty-
two, just out of some California college, and she had been working in the Esalen office until Bo insisted she be admitted to the
Residential Program. She didn't usually say much. I suspected
she was dumb and wondered why a Ph.D. like Bo bothered
with her. She went into the adjacent bathroom where she proceeded to set her short, dark hair with blue plastic curlers, leaving the door open so she could hear, and in full view of all of
us.

I became quietly angry. First, because she had become
bored with me, and second, because she showed it. No manners, I thought, and no manners in setting her hair in public.
That was what I meant about this group; no sense of decorum,
one doesn't make-up on stage, one just doesn't wear curlers in
public. She went on curling her hair. I restrained my comment.
Surely she knew how lower class, how American, how common
and cheap she was being. I was embarrassed for her—she had
just gotten careless. She would stop soon, I thought to myself.
But she didn't: middle and forefinger lifted a wet lock and the
other hand snapped the plastic into position. At last, embarrassed for her or not, my disgust erupted—there was little I

needed to say, I thought, so charged was I with a sense of the obviousness of it all. She would wither at a hint: "Susan, one isn't supposed to curl his hair in public. It's offensive."

I was amazed. She didn't miss a beat. Susan calmly faced her mirror, not even bothering to reply to my comments about her bad taste, blue curler following blue curler. How could she not listen to me? How could she not conform to those rules I had so painfully learned myself and so clearly passed down to this heathen? It was as if she was saying to me that there were things more important than *style* and *manners* and *propriety* and being concerned about what others thought. One's own daily ease and comfort were more important. Even my silent hard stare had no effect. Susan wanted to curl her hair and she wanted to listen to what was going on. *Voilà*—the curler and the open door. One could suit oneself. And, if one decided to suit oneself, I thought, then to what end my painful learning of the scale of behaviors? To what end my labor in climbing the ladder of manners? How was I better than others, more highly placed and therefore more secure, if the only person I had to please, most of the time, was myself? If curlers could be made public, consciously public, then most of what I had to call my own was worthless. The absurdity of it. There I sit, in an ugly brown cabin in Big Sur, naked, unfed, tired, being rat-packed, a character out of *The Rape of the Lock*. It is no wonder that I got very confused and the other participants handled the situation very badly.

Robert and Martha and Bo attacked me continually. Most of what I remember about that evening was the exasperation of all of them. They wanted an emotional response and they baited me endlessly to get it and I got more and more determined not to trust them because they seemed so angry.

I was sitting up on the mattress, very tired by now. The general exasperation of the group was reaching its acme when Martha extended an arm, pointing her finger at my crotch, and shouted, "Look, Robert, he's got an infection."

Two weeks before, shortly after I had been to bed with
Catherine and Martha, they both came down with vaginal in-
fections. They had surmised and it had become public knowledge that I had some sort of infection. I thought nothing about
it, continuing to fuck other girls. Once before, about a year
previous, I had given a girl vaginitis and gone to a doctor about
it. He had told me that there was no way short of laboratory
tests that one could tell if a man was transmitting vaginitis—it
didn't affect the man, only the woman, and it came and went so
quickly that by the time the woman had it, after five days or so
of incubation, the man might have been cured. When Martha
shouted, I looked at my penis.

I was ashamed that it had been the focus of so many eyes.
There were red splotches on it.

Martha said, "He gave me the infection, Robert, and he
knew he had it."

I protested. "I always have those red irritated patches, from
masturbating," I admitted, ashamed still more to have to admit
that. But even my embarrassment and shame were not enough
for them. Robert demanded to look more closely. He wanted
an explanation. I explained again: I generally had those red
splotches but they didn't mean I was infected, the doctor had
told me one couldn't tell by physical inspection if a man was
going to give a woman vaginitis, he had told me that.

Martha practically shrieked: "Why didn't you go to a doctor
this time if you had those red marks? Maybe it was different
from last time? Why? I hurt so much I've cried every time I've
peed for two weeks. Robert and I haven't been able to make
love since you fucked me. Catherine is sick and God knows
how many of your other girls!"

I was amazed at the anger. I felt wronged. Unjustly accused.
I protested again. But Robert and Martha were furious at me,
furious. Part of me reasoned that they were angry with me,
really, for having fucked Martha in the first place. But a part of
me found something, some element, hard to explain away;

there was something they were saying that was hard to excuse, but I couldn't quite get it.

Martha was weeping in memory of her pain. Robert leaned over me: "If she doesn't get well, I'm going to cut your balls off."

I tried to smile him down: "Come on, Robert, you're not going to do anything to anybody." But his eyes bulged in a way not entirely melodramatic. He meant it. "I'm angry at you, really angry, and if you hurt Martha again I will cut your balls off." Then he asked: "Can *you* really be angry?"

"Of course," I said. "You've seen me be angry with practically everybody in the Resident Program."

"NO, I don't mean sniping. I mean anger. Anger you can feel in your body. Do you have the slightest idea of what I'm feeling?" His face turned red with the strain.

"But, Robert," I said, "I didn't do anything wrong. I told you what the doctor said."

"If you had red marks on your prick, you should have gone to the doctor to check. You knew you had gotten two girls sick."

"I didn't think it would mean anything, those red marks. I always have them."

He looked at me, more calmly, almost clinically: "You just didn't want to take the trouble. You didn't want to miss a fuck" —a bit with wonder—"you're a sociopath."

I was even more confused by that word. I didn't know what it meant. And it was further embarrassing to admit that I didn't know.

Robert hissed the explanation: "A sociopath is someone who hurts society, hurts people, wants to hurt them."

There was something overdone about all this, I thought. Robert's emotions were always just a tiny bit hard to believe, they seemed slightly worked up. But I felt, nevertheless, the force of his hurt and anger. And I felt the force of the word "sociopath." Apparently, there were things I did not know, about biology and medicine for example, that I should know. I should have seen a doctor about my prick, they were saying. And I had no compassionate regard for the sickness of these girls. I was willing to let the girls after Martha and Catherine take their chances because I had had one experience with a doctor. I began to see that in the eyes of these people, far from being the reasonably decent sort that I saw myself being, I was selfish and all too careless with other people's bodies. They couldn't understand how embarrassing it was for me to go to a doctor and say I had been fucking and haul out my prick—what would he think? They were so angry with me anyway that they wouldn't even listen to what my first doctor had said.

I went round and round in my own mind, defending myself, arguing my case again, reasoning that I wasn't that bad. And yet, at the end, some vague dread remained. Were they right about me?

A little while later, as I put on my clothes to leave, I thanked them, imagine that, for the evening. The next morning I told Herbert that it had been a good thing though I was too confused to know how to specify why it had been so. Herbert waved aside my praise. "That group," he said, "they have nothing to teach you—they mind-fucked you." I wasn't sure, myself, but in the next few days I remembered more of the hurt than the insights, the shouting at me, the pushing on me. I began to fear that group—they were unreliable, experimenters with people, not to be trusted. That sociopath stuff was nonsense: Robert was angry at me because of my fucking Martha and Bo hated me for exposing his incompetence.

When, in succeeding days, I returned to the Residential group, I found the atmosphere hostile; not just toward me, generally hostile. More fights, physical confrontations. More sniping. Bo and Robert and Joseph were grumbling about the lack of imagination in the group, the lack of a religious or mystical cast, the lack of real daring. They wanted more. Herbert Retter and Marvin Handleman, the two men whom I considered the most mature and solid of the Residents, were more and more withdrawing from the Program: they considered it childish. I found Schutz's leadership already clichéd. He admitted that the group had already gone beyond any group he had ever known before as far as intimacy, self-disclosure, and risk-taking went. Yet he was running it like groups he had known before. It made no sense. He seemed a clumsy and heavy-handed Prussian, working us too hard, too relentlessly, too simply relying on the brutal confrontations of encounter. The pace was exhausting. He was driving us, driving me, beyond what was comfortable, what seemed endurable. I needed help from others. I had not been able to get it from the group of twenty-two; I had not been able to get it from a smaller group of some of the most talented; I was definitely not going to get it when the larger group had become factionated and bogged down in discussions about how the group should be run or what the program should do. I began missing group sessions. Driving to Berkeley in my car, visiting Diane, just staying away.

I entered the lodge a crowded, smoky Friday night after missing two days of encounter. Lots of new seminarians; the usual disorder of the beginning of a weekend at Esalen. The seminarians came to the weekend seminars or to five-day workshops from Monday to Friday. There was always new excitement when a new group of them arrived. My absence had increased my anxiety but I was also curious to know what had happened with the Residents while I was gone. Ken Barker, a slightly malicious smile on his face, asked, "Haven't you heard about the death trip?" He grinned across the table at Linda: "We're all going to die on Sunday."

I pretended to be amused but I didn't find it funny at all— what new madness was this? Herbert, it seemed, had convinced the Residents to try something that he promised would break our stalemate, our bickering, and our uncertainty about what to do since we had apparently exhausted encounter. We all wanted to change, he had said. Well, he had already had his change—his mystical experience—a week ago. We would get nowhere in an encounter group, he had said. There we paid attention only to our faults, and we struggled to rid ourselves of them with a manic fury: pathetic and laughable, twenty-two adults sitting in a circle each trying like mad to bend down, pull on his bootstraps, and raise himself to unknown and vague heights of humanity. We had to go "way out," Herbert said. He agreed with Bo and Robert and Joseph. They talked about taking risks. O.K. Let's get to it—let's die and see if we can be reborn.

I listened with artificial enthusiasm as Ken talked. At least it was an alternative to the encounter group which I had repeatedly attacked. When Ken explained the rest, I could hardly believe it: Herbert had persuaded the group to let him lead them to where he claimed to have gotten in his experience. We were all to spend the weekend preparing for death, saying good-by to life and imagining that Sunday night we were to die. That night, we would descend to the baths. Each of us would be wrapped in a wet sheet at midnight. Herbert would be assisted in wrapping us by Robert and Joseph, younger wizards. Then he would wrap them. The sheet would keep us warm. It would be impossible for us to get out of the sheet or even to move because the wet sheet would stick to itself so that no force from within could budge it. Through the night, we would struggle or lie still, piss and shit in it, scream, go mad, change our minds—no matter. There would be candles and drumming. At the beginning I would read poetry about death. Herbert alone would be free to move and he, master of these grisly ceremonies, would carry a long knife, for symbolic purposes and maybe more. He would unwrap the sheet when he judged each of us ready.

Herbert had come up as they were explaining this to me: "Quite a scheme," I ventured.

"It's no scheme. You really will die that night. I've got some surprises in store. Spend the weekend preparing—I want you to read death poetry." Then he got up and walked away.

The scheme had seized the imagination of my fellows, and they enthusiastically unfolded it to me, with all the glee of slightly older children telling a younger one about some imaginary monster that would swallow him up. The social pressure was considerable. And indeed, it was intriguing: like a ghost story. I never really expected that I would have to go through with it: I wouldn't. It was too scary, too uncomfortable, without plausible rationale, too dangerous. And I was not about to trust myself so completely to anyone, especially to somebody who was hinting that he really might kill some of us. After all, suppose I wasn't one of the lucky ones who could persuade him of their right to survival? No, they couldn't really be serious about it.

On the other hand, the group had never been so welded together, never so uniformly enthusiastic about a plan. Maybe here was a scheme to give new life to the program, maybe we could become a group through this wildness and I could get what I needed, whatever that was.

I put aside my fears, from time to time, and tried to get into the thing. But, by Saturday afternoon, I heard gossip. Robert Portman had approached Bill. The death trip idea was a good one, said Robert the psychic adventurer, but he didn't trust Herbert to be the person in charge. He and Joseph should be free, too. Herbert had become too freaky. As soon as I heard that Robert was objecting to a part of the procedure and urging the calling of a meeting, Sunday night, before the death trip at midnight, to discuss the details, I was relieved and glad. I became smugly certain that our group, warring once again with one another, would never go through with this experience. I think *I* told the rumors to Herbert, personally, partly to defuse his energies for I did not want to die, in any way, and partly to enjoy his defeat (that was all our styles then).

By this time, my own attitudes toward Herbert were completely mixed. I felt respect for his having so much experience of the world—he could teach me. I was also impressed by his mystical experience; I knew that he had contacted some basic knowledge and that it had given him special gifts. Furthermore, he had defended me in the group. I remember when I was being universally attacked for being some variety of "bastard," he had dismissed such comments, affirming "Stuart is a sweetheart." There were times when I needed the protection of this big guy. On the other hand, I was frightened of him. He had become very arrogant after his "experience." When you challenged one of his statements he would merely fix you with his bulging eyes, nod slowly, several times, and simply say, "I know." This was weird but somehow Herbert, the Jewish boy from Brooklyn turned novelist and guru, was not as weird and frightening as Robert and Joseph. Herbert and I, it had turned out, had both gone to the same high school: one of those public schools reserved for bright members of the New York middle classes, nearly all Jewish, who couldn't afford to go to private school but who would make it to college, somehow. We had striven over the same paths. Robert and Joseph and Bo were goyim, naturally prone to madness and excess. If Herbert seemed crazy at times, I knew nonetheless that deep down he was safe.

In fact, once he got the news of Robert's resistance he wanted to abandon the freaky death trip completely; he became quiet and seemed to look his normal self—a silly looking, big, nice guy who had recently had an unusual experience.

As Sunday night approached I knew what I wanted. No death trip. And no encounter. That method was clearly bankrupt—we would never become a group by personal confrontation. I needed room to breathe: let's have a program but let it be more individualized, let people find their own way. Encounter meant only more bickering. As far as I was concerned that one experience at Old Westbury was enough.

On Sunday night discussion began with Robert voicing his hesitation about Herbert being the only leader of the death trip. It took only a few minutes. When parts of his scheme were objected to, Herbert did not defend himself. Instead, he condemned the group for being afraid of truly taking risks in the interest of getting somewhere special.

"Do whatever you want, I'm not going to participate in anything. I'm out of it." He sat there silently while many of the others implored him to lead the death trip with modifications. We were back in the old impasse but at least now, I thought, we had rejected plunging into super-weird mass experiments. I didn't know what it might be but maybe now we could begin again, begin the program more gently and more reasonably, somehow. We sat there in ragged discussion about what to do next. "Aw, fuck it," said Ken, and sulked. Robert and Joseph were silent. Catherine joked with Ned. Bill sat talking to Bo and Susan in whispers—you could feel his discomfort.

At last Linda said, "Let's have a marathon. We were going to stay up all night anyway, let's see if we can break through to something at last."

"Why not?" Martin said. "We'll encounter until something happens."

There were a number of acquiescing nods. "A marathon!" I exclaimed. "This group isn't capable of having a cocktail party and you want to have a marathon. Look, it's time to reconsider the whole program, back off, start again. Nothing can come from insisting [I glanced at Bill] that we keep pushing toward intimacy. We're all scared of each other."

They didn't agree. They thought it worth a try. They said they were ready for a big experience tonight. "Let's go to the baths, do some ritual chanting, get our heads clear, and then come back here for a marathon."

I sat there with Herbert, full of contempt. I began to use

Herbert as cover: these people were trivial, not serious, I, Herbert, am serious—I would have led them to death and rebirth: look at them trying to chant themselves into idiocy.

Herbert was withdrawing and I wanted to: the terrain was too uncertain, too scary. He had the cover, he was the wise man; if I were his student, then I could consider myself wiser than the others, I could save myself from them and their incessant experimentation.

And, after all, they were so absurd—so spiritually pretentious and yet so clumsy. They would storm the gates of paradise one way or another—by chanting, encounter, meditation, hypnosis.

Seated in our chairs, Herbert and I sneered as they treked out, all twenty of them, to be good soldiers of the human potential. But we did not leave. I don't know why Herbert stayed but I could not leave. It was too enormous a step. To leave would mean to be left alone. Besides, we had assembled in the room for some awful ceremony and, who knows, there was a chance that it might happen. Perhaps the marathon would change things. So, we sat, teetering on the edge of decision, both of us, with our different reasons.

And we teetered for half an hour, in the redwood-lined room with the windows on the ocean, FIRO named, after Bill's first book on the theory of interpersonal behavior—the setting seeming to sum up the contradictions of the experience: the magnificence, the amplitude, and the drama of the Big Sur coast, and the faintly cheap quality of a room named for another neglected volume in the pseudoscience of psychology. Esalen was a contradiction: vulgar: the pursuit of the spirit without adequate traditions: a wild California chasing of the eternal—you know, Aldous Huxley in Hollywood writing the *Doors of Perception*. And, make no mistakes about it, there was, to the gaze of the naked eye, not even an Aldous Huxley in this group.

After half an hour they returned, straggling in slowly; they chattered, giggled, looked askance at us as we looked the same back at them. I remember feeling left out, a bit cowardly, and yet determined, determined, not to go with the foolish herd. Eventually, they all found their places. Let the marathon begin.

A marathon, in case you are unlettered in these terms, is a nonstop encounter group. The principle is to run the group, night and day, not allowing people to withdraw by leaving, either to sleep or to eat a meal. Food is brought in. The hope is that by breaking down defenses with these devices, people will become more open, more honest, more in touch with their true feelings, and that they can then work through to new levels of intimacy, self-awareness, or something. Besides all this, a marathon is a very serious thing, a muscular form of encounter, going for broke.

The group settles down, becomes solemn, tonight we will break through. I was startled to see Bo Cahill manfully rise to lead the way. The paid expert; it was obvious that he was going to try, by courageous example of self-disclosure, to lead us to new heights. There began what seemed to my eyes the most ridiculous and pathetic effort since the abortive hike to Tassajara. It was Bo, Bo the psychic adventurer, Bo the barefoot boy with cheeks of rose, soft like Caravaggio's juvenile satyr who hangs in the Uffizi. This Bo rose to tower over his superordinary girl friend, as I thought her, Susan, she of the curlers. Susan of the short muscular limbs, the slightly too thick ankles, the ignorant whining voice of a California car hop. And while my startled eyes gazed, the delicate and rosy satyr and the car hop encountered. This was the route to the human potential! Bo would explore his aggression toward his girl friend—like watching a lamb trying to snarl at a mastiff. He stood over her, she gazing at him with the same apparent blankness that had endured my remarks about her curlers. Impassive, she endured. He stood over her, nearly astride her as she reclined on the floor, her head propped up on one elbow and he tried, as he put it, to "get in touch with his anger." An endless monotone was what he produced, nearly a whine: "Susan, I hate you; I want to kill you; I despise you; now [at last, an original thought, we wait with expectation] I want to strangle you [a pathetic attempt at Stanislavski acting follows as he feebly grips the air with his fingers—Bo the strangler]. I hate you; I want to strangle you. I hate you; I want to strangle you." And it went on for nearly an hour. I was unable to tell in the face of this spectacle whether Bo was the madman or I was. No matter, by two o'clock, the entire group of psychic astronauts— with the exception of Bo, me, Herb, and Susan—was fast asleep on the floor.

I had been right. This group of Schutz's was a bust. There was just a chance that we could treat each other well enough to have a cocktail party in, say, a week. Then, we might try to go on. Schutz had made a mistake. The evidence was before me: eighteen sleeping adventurers. What would have happened if the Beast in the Jungle had sprung now?

CHAPTER EIGHT

wallowing

i couldn't see any other choice. I was going to have to drop out of the Residential Program to which I had come with so much hope. Imagine that. Dropping out of Esalen. It was an uneasy prospect to be so utterly out of things as that. I went up to Marvin Handleman's house. Handleman was unique in the Program because he had a family. He was forty-two, manly, kind, and he had a wife and three daughters. I was glad to get there, to find the warmth of that family scene for my sense of loneliness. And also my sense of freakiness. Dropping out of Esalen is pretty freaky, I thought. It was getting hard to trust my own judgment. Finding fault with the Residential Program was one thing but dropping out entirely was something else.

Their kitchen was warm, the three girls, nine, ten, and

twelve years old, gave promise to all the rooms. Cecilia Handleman had an independent income and the prosperity, the settled, tribal quality gave the dwelling an air of security and permanence—struggle over. I took the coffee cup which Cecilia handed me smiling and watched the girls making some clay design on the kitchen table. It was good to be there: like most bachelors, I enjoyed being adopted by a family. I sipped at the hot coffee while the thought crossed my mind that these people would take care of me in case I really did go crazy at Esalen. Marvin held out his arm: "Want a cigarette?" We smoked. He was full of annoyance and criticism. He thought the group extremely lightweight—we agreed on that. And, he didn't quite know what he thought, for he was not an articulate man, but he was deeply annoyed. He was going to drop out of the group, if not the Program, altogether. I was pleased to hear this news —at least I wouldn't be alone.

Handleman went on. He was annoyed with the animosity toward his family at Esalen. In those days there were virtually no families among the staff. Many people came to Esalen to experiment with many sexual partners; stable monogamy was an embarrassing sight; children were few and their innocent eyes, looking at the spectacle of sexual indulgence, further embarrassed everyone. Handleman felt this resentment and it made him angry. He condemned Esalen as being immature. It was a sterile place and he was sorry that he hadn't realized it before.

I lingered over the hospitable cup of coffee, savored the comparative comfort of their nest, and listened to the complaining. I joined in with my own refrain.

Herbert arrived and got himself a cup of coffee too. "Gutless wonders. They aren't serious about breaking through to anything."

"They're kids," said Handleman. "They're doing their sex experiments and their group experiments, and God knows what other experiments. I've done all that crap." And I believed he had.

"Me too," said Herbert. "But the worst thing is that Schutz. He's dangerous and reckless. Particularly the physical violence. He shouldn't let people fight in those groups. I hate it. Somebody's going to get hurt."

I could see Handleman look at Herbert a little hard for Herbert had boasted to us how successfully he had studied karate —he claimed he could take a man's eye out with a kick. It was strange this condemnation of violence coming from him. Schutz, it was true, made people who were angry at one another in the group wrestle. It cleared the air, he claimed, and it often led to a greater awareness and frank revelation of what was causing the conflict. That seemed to make sense to me but Herbert insisted that we should condemn Schutz for violence. I think that both Handleman and I went along with this because it was part of the case against Schutz; it was a point that could plausibly be made.

We were beginning as a splinter group to try and finds ways to justify our separate withdrawals, and we were willing to get our justifications where we could. It was an alliance of necessity, for all three of us were unsure, disappointed: we had come with enormous expectations but suddenly we were out of the Program with nothing to do. We sensed, each of us, that the Program was not right for us, but it was necessary to justify such a decision and it was necessary to release the anger: we were being cheated—we had come for the Program.

After an hour's talk and coffee and cookies and daughters and wife and domesticity, the bachelors had to leave—it wasn't our lair, even though we could find comfort here. I wanted to stay but after a while it creeps up on you: what they've got is theirs, not yours. It had gotten cloudy outside. I remember how surprised I was when we left that Herbert, who had seemed to agree so much with Handleman's arguments about the imma-

turity of the group and the insensitivity of Schutz, explained:
"Handleman withdrew from the program because he's afraid
for his marriage." I asked what he meant, they seemed to me to
have a good, stable marriage, what did marriage have to do
with anything? "They have a shitty marriage, and Handleman
knows it will come apart if they get in the group and expose
themselves, particularly to the sexual experimenting. Handleman is running scared. I know."

I didn't like Herbert saying this about Handleman. I wanted
the three of us to be friends, stick together. I thought to myself
that Herbert was just projecting some of his inadequacies in
the situation—his marriage had failed in divorce. Still he insisted. I felt torn between Herbert and Handleman. In the
afternoon I went back to visit the Handlemans but they had
gone off, their neighbor said: "They've gone to visit friends in
Carmel." Fifty miles away, I thought.

I wandered around that afternoon, looking for Herbert.
Once or twice I climbed up to the Handlemans' house to see if
they had come back, but their car was not in the driveway.
Even after six o'clock, when it was dark, there were no lights in
their house—they were going to sleep over somewhere, I
thought.

It began to get cold and I went into the lodge. Herbert was
there sitting by himself, drinking a glass of wine, and waiting
for dinner to be served. The lodge was almost deserted. We
were over an hour early.

"Where ya been?" I asked.

"I was around. Actually I was looking for you. I looked in the
baths, up at the Handlemans', all over."

"We must have missed each other."

"Yeah."

We sat for a while and watched others come in, and we had
our dinner among the first. We were barely speaking to the
Residents at this point. We got up to go at the same time. "Let's
go up and see the Handlemans," I said.

"Sure."

The lights were still out. Herbert was chewing carefully on a toothpick: "You know, I heard they're going to have a meeting tonight to discuss the Residential Program." I looked at him and wondered what he was thinking. I didn't want to go to such a meeting. I was fed up. I felt such contempt for Schutz and the docile group he was pushing around. And I felt fear of those mad experimenters, too. It was as if they all had nothing to lose and could take any risks offered. That they might be suffering fewer fears and pains than I, might even be getting a lot out of the Program, never occurred to me. *I* thought they had no brains and so would follow the suggestion of the appointed leader, no matter what.

I looked up at Herbert. "Let's go," he said. "Maybe they'll listen to us after last night's fiasco."

I wondered. Why not? "It's worth a try," I said.

I climbed the path to FIRO through the dark October night. It was exciting to think that we could devise a new program founded, above all, on individual differences—we could use the nine months and the environment of Esalen to conduct our individual search at our own pace. We needn't be all herded together like animals.

We were out of breath and a half-hour late when we got there and I was surprised, collecting myself, to hear no sound of talking coming through the closed door. I opened it. The room was absolutely without light. I couldn't make out what was happening at first but I dimly began to discern bodies moving around the floor, and Bill, seated in a chair near the door was saying, very gently, "That's it, wallow into one another, just wallow."

The fucking herd, I thought, the only companions I had, had literally shown themselves to be dumb beasts—a herd of pigs wallowing at the direction of the master pig. My voice, the voice of reason and learning, could never be heard here. They were wallowing because Bill thought that wallowing might bring the group closer together. They could wallow forever and never form a group. The lack of dignity, of elementary human dignity! I raised my voice above a level that was genuine, for despite my anger I was afraid of them and said to Herbert, so that all could hear my contempt, "Let's get the hell out of here."

Without ever having taken my hand off the doorknob, so brief would I let my participation in this madness be, I slammed the door shut. I was finished with the Residential Program.

CHAPTER NINE

✣ where to turn? ✣

over the next week I wondered what to do. I talked a lot with Herbert and Handleman, especially with Herbert. Finally, on Thursday, ten days after the wallowing, something happened. I ran into Herbert in the late afternoon. He asked me if I had heard what had happened to Jim Bugle. Bugle was a clinical psychologist from San Diego State College, a man in his middle thirties, with two daughters. He had recently left his wife. I had never liked him. He would come up in the dining room when I would be nursing my wounds and confusions from the group, trying desperately to keep my calm perspective and tell myself that I was all right, the Residents were the sick ones. He would come up from behind and lay his hand on my shoulder. I looked up to see his teeth grinning around his pipe. "How's it going?" he says.

"Fine."

He pulls up a chair to sit next to me and puffs away, looking at me with the practical detachment of the professional "people-helper." That's the way he saw himself, a nice fellow trying to help others less fortunate. I was still a little shaky but I continued to munch on my sandwich—glaring back at him.

Puff.

Puff.

Puff. "You know, Stuart, I think you're getting upset here." Puff. "Let me know if there's anything I can do. I'd love to help but I don't want to bother you now." Pause. Puff. Stare.

"See you later."

Pat.

He did it to everyone. He had a marvelous knack for mentioning, in your interest, of course, the very thing you didn't want said. Soft-voiced, he blandly told everyone he liked them. His lack of self-insight was total. We had tried to break through to him (we had all become very adept at breaking through). One day Jim was under attack from the group for being hostile and not knowing it: "Show it, show it!" they cried.

"I'm not hostile," he insisted quietly. "I like everyone here." But even the sentimental Sylvia, she of the Peace Corps and the constant smile, was screaming at him. Clever lad, I whispered to her, "Take his pipe and break it."

She lunged at him. Snap. It was good for the phony Sylvia to get angry and malicious, I thought afterward, but Jim, slightly shaken, fingering the fragments of his pipe, hadn't changed.

"Why did you do that?" he whined. "I don't dislike *you*."

I was not surprised when Herbert told me he had just saved Jim Bugle's life. Herbert had been coming from visiting the Handelmans and was walking down the path to the lodge, when he heard the shouts of the men in the group who were tearing out of FIRO. They were after Bugle and Bugle was running and yelling for help. Herbert had intervened, taking up a stick he had stood off the whole group, a detail that he recounted with pleasure. "I told them I would club the first person who touched him. Nick Moskowitz began dancing around me, asking me to fight, but I stared him down. Then Bugle—that dumb brain-washed Bugle—went back into the meeting room with them. I told him he was a fool but that if he needed help again to yell."

I forget how I learned the sequel, but less than an hour after that scare on the path, goaded beyond control, Jim had broken through. In the process, he had taken one of his goaders, Bo Cahill of all people, and thrown him through a large plate-glass window with such force as to bend the aluminum strut in the middle of the window into the shape of a U. It had been a miracle that neither Bugle nor Bo had been badly hurt or even killed.

I had seen enough. Was it worth taking such risks in the name of some vague "human potentiality" that the likes of Jim Bugle and Sylvia Dalton were supposed to realize? I determined to go up to the city to talk with my friends, Mike Murphy and George Leonard. I was not just an ordinary nobody like the other members of the Program. I was a hotshot in the field of educational reform; Mike and George knew my talents, they had given me a place of honor, albeit a tortuous one, at the Ali Akbar Kahn concert. They would listen to me. There was no sin in having made a mistake and trusted Schutz: after all, this was a new field and the Residential Program was an experiment. Let us all acknowledge the mistakes and restructure things. Herbert would take over the Reservations Desk of Big Sur, an important post in the running of Esalen. He would replace Joe Harrison, a nasty person. Handleman would take over the Residential Program, replacing the nasty, mean, coercive Schutz. I, it was Herbert's suggestion, would become Program Director of the entire Big Sur operation. It was an excellent scheme, I thought.

I managed to bury any doubts as to my suitability—after all, how was I to become Program Director of this center when I had virtually no firsthand knowledge of the existing program? No matter. There were things I knew and that people here needed to know. We would have seminars on manners, for example. Everyone here thought good manners were "phony"—a quick course in Jane Austen, one of my academic specialties, would show them that "reality" could be perfected by manners. Unbuttoning wasn't everything. We would unite the Apollonian and the Dionysian, as Maslow had proposed to do, rather than spend our time trying to cure neurotics like Jim Bugle even if we had to kill them to do it. There would be dignity. There would be safety. Esalen had gotten too far out, irresponsible, and foolish.

I arrived in San Francisco and went to see George Leonard. I met him at the *Look* office, which he managed, and got the usual flattering big hello from him. I was wearing my most elegant suit: a rust linen job, which I had bought in Florence years before, and that I fancied was, at the time, the most elegant suit in the west. I had wanted to be well dressed for George; we were both successful men and I wanted to reflect that. I had started to feel very upset but I determined not to betray myself, to hold on. In part, I relied on my clothes, they would bring me through. He took me to the Sheraton-Palace for lunch. But when we entered the elaborate dining court with its marble pillars and vast ceilings of frosted glass, I couldn't help but feel I didn't belong among the other well-dressed people. Apart from being Jewish, I was poor, on a low salary this year, and I was without vocation—I had come to Esalen an academic reformer and I had staked my reputation on Esalen's being able to deliver a solution to the educational problems of the century. I had found it, instead, a bankrupt institution. I tried to explain this last point to George, as I ate my tomato stuffed with crab meat and drank his brand of beer, Lowenbrau. I was very nervous, pressed between the expensive and intimidating social situation that we were in and the weird funny farm haunting my mind which had brought me here. I didn't even know to which world I thought I belonged, now. I began to have the sensation, that became a constant theme through the next months, of belonging nowhere.

George had just finished writing a book on education in which Esalen played a major role. But I recited the bill of particulars, calmly, one successful problem-solver talking to another: the Jim Bugle event, the trip to Tassajara, the abortive death trip, the mediocrity of most of the participants, the reckless experimentalism of a few. Something must be done, I said. George's reply: "Well, I've just finished my book on education and one of my principles is the principle of the 'free learner.' You shouldn't have to do anything you don't want to and alternative tracks should be provided for different kinds of people. Maybe you and Handleman and Retter should do a little program of your own."

I was stunned. "The free learner!" "A program of our own!"

"No, George," I said, trying not to show all I was feeling. "I think those guys running the place at Big Sur are dangerous. You're Vice President of Esalen; isn't there something you can do to clean house?" He stiffened and poked at his salad. "Well, I hope Esalen isn't that bad," he said. "It is, after all, a place for experimentation and, besides, I don't have a lot of real power you know. But I'll talk to Mike Murphy. How are you doing, personally, I mean?"

"Oh, just fine," I said. "Can I get another beer?"

"Sure!" he said.

I was puzzled and disappointed I didn't feel better after seeing him. I had expected that his tall, successful presence would rub off on me, as it had in the past. When we went back to his office, he insisted that I read or rather look through the manuscript of his new book: *Education and Ecstasy.* The book was very optimistic and it read the way I had talked before I came to Esalen. I read how man had gone off the path when he stopped being a hunter, how pleasure was thereafter postponed, how repression ruled. I read how this was ending, how technology would save us, how encounter would save us, how man could experiment with his life and learning would be a joyous adventure. It was a sweltering hot October day and I longed to scream: "What about my pain, George? What about the pain?"

But I didn't talk about myself. I talked about the issues. I told George that his book was too easily optimistic, that he left out the great tragic vision of Western literature and he had not borrowed the wise irony of our literary tradition. Those criticisms of his new book hurt. He pulled himself up to his full height and shouted through the offices: "Damn irony. Damn Western literature. Damn the New York literary intellectual. It's time for new things." I mumbled some reply. We talked for a few more minutes, then George's phone started to ring. I thought it a good time to leave. I was shocked at the shouting and the whole reception. George, whom I had looked to for help as to a father or older brother, didn't believe me. He didn't believe me about Esalen. He was one of them—not realizing the dangers of "breaking through." He was one of them.

"Good-by, George," I said.

"Let me walk you out to the elevator," he said. "Call me when you're in town, Stuart."

I put on my jacket, my shirt was wet from the warmth of his office, and we walked into the hall toward the elevator. I had come to the wrong place for comfort.

I turned to Michael Murphy. He lived at that time in a high-ceilinged room and a half. Its bay window fronted on the back garden of an old wooden house in the Negro district of San Francisco. There was a bed, a few pieces of furniture, including a desk, some pillows for Zen sitting, and a telephone. Painted white, the room was clean and austere.

I was relying on Mike. George had introduced us and we had liked each other extremely when we met at the seminar on "From Dream to Reality." After the micro-lab that had left me so euphoric, we had simply giggled with each other for five minutes. I said to myself then, here is a soul brother, a man who can laugh as I can. No pompous Bo Cahill mouthing irrelevant truths like: "You're life-positive." Mike found life delightful. He was the very symbol of the joyful Esalen that had brought me here. I wanted to be like him and part of me, my joy, the playful joy that was also an ingredient in my Corvette, my Tom Jones escapades, my carrying on, my girls, my costumes, my joy was already like him. Mike would help me.

I listed my complaints, going once again through the litany of the dangers of entrusting a significant institution to mediocrities with no sense of limits. Again, I described the Jim Bugle incident with its near mayhem.

"Well, I can't understand it, Stuart. Bill Schutz was always so nice to me. (Pause.) And you say he's this monster. (Pause.) He always gave parties for me when I came to New York."

So big deal, Mike, he always gave parties for you—it's me we're talking about. Me. Me. I'm going nuts down there and I think you've handed the place over to nuts.

Mike pondered some more: "I do think it's bad that everyone has to do the same program. Why don't you think of a program of your own?"

Mike, if I have to think of a program of my own, I can't help but feel there is something wrong with me, and I don't want to think that. Can't you take my word for it? Schutz is no good. The Residents are no good. Can't you give me the place? Save my pride, my self-respect? Make me think that I am as important as I try to believe I am. After all, didn't you invite me to Esalen? Didn't you urge that I be in the Residential Program?

"I can't just interfere with everything in Big Sur. I'll have to talk this over. I'll talk to George. How are you doing personally?"

"Oh, fine, I guess."

Murphy is just like the others.

When I got back to Esalen I began turning toward the people at Old Westbury. I had persuaded the Provost, Harry Galtzer, to send me to Esalen during the first year of my tenure. Galtzer was a nice man. Of all the words that come to mind, nice is the first and most important. It was he whom I had finally trusted to catch me when I fell over backward in that first encounter group at the college. He was a sort of people-helper—labor organizer, director of a psychiatric clinic, things like that. And kind, sweet of character, well-bred: a Jew with money and family and taste. Not too well trained in an intellectual way, an inferior, in the last analysis, I had thought to myself, but still a nice man. I was supposed to write him about my Esalen experience so as to keep the college up to date about what I was learning. It was understood that what I was doing was at personal risk, it was understood that I might get upset. Harry would be my anchor man.

I wrote to him often. But, Big Shot that I was, I did it electronically. I had one of those IBM dictating machines with me; the college had furnished it; one of those little black jobs you can hold in the palm of your hand. The executive fasces, symbol of authority. Imagine the sight, Stuart sitting on a rock, on the path to the baths at Esalen, staring at the Pacific, the sunset, the gray-brown cliffs and the blue-black swells, dictating personal letters to his boss into his IBM executive machine. No sir, they would never trap me. I would have my IBM in Big Sur and once back at the college, I would be the bold, sexy kook who went to Esalen—who could trap me? Who could find a box for me?

So I began dictating long letters, three, four, five plastic-rubber-tape letters to Harry. They were typed at Old Westbury and he would circulate them. Elegant letters, logically organized. But, what I was dictating was my disillusionment with Esalen, my disillusionment with the hippies, my disillusionment with Schutz, with the whole human potential movement. This complaining would undercut me even more, I realized. I had persuaded the college to spend a lot of money sending me to Esalen, and I had told them that Esalen was the hope of education, and I had told them that any claims to running any experimental college without getting deeply involved with the Esalen style of affective education was a sham. And now I was saying Esalen was bad.

Maybe not. My criticisms of Esalen could be to my advantage if they weren't too fierce. A lot of my colleagues had been skeptical about Esalen in the first place. Maybe they could now say, Stuart is maturing, he is not the zealot we thought, he is balanced in his views and critical.

No, that wouldn't work. Those people at Old Westbury would never like me. I had learned that in the encounter group. There was something they saw about me as trivial. I didn't know what it was but I felt it. They thought me young. They thought me arrogant. I thought them slow and square and unadventurous. They wouldn't have come to Esalen. They weren't interested in changing themselves. They pretended to be happily married. They didn't take me seriously, whatever the complex reasons.

But I increasingly needed someone, someone to confide in outside of this painful place. I began to address my letters to Harry alone. Letters that became more and more pleading. He would be my outside friend. I told him to stop circulating my letters and to keep them only for himself. I demanded that he write me as frankly about himself, his life, his marriage, his worries. Encounter me by mail, Harry. I blackmailed him: if you don't reveal yourself, you are a coward, like the other academic cowards. I sucked on him—I wanted his strength. He must have known what I was using him for, nice guy that he was; though he tried to respond, sensing my pain, he didn't. His letters (which I kept) all began with an apology for being so long in answering. They alluded to his personal life but he wouldn't tell me about it. He wasn't sure, he said, "whether it was helpful to discuss everything with colleagues." Another disappointment. Another person on whom I could not fall. I got angry at Harry's evasions. I grew silent. My letters became fewer. I was getting more and more alone. Who would support me? Who would tell me I was good?

CHAPTER TEN

✳ i assume my role ✳

i turned more and more to Herbert. He needed me, too. For all his bravado and strength, he also was alone.

We began spending a lot of time together. Breakfast would be over at Esalen at ten a.m. The long-skirted waitresses without brassieres, their nipples peeping against jersey blouses, would have cleared the tables in the main dining room by then. Maybe a last glass white-stained with the milk it had held, some crumbs, a stray saucer or two—only these left to remove. The sunlight was bright through the large windows. The wooden tables glistened slightly where they had been wiped down with a mixture of warm water and ammonia. Life and noise were gone, an antiseptic smell in the room that had held a hundred people an hour before. And the warm sunlight through the windows, the grass of the lawn, decks of faded redwood. Swallows dipped over the pool and, beyond, the sea gleamed, dark blue, nearly black. Everything pointed toward the outdoors. The vastness of that panorama, the sense of the mountains at our backs, that enormous landscape where it was so easy for people to come to Esalen and experience emotions and insights greater than they had known in the cramped city.

But Herbert and I lingered inside. The others had gone to their meeting rooms: seminarians had gone to hear some famous intellectual or to try Yoga, the staff to their work, and the Residents were dutifully pursuing their herdlike activities, whatever they were that week. But we two lingered.

We would talk about various things. Women. A lot about the women currently at Esalen. We began a kind of competition to see how many women we could fuck. But, between mealtimes, all the women were engaged in one activity or another so there were no women to be had.

We talked about literature. Herbert had gotten interested in cultivating my good opinion of his work. One morning we even worked up a scheme for us to discover one another. I would write a great critical appreciation of his work, coach him with my knowledge, introduce him to my authors—Flaubert, Conrad, James—and in so doing we would both become famous, I for my critical acumen and he for his work.

Driven at last by our superfluousness out of the vacant dining room toward the air, we went to the porch in front of the lodge. From it you can see people enter the office opposite and you can hear the noise of automobile wheels on the great coast highway, two hundred feet above, and occasionally catch a glimpse through the trees of tourists speeding north or south. We sat on the bench by the porch.

The bench was for the early part of the morning. It was cool there then, the porch shielded us from the sun. The bench is twenty feet long and we could lie on it, propping our heads up to see what there was to see. And we could sit on it, with legs dangling. And we could prop our backs up against one of the poles that support the bench and the porch roof, extending our legs outward. Or I could tuck one leg under me. And we didn't have much else to do but talk and try out these various postures, maybe filling time up a bit more by sipping on the thick white coffee cups, the kind you get in old-style diners, which we took with us from the dining room. Occasionally, a seminarian would arrive late and we surveyed him closely, playing a game of psyching him out, reading his character, looking for signs that betrayed his nervousness, his anxiety about coming and about being late, his fear of us who were so obviously comfortable at this strange place, his discomfort at not knowing how to adapt to the easy-going quality of the staff. If it were a woman, we could share our fantasies, plot strategies, be helpful with suggestions to her as a way of making a first move. But such things were rare.

Usually, it was just the staff, people we knew, more or less. The girls we treated as possible lays, we flirted, each in our separate styles, a competitive thing. With them I would be ingratiating and tough by turns—a bit of manipulative judo that I thought worked pretty well. I would look relaxed, stretching out my legs in their expensive pants, the high brown leather riding boots showing at the bottoms. I was still wearing my shirts, starched, and my ties. I would play with my tie and banter with them; here I am, dear, a nice young fellow, not one to hurt you, but substantial, a good and even sweet person, clever, and cultivated, and even upper class in a way. Come, wouldn't you like to know, to fuck, someone like me? Come, you're only a penniless hippie, probably only nineteen or twenty, try a straight guy for a change, one with a little mystery for you, a little glamour.

Herbert's style was different. He would fix them with bulging eyes. He was usually picking his teeth with a wooden match or something. Down home, but big, six feet three or four. And strong. See that unswerving glance? Sense the psychic power, imagine the size of the prick, imagine it. You wouldn't get anything phony from him. Just a regular Joe, but an author, and a kind of adventurer; he would tell you stories, about the days in the unions, in the Communist party, in the ghetto, the prisons, he would tell you, he would take you on an adventure.

But the staff girls were resistant—we didn't seem able to interest them. Probably their prejudice against Residents, we thought. We would have to wait for mealtimes or after the evening sessions when the seminarians were through.

I didn't know what to do with myself. I could drive to Nepenthe, a splendid restaurant and bar eleven miles up the coast, where I had opened an account to make me feel at home. In the morning though, the bar was closed. I would save my daily trip there for a martini or two until late afternoon. Besides, there were more people to look at in Nepenthe then. I could always go up to Berkeley. Diane was there and other friends, but I couldn't do that every day. If for no other reason, there was the college's money to consider.

After about an hour of sitting, maybe having gone back to the dining room to refill our cups once or twice, it got chilly and stale on the front porch. We went to the back deck. It was different there. We didn't face the office. We faced the ocean and the great mountains that came down to the sea. The coast was visible for miles. More space here. The sun was warm. Take off your sweater. Stretch out on other benches. Look around. Listen to Herbert philosophize.

He always had a new revelation. His "experience" early in the Residential Program had given him basic insight into things, he said. He was working out the details. His speech would get aphoristic: "There are no accidents."

"What do you mean?"

"I mean there is causality, motive in everything. Look carefully, under the surface of life, underneath what people try to hide. See what they're after. Then your eyes will open."

I was puzzled. "What does there being no accidents have to do with seeing into people's motives?"

"Look at Harriet. Her husband was climbing one of the hills, he slipped and was killed in the fall. No accident. She killed him. She wanted him dead and he got the message."

I knew Herbert's sense of being endangered around women. After he fucked them, he wouldn't even let them spend the night with him. "How do you know it wasn't an accident?" I asked.

"I saw when she read the autopsy report, she had no feeling. There's a lot you don't see here."

I would puzzle over what he said. I wanted to agree with him, he was so experienced, he seemed so sure of things. But so much that he said didn't make sense.

"You'll learn," he said. "You're coming along fast."

I sat in silence, thinking. Then I stood up. "I'm going to take a ride."

"Go slow," he said.

"Yeah, sure." I grinned.

I loved to drive fast those long, warm mornings. "Fuck driving slow," I thought. One of the reasons I had come to Big Sur this year was to drive fast. The adventure of it—no police—beauty and danger as I speed along the cliff edge.

Most people at Esalen hardly left the place. Most of the Residents didn't even have cars. But I was on the road often, at least once a day.

I would get into that wonderful machine, for all its vulgarity kind of luxurious, and would take it slowly to the top of the driveway. Then, swinging it sharply northward, I would hit the accelerator, the rear end digging in—not a nimble dancer, like an Alfa or a Porsche, but a home-grown American monster—the tires would break loose and we were off.

I particularly enjoyed picking up hitchhikers. I would be considerate, asking them if they minded going fast and telling them that I would slow down if they wanted. Then, I would tear along the curving road, braking before the bend and then accelerating into it, the rear tires sliding slightly outward as the car rushes round the bend, the squeal, and then a mash of the accelerator to the floor on the brief straightaway, braking as the next curve is quickly upon us, the weight of the car thrusting forward. I reach down to flip up the four concealed headlights and turn them on in daylight to warn other cars out of the way. I downshift one gear and then with a slight jerk of my wrist on the wheel I am in the left lane out from behind the ponderous line of vague tourists, too timid to pass each other on the mountain road. I push the accelerator down as fast as possible and rush forward to where the first oncoming car appears, then, driving hard up to the hole in my line of traffic, the front edge of my car just at the right rear bumper of the car before me, I twist the wheel slightly and the car nestles with a quiet roar of the downshift behind the startled tourist who eyes me in the rear view mirror, my four-eyed electric monster breathing down upon him. It is scary for me, too, but I stifle the fear, preparing at the first opportunity to move over and then the jolt of the accelerator again, always traveling two or three times faster than the road apparently allows, shifting decisively, my attention fully engaged by the car and the road, the surface, looking for fallen rocks, peering, as I round one curve, to see if there are any cars three or four or five curves ahead as the mountain road stretches forward, and seeing none, using both sides of the road to allow for more speed, always, more speed, enjoying especially the long sweep of the curved bridges over the canyons, the tires squealing all the way through the two-hundred-foot curve, and my companion, obviously wanting to protest, petrified, but too thrilled by the adventure and the sweep and the skill of it all, and hapless tourists in their spongy riding sedans throwing up dust from the shoulders as they leave the road in panic.

But how much time could I spend on the road? Not all that much, really. Then I needed some excuse, some errand to get me out there, and most of them didn't extend farther than Big Sur. And, besides, it was exhausting driving at that pitch. The whole organism is keyed high, your eyes are looking hundreds of yards ahead, studying to see exactly where the pavement ends as you cut across a curve; your body is slouched into the seat, arms extended stiff toward the wheel so that you can *feel* the car sliding and adjust if the rate is so perilous that the car might spin with the sea on one side and the cliffs on the other; your neck gets stiff with paying attention, and time moves incredibly slowly, the effort seems enormous, and your breathing gets shallow. So, after I have raced myself for even a mere fifteen minutes, thrilling though it is, I am exhausted, and I realize each time that there can be no real triumph: the road, as I turn into whatever driveway is still there, unconquered; there is no one else in the race, no trophies, the whole thing a kind of illusion; and there is no one to share it with.

The dullness and the monotony and loneliness persisted. Most people had no idea that I was becoming very confused and I tried to conceal it from myself. I came on hard and aggressive. I held firm opinions on things, I differed with people about how good a place Esalen was, and unlike the herd, I was not afraid to say so. I have a long letter I wrote to Harry Galtzer at this time in which I make my criticisms in the broadest possible terms. I see the human-potential movement as one reflex of a civilization desperate for meaning. Desperation is the central datum, I continue. In a society where meaning has departed, one may be willing to try any experiment, no matter how personally risky, to find meaning. So, one might decide to throw and be thrown through a window on the *chance* that something helpful might come of it. We can see the same recklessness in the daily newspaper: war, civil commotion, gratuitous crimes, student uprisings, right-wing assassination plots. It is clear that we are living in times of unbearable stress for much of the population. The whole culture is going down the tubes. To meet such stress would require people refined by culture and stiffened by self-discipline. Naturally, a Jim Bugle would lend himself to suicidal experimentation. This was the kind of situation Hitler had moved into. Only a self-conscious elite, one aware of history and tradition, would have enough detachment to see the difficulties of the times in which we lived and the consequent necessity of staying in touch with our Western traditions, our rationality, our sense of limits, our sense of decorum and order. Myself, for example. And this was the special pathos of the human-potential movement, for it had been constructed, so to speak, in order to provide an alternative to our suffering civilization, an alternative to the repression of the nineteenth and early twentieth centuries, but, like the hippie movement, it had gone wild. The good impulse had been perverted.

So I wrote placing our little rural retreat in the perspective of civilization, its discontents and its decline. Ortega y Gasset had warned about the revolt of the masses, said I—here it is; with the standards gone, a robot-like Schutz, a man without culture, becomes a leader.

"I think encounter groups are more interesting and more real than literature," he told me once in the baths.

"You don't know our literary tradition," said I.

"Maybe, but I once bought season tickets to a repertory theater—Arthur Miller, Tennessee Williams, Shaw—and I found it bored me."

What had such a man to lose? What can he know of preserving the good in our culture? Everything to the winds, he would say, onward, onward, there is nothing to be saved.

Then I went on to warn the people at Old Westbury of the dangers our whole civilization was facing at this precarious time. It wasn't as if, to hear me talk, *I* was really in danger. I was simply doing my duty as a certified humanist and trying to save the culture from the latest wave of barbarians.

Dr. Gerard Engle arrived to lead a workshop shortly after I wrote that last letter. Schutz had spoken of him earlier: Engle was to be the chief person to lead the Residents in "body work." The name for Engle's approach, "Somantic Dynamics," smacked of snake oil to me. Engle arrived with a number of assistants. They all wore sport jackets and ascots, city fellers trying to look comfortable in the country. I remember thinking they looked absurd but feeling put down by the apparent class.

Herbert warned me about Engle. Engle was another false guru, according to him, like Schutz and Gunther and all the rest. I ran into Sandra in the dining room and she said differently. She was working at the Reservations Desk now and had signed Engle and his party in. I was surprised: generally she shared the hippie staff's scorn for the Esalen program: too square, too contrived—let it happen, man, let it all hang out, let it flow. But Engle was an exception, she said. She drawled it out in her elegant Southern accent. "He *really* seemed happy, unlike most of the grim-faced psychologists around here. There's something vital about Engle. I might take the workshop myself."

Who to believe? Naturally, I inclined toward Herbert, but Sandra wasn't exactly like the rest of the Esalen people. I knew, deep down, that she still preserved some of her aristocrat's sanity. It had to be so and her judgment was hard for me to ignore.

The following day I had my chance to judge. Engle began working with a group of about twenty-five seminarians, Residents, and staff and for that day and the next two, Herbert and I had to share our deck and our back bench with others. It was a sight not to be believed—the normative hero of Sandra; he, the best, happy, and healthy group leader of the human-potential movement, spread before my startled eyes a scene like bedlam.

In our mountain- and sea-draped setting, twenty-five adults, the men wearing jockey shorts, boxer shorts, and swimming trunks, the women wearing a motley variety of leotards, bikinis, bras, and panties. And this group, in these states, open to the elements, not simply standing around or doing something vaguely resembling the normal but contorted in the most strenuous and apparently painful activities: some are placed in strange positions over stools, their upper backs against the heads of the stool, their legs spread out in front of them, bent at the knees to support them, their heads hanging over the other side of the stool; others are coaching these, pressing down at points on their bodies with hands, or simply instructing them to breathe deeply; still others, having finished the five or so minutes required breathing over the stools, are bent over, from the waist, their arms hanging loosely in front of them, their knees bent slightly, their toes turned inward, their legs spread apart, their fingers just touching the floor. "Keep your head loose on your neck, let it hang, try to find the place when you bend and unbend your knees where the tension is, let the tension rise, let the vibrations come. You've got to experience the tension and the energy it's blocking." Another group, having progressed through this exercise, is standing erect, again with knees bent and the toes pointed toward one another, but legs farther apart: "Put your fists in the small of your back and push forward, push your jaw out, make noise, allow the vibrations to come up your legs." Someone else is being marched to the bathroom by another assistant who will teach him how to vomit voluntarily. The whole scene has a peculiarly sexy but decadent quality to my eyes. Herbert was right when he said wait until Engle comes.

I am stupefied and amazed. What in the world are they doing? This is the most bizarre and pathetic attempt at self-help that I can imagine. It looks cruel and yet the Residential herd is so faithful to their masters that they throw themselves into it. There is much talk of "getting into your body" and "mobilizing blocked energies" "of reliving childhood traumas in supportive surroundings" "of learning to express repressed aggression." For what, I wonder? But I can't hear everything—they shoo me away because I am not participating, and I don't want to get too close, either. The whole thing offends me. Engle himself demonstrates an exercise. "All right, one of you lie down on this mattress. Now what I want you to do is kick your legs up and down, one at a time, bringing the leg down as hard as you can on the mattress and, as you do that, do the same things with your arms and fists. That's it, good, that's it [he smiles]. Now scream 'I won't!' as you come down each time. Excellent, excellent; [he smiles throughout] keep it up." The assistants help other Residents to do the same thing.

I turn to Herbert, at last, and ask what is going on. Herbert: "Simple. After they are allowed to stop, they feel better. If I twist your arm and then stop, don't you feel better?" The explanation didn't make perfect sense, but it was a better explanation than any I had of what was taking place. I sat on the bench by the fireplace, my back to the vast ocean, looking at those gyrations and listening to the screams: "I won't! IIIIIIIIII won't! IIIIIIIIIII won't! No! No! No!" For three days it continued.

You couldn't get away from it. All over the property I heard the induced screaming, all morning, all afternoon, the thin wooden doors of these cheap cabins couldn't keep it out. There was no retreating.

"An abattoir," said Herbert, his contempt at the acme being indicated by his use of such a recondite term in that unsophisticated setting.

I became angry at what I saw, angry at Engle the monster, angry because I couldn't understand how I could be so sane and clear-sighted and all these people such stupid dupes, angry at the incessant yelling that had disturbed the place. The pounding and screaming and crying. How could people let themselves be so undignified, how could they put themselves in other people's hands like that? And Engle, so pleased with himself, bouncy, wearing his ascot while the Residents and semi-narians sweated and suffered.

The second night, Engle was going to show some movies. Anyone could come. The place was packed. The audience very respectful. A lot of the Residents had told me how much they were getting out of the workshop. I found a seat and waited. The lights went out and the movies began. As weird or weirder than what I had already seen: a girl in a leotard, well-formed, lying on a mattress; Engle wearing a coat and tie sitting near her; an air conditioner; office furniture as the camera pans the room. Engle: "Now I want you to do some kicking." She nods, kicks for quite a long time. Engle, briskly: "Tuck your head back, tuck your heels under your bottom, grab your ankles and push your stomach up." She obeys, begins to vibrate through the pelvis, through her thighs. At last she stops. "Now, how do you feel?" "Good." "How has your sex been?" "Much better since I've been coming to treatment."

Ahah: I get it at last, I think. The man is a therapist for people with sexual problems, like the girls in the Residential Program who can't have vaginal orgasms. And the idiots in the workshop are being treated like patients. And of course he's a quack—anyone can see that; he gets a hold on people by making them do these ludicrous exercises and then they're too embarrassed to admit that something isn't happening. Herbert is right about him.

He answers questions after the film. He is very moral. Sex is for marriage, says he. People who screw around are kidding themselves; they don't get real sexual satisfaction. I get even more furious at him. Earlier in the evening he has answered a question on child rearing. Child-rearing instruction is a waste of time, he said. People must be healthy first. Healthy mothers have healthy children, neurotic mothers have neurotic children. In the middle of the evening, he happens to mention his own mother: "My mother was a sadist," he remarks casually.

I've got him. I explain it to Herbert. Shall I spring the trap, expose him in front of his dupes? "Sure," says Herbert. But I am afraid. I am taking on the whole place and one of its idols, in public. I hesitate. I wonder. Yes, I will. I will strike a blow, make a stand, enough of conformist acceptance by these soft-minded nonentities. "Dr. Engle," I say rising, "I have a question, only a brief one." "Yes, what is it?" "Dr. Engle, was Reich's mother a sadist, too?" I sit down.

He looks around, puzzled. Of course the unself-conscious fool wouldn't get it, I think. "What do you mean?" he asks. I get up again. "Well, you said earlier in the evening that children were like their mothers. Then you said your mother was a sadist, a bit later. It's obvious that you are a sadist—you enjoy your work so, grinning as these people scream [I wave an indication of the crowd]. I was just wondering if the mother of your teacher, Reich, was a sadist?"

Engle is slightly stunned. He tries to go on to another question. Nick Moskowitz, he who dismisses me, most pathetic of the pathetics, a man who has been to seventy-five Esalen workshops before the Residential Program and still hasn't gotten the help he wants, looks at me in scorn and laughs me off: "Awww Stu, sit down and quit it, will ya?" But I go on: "It's obvious you are a sadist, Dr. Engle. Take what's happened here this evening. When the evening started, the room was full of girls; it's Saturday night and everyone knows people come to Esalen to get laid. Then you began all that stuff about fidelity and how people would only get to the heaven of a Reichean orgasm through fidelity. And have you noticed? The girls have been leaving all evening. You *are* a sadist. You're going to leave everybody feeling frustrated or guilty tonight."

I get a laugh. The audience warms toward me. A well-built girl at the door, on her way out as a matter of fact, for my observation was partly correct, says: "Don't worry, Stu, some of us are still here." I ostentatiously walk toward her. I am proud of myself. It is full warfare now. I have made my open stand, not just to the Residents, not just to Michael and George, the officials, but to the public, leaders and seminarians alike.

The rest of the night wasn't so good. The girl saved my face by walking out of the room with me but she wouldn't go to bed.

Still, that night gave me relief. Whereas during the first few weeks I had been self-confident and fearful by turn, strong and uncertain both, now I had found a way out of the confusion: I had a role. From now on, I would be the Esalen rebel. By deciding to take on the place, its ethics, its language, its mores, its programs, its heroes, I could put an end to the doubts that nagged at me. Before, my disappointments with Esalen had led me to a dead end but now I could make a career of proclaiming that *Esalen* was a dead end. Once more, I was critic-in-residence, but in this freer atmosphere I need not pull my punches as I had in the academy. I had taken on one of the local heroes and, I thought, made him a laughing stock. I would be the rebel, the village atheist, the one honest and rational man. And Herbert would help.

It was shortly after the Engle evening that (cheered by the realization that I now had a place, and an honorable one) I celebrated in the bar with Herbert. It was after dinner and the room was crowded, the one table in front of the bar being full of after-dinner lingerers. I had had a few beers and thought of a great idea: "Herbert, suppose we design some Esalen programs ourselves, but instead of these half measures, like Engle's screaming and kicking, let's go all the way. Take some of the basic principles like 'going into your fears' and 'reliving painful childhood situations in supportive circumstances.'" Some of the other local gurus had made much of these. "If you were afraid of homosexuality, go into the fear," said Schutz, "try talking it through, touching some other guy's penis, even try going to bed." Or, if you had been beaten up in childhood fights, try it again this time, and grow: that's presumably what was behind the baiting of meek Jim Bugle into throwing Cahill through the window.

"Hey, Herbert, what do you think of this: 'A Weekend of Piss.' Here's the Esalen write-up: 'Many people have unconscious hang-ups derived from bad childhood experiences. One of the most common of these is the discomfort from being allowed to lie wet in one's crib; memories of this discomfort become associated with urine and therefore with the genital area. This can lead to all kinds of difficulties, including impotence. By re-entering the scary world of childhood we can hope to right this wrong and free new energies for adult enjoyment. The seminar will take place in the Esalen swimming pool, which will be flooded with human piss instead of water during the weekend. We expect big breakthroughs from this one.'"

Herbert was delighted, he gasped through his laughter: "The following weekend we can do it with shit! The possibilities are endless! Ha. Ha. Ha."

"Hey, Herbert, why not this one for 'going into fear': 'The fear of falling is almost universal in man. We may suppose that falls during childhood, the result of careless but perhaps inevitable neglect from time to time, are what cause this fear. The only way to conquer this hang-up and break through to fuller human potential is by falling. In this weekend, seminarians will discuss their fears of falling and share reminiscences of early childhood; in group fantasy we will try to live out our fears of falling and turn fear into delight: then, as the climax of our explorations, each seminarian will be required to jump off the cliff.'"

We went on. "Afraid of getting beaten up as a child? Try our weekend of beating. Each member of the seminar will be beaten by the other fourteen members for one hour. Discussion will follow."

"Adults suffer from repressed aggression. The adult must learn again to mobilize his aggression, so say both Fritz Perls and Dr. Gerard Engle: a weekend of flogging."

"A weekend of drowning."

"A weekend of dying. Ha. Ha."

Endless, truly endless ways, by applying the few basic principles that then seemed to me nearly universal among the ex-
periential workshops at Esalen. "Thought destroys flow; people
must learn again how to let/allow themselves to be. A
weekend of nothing."

It seemed very funny at the time; Engle had left the whole
place nervous and a little hostile. We had our table laughing
for well over an hour. Various people joined in—there seemed
to be a well of cynicism about the Esalen thing that one could
tap. People could laugh at it I was discovering—here was a
point of attack. After a while, though, all the others left. Some
were going to bed, others sheepishly admitted that they were
going to their evening workshop sessions. I was surprised—
they had laughed so hard. I felt betrayed. Fuck it. Only Herbert and I had the strength of mind to keep ourselves from
such degrading nonsense. Enough that the others had listened
to us for an hour. Now to regroup and refresh ourselves, it was
going to be a long fight.

We left the bar that night with a strong sense of mission and
set out for Herbert's house. It was very dark and we stumbled
through the path bordering Bo Cahill's garden—Bo trying to
lose his mind by raising a few heads of lettuce: neoromantic
pseudoagrarianism. Then, past the fence that announced the
entrance to Dennis Murphy's property, where Herbert lived. It
was black under the trees and I was afraid to proceed but Herbert confidently stepped forward through the darkness. At the
bottom of the broken asphalt road there was a bridge under
which rushed the Hot Springs Creek—the sound in the night
was frightening, that rushing water, and dogs guarding the
other side of the bridge began to bark fiercely. Herbert wasn't
afraid of the dogs, though: "Stay," he shouted. And they did. I
had always been afraid of dogs and was impressed. The least
thing he did began to impress me.

Herbert's place was special, a sanctuary off the Esalen property. He alone of all the Residents lived with a view of the ocean, and a fireplace. He had, also, sequestered there a few bottles of brandy and other liqueurs, and from time to time a cheese and a Jewish salami. He produced these with all the flourish of a grandmother. I was grateful for his provisions, his old-maidish bachelor ways, keeping a secret store of goodies, apart from the meals in the dining room or what one could buy at Nepenthe. It helped to have a friend who could give me a sip of brandy. It helped on those cold nights when, after the humor, those unregenerate morons would listen to reason no longer.

CHAPTER ELEVEN

✠ experience ✠

the eighth week of the program came round and the Residents were going on their practicums for a week. I had been looking forward to this part: we were supposed to go off campus as consultants from Esalen and teach what we had learned. I hadn't learned very much from Esalen, I thought, but it was a chance to get away and consulting was my thing. I was a real consultant, not like my fellows who were doing it for the first time. I reasoned that it would be good for my education—I was going to go with Marvin Handleman to the children's home in Sacramento from which he was on leave. I had never been to any such social-service-type place and I had always felt a little guilty about that. It was like I had been avoiding something—the sight of the poor and the homeless, my responsibilities to them as a human being. That kind of thing.

We drove up in the Corvette and I was pleasantly surprised when we got there. The physical facilities were pleasant, a number of detached small buildings, lawns, trees. The kids were very lively-looking. "I guess I imagined kids with hang-dog looks, shaved heads, staring at me with hungry big eyes," I said. "These kids are fine."

"Yeah," Marv said, "aren't they terrific? Fantastic energy. And smart! The psychologists test them and they say they have low IQ's but you can see how shrewd they are. Little hustlers." I watched the boys in the grassy playground fiercely trading cards with ball-players' pictures on them. In the dining room, dinner was pleasant and wholesome—no worse than at my college, I thought. The "houseparents" who slept over with the kids in a number of cottages were bright and decent—no Dickensian monsters here. I was with the senior boys, aged fourteen to seventeen. One of them was trying to embarrass the houseparent, Mike, a young man earning his psychology degree at some nearby college.

"Get laid last night, Mike?"

Mike was cool. He leaned over and whispered with mock condescension, "It's very bad manners to talk about fucking at the table," and he continued to ply his knife and fork. It was funny and real. I felt alive. A good place.

As the first few days wore on, however, I began to see more. There was always a big to-do at mealtimes to make sure nobody left the dining room with extra food.

"Where're you taking that bag of food?" Mike asked.

"No place."

"O.K., O.K. Put it down."

It was for the runaways. The kids who would just take off, in the middle of the night, and hitchhike through the city back to their old neighborhoods. If they stayed away more than so many hours the houseparent had to call the police. If the kid had a record, and most did, he was sent to Children's Prison. Usually, after the kids had run away, they came back to the

Home, to hide out with their friends until they could think what to do next, if they could. The food was for them. The kids came from broken homes, I learned. They'd been raised by uncles or aunts until they got into trouble or everybody died or got tired of them. Then they were sent to the Home. They were one step from prison even though they lived here, and every month, of the fifty or so, two ran away. It didn't seem right to me—these people weren't doing their job. These kids ought to be getting a better break.

Susan and Linda, who had come with me, agreed. Linda had worked in such homes before, I learned. It gave me a new respect for her—this was a good thing to do even if she wore her husband's BVD's. We talked about how to "turn this place on," give the kids a fair shake. Susan, it turned out, had been raised in such homes. I appreciated how much she must have suffered. I felt sorry for her and thought it was marvelous that she was here trying to pay things back. She and Linda got very involved in the cottages, actually helping out the houseparents at night—reading to the kids, talking to them. I saw myself more in a consultant role. I liked the kids but I didn't want to get too close to them. There would be, I felt, a lot about them that I couldn't handle: I wouldn't know how to be with them. They would sense my pity, my reserve, and they would puncture it—I knew how good they were at that.

The third day I was ready to make my contribution, though. I had thought things through. We had our first meeting with the director, a man whom Handleman had dismissed as being "very good with the board." In essence I told him that he was doing everything wrong, that he was wasting the resources he had, that the state allocated twenty-seven dollars per day per child to him and all he was doing was feeding them and giving them a place to sleep, that he wasn't using his staff to capacity, to their potentials, and that he had a priceless opportunity here to have a model residential school and release the potential of these kids. Instead, all he worried about were runaways, his "responsibility" not to lose kids. I added further that his entire staffing setup was faulty: the two young women who were the "social workers" and were seen as professionals supervising the "houseparents" were not really professionals and besides, the "houseparents" were more intelligent and more real anyway. The two "social workers" were present as I delivered myself of these remarks—I was not a consultant to mince words, not me —only the truth, man. Handleman more or less agreed with me, as did Linda. And my advice, in a theoretical way, was excellent.

I tried hard in the succeeding days to press my original points and Linda backed me up, but it wasn't clear to people what I was recommending. "I just think the place should be more positive, give the kids more what they need. They've got so much energy, so much life."

"What would we do?" they asked.

"Well, the Esalen kinds of things." (I was startled to hear myself say this.)

"Just what do you mean?"

I lapsed into silence.

"Will you come and do it?"

It was getting confusing, somehow. I wanted to help. I saw what was wrong, but I didn't help and I didn't know exactly what I was recommending. The director is so stupid, I thought. Handleman was thinking of leaving, himself. God, those social workers. It's hopeless. I looked out the window and I saw Susan alone on a swing by herself instead of helping the kids with their studies. It was a relief—even the orphan had given up. I went out and flirted with her, but my feelings were heavy.

The day before we were to leave I met a tall blond girl, a hip inmate of the place, about sixteen. She was pretty and very suspicious. She was one of Marv's favorites and he introduced me to her saying she wrote poetry. I thought it would make her feel good if I read and discussed it with her. It was very good poetry and she was delighted with my praise. I got excited about helping at least this one, with her faraway look. Next year she would leave the protection of the Home and I thought that with no outside support and with her imagination she would head straight for drugs. I told her I would try to get her into college, into Old Westbury. She brightened a little bit out of her usual suspicious depression. I remember her faraway look and her too thin arms and legs.

But by the time I got back to Esalen I didn't want to think about the Home. Linda called meetings of the four of us who had gone there and were supposed to go back. I was very lazy at the first one, lying on the grass and staring at the clouds.

"You write our report," I told her.

I didn't go to meetings after that and I was glad the others seemed to lose interest. This was our year to work on ourselves, I thought. Though I thought about the poetess, from time to time, I never wrote to Harry about her; after a time I even forgot her name and I never got around to asking Marvin. I wanted to put the whole thing out of my mind.

I was very glad to see Herbert when I got back. He had spent his practicum keeping his eye on the place, he told me, looking at the way things were managed: "The same crap as the Residential Program," he said. "Joe, the reservations director, is lousy. He treats his staff badly and he wastes money." We lounged on our benches and patrolled the place with our eyes. We wouldn't let anyone get away with anything—they would know that we saw them.

One sunny morning in the middle of the week, in November, when there was nothing for us to do but lounge, the girl in the office rapped her knuckles on the window that looks out on the porch bench and beckoned to Herbert to come in for a telephone call. There is only one telephone at Esalen and it is always exciting when you happen to be around to receive a phone call. Usually you only get written messages saying somebody has called and asking you to call back. Herbert went inside and was in there quite a while. When he came out I asked what was happening. "An old girl friend of mine in the city is finally breaking out, finally realizing who she is, all that stuff I have been talking to you about. Naturally, they are trying to make her think she's crazy; she is really only coming alive. Very high-energy girl. She's a schoolteacher, divorced with two kids. She called me for help and I told her to come down here and in this free atmosphere she can do her thing. You've got an extra bed. I'm going to put her in your room."

"You are? How do you know we will get along?"

The voice of absolute certainty, the guru: "You'll get along. You'll like her. You'll be good for each other. She's lots better than the girls you've been fucking; this is one of my old girl friends. A high-energy girl."

She didn't arrive until the following morning. That was surprising, when I heard it, because she was supposed to have been desperate to get away. Herbert, whom I met on the porch and who had already received her, told me she was a little upset; she had started early the morning before and it had taken her a whole day to drive the four-hour drive. I thought nothing of this; Herbert had said she was "high energy," a phrase he used to designate people who were especially alive, and she was obviously going through something. I was intrigued. Perhaps I was going to get a little of the life experience that Herbert had.

A few minutes later she emerged from the ladies' room and joined us. We all sat down to lunch together. She was a neat-looking little person, not pretty, but pleasant-looking, with a little Irish face, ruddy complexion, blue eyes, and a trim figure. She was wearing a plain white blouse, plaid woolen slacks, and her hair was in pigtails. Despite her clothes and hairdo, I was surprised when she told me she was twenty-nine, she looked several years older; also, there was something funny about her eyes. Herbert had introduced us and told her she was going to stay with me and that I was a very good person whom she would like and who would be good to her. We looked at each other and smiled.

I ate my lunch and thought about whether she would make love to me, eyeing her from time to time.

Herbert and she talked about various matters; her mother didn't approve of the casual way she was living and her ex-husband was trying to take away her kids. "Karen, you're all right, don't worry about what they think, stay with yourself." It was becoming a cardinal rule of Herbert's emergent philosophy to avoid the negative probing of people like Schutz and to accentuate the positive. Tell people they are beautiful and they will be, he had said to me.

After lunch Karen said she was very tired and that she'd like to take a nap. I showed her to my room and gave her one of the beds. She brought in a suitcase. Then, I left, to go do something. I needed to kill some time. When she got up we could get acquainted. I was very excited—a strange woman sharing my room. Anything could happen. Maybe we could become *real* lovers.

When I returned, the door was locked. I was surprised. I knocked and waited. Suddenly I heard footfalls behind me, someone running. It was Karen. And, to my astonishment, she was wearing only a pair of red nylon panties and a black bra. There was sweat on her upper lip. She had been running around outside gathering flowers, she said. This was pretty strange, I thought, but there was something electric about her.

"Come on inside," she said. We sat on the bed.

"Do you feel rested?" I asked.

"Oh, who needs rest?" she said. "I feel great now that I'm here—and with you." Her eyes looked at me very big. I touched her and she opened her mouth and pulled me to her. She pulled my clothes off passionately. We made furious love. She screamed "Come in me, come in me!" When it was over I glowed: I was especially pleased with myself because she told me it was the first time she had come.

I closed my eyes to relax and heard her leap up and go into the bathroom. Rushing water, rattling of pans. "I don't have any pans," I thought. When I heard her return to the bedroom I opened my eyes. She was carrying one of those round-bottomed stainless steel camper's bowls, full of soapy water. I looked wonderingly at her. She motioned me to lie down and close my eyes. She stroked me with a loving hand, worshipfully. Almost instantly, after I felt it, I looked up and saw her, her loose red-brown hair dripping with soapy water, applying her hair to my genitals and washing them. It was a fantastic sight—a little frightening at first. But there was a dreamlike quality too, if I let myself enter it. Herbert had said she was acting a little strangely. I would give her the love she needed. I drew her to me and petted her. I felt very manly, and adventurous.

The evening was calm and we went to bed and slept. The following morning I went off to town, unconcerned. When I returned cheerful with expectation, just before lunchtime, I found both of the beds covered with books. There must have been fifty. I asked Karen about them. "I'm reading them," she said.

"Really? All of them?" Then I laughed.

"I have a lot to learn," she replied solemnly. "There's so much I have to learn."

I felt slightly uncomfortable—all this overstatement and prophetic intoning of the obvious. It didn't make sense. She hadn't seemed dumb before. I glanced at the titles as I mused. "That's my copy of *The Aeneid*," I thought, "but I lent it to Marvin. I recognize the rest of the books. They were on the shelf in Marvin's house, next to *The Aeneid*." Slowly I looked up at Karen. "Where did you get these books?"

"They're mine, I told you."

"No they're not," I said.

"Please don't tell," she said. "They really are mine. I need them. You help me—I need them to keep up with your books. You've got a lot of books so I have to have some too."

I looked slowly around the room. Fishing tackle all over, clothes, a sleeping bag, children's toys, a Raggedy Ann doll. I wanted to run out the door. But it was my door so where was there to run? I felt sorry for her and very helpless—almost petrified. She was going crazy and I had no way to reach her. "Look," she said, "I wrote it all down," and she came up to me and put a hand on my shoulder and showed me what she had written. I shuddered at her touch. On the pad, in large childish letters:

> "WILL YOU SHARE YOU WITH
> ME THROUGH YOU BOOKS
> IT
> WILL HELP
> ME TO KNOW YOU IF
> I CAN READ THEM."

She wanted me to go crazy with her.

My mind raced to think of what to do. I could play along—but that wouldn't help. I didn't want to get more deeply involved. She was Herbert's responsibility, I told myself. But maybe I could help her by being firm. I would try. This thing had gone far enough already. "Karen," I yelled, "stop it! Put those books back where you got them. And clean up this mess you made. Put those children's toys away, somewhere. You're not a child: you're a woman and you're my guest."

She looked at me, almost whispering, apologetic, very concerned. Then she wrote on the pad:

> "I NEED ORDER IN THIS
> ROOM. WHO KNOWS ORDER
> I NEED IT TO CONCENTRATE."

She smiled.

I was too nervous to stay. I went down to the lodge but Herbert wasn't there. I felt helpless. She was in my room, I had no place to go and I didn't know what to do. I decided to wait until evening. That would give her a chance to calm down and put things in order.

I returned to the room late, with Herbert. About seven o'clock. It was dark. All of the furniture, including the two beds, were piled outside. Karen was in the corner kneeling among many pieces of wood about four inches long and an inch wide that she had gotten from the scrap box in the tool shed. "I'm making a bookcase," she said. "What should we do?" I whispered to Herbert. He just looked at me. I went and asked the Handlemans if I could sleep at their place.

Late that night the noise began. We had kept close to the cabin and I found Karen standing in the middle of the large bed, which had been moved back into a corner, with a broom in her hands, swatting at hundreds of black flies which had entered when the door had been left open during the afternoon. She was screaming at them. We looked through the window and tried to enter, but she rushed for the door and locked us out. Herbert seemed paralyzed—he had nothing to say. I went looking for Joe, the Reservations Director. He came up and looked at her screaming in there, talking to the flies and across the room to another Karen we couldn't see. I felt terrible. I wanted her to stop, to be well, to stop screaming in my room. Couldn't we call the doctor in Big Sur, have him give her something to calm her down?

We sent someone off in the dark to make the phone call. We waited outside, looking through the picture window at the madwoman, Herbert helpless.

The doctor wouldn't come unless it was absolutely necessary. I was furious to the point of tears—dolt, of course this was serious, Karen might kill herself, it might be my fault. Joe sent someone to call again. He returned. The doctor would come.

But time was passing. To my surprise Joe decided to intervene. He knocked on the door and called her softly, "Karen, let me in, it's Joe, I want to talk to you." She refused at first but after he persisted, she opened the door, still standing on the bed with her broom. He left it open, but we didn't want to startle the woman and so we remained just at the edge of hearing distance, able to make out some of what he said, but not everything. He was reasoning with her, persuading her that everything was all right and that she should go to sleep. To my amazement, she seemed to be going along with it. His voice was reasonable, firm, and comforting. It took a long time, maybe half an hour to even get her off the bed, but finally, she did get off and at last she went to bed, with the lights on—she didn't want the light off—and Joe exited. Then, and only then, of course, did the doctor show up.

The next morning, having slept badly at the Handlemans' house, I was exhausted. I told Herbert that he had known Karen, she was his friend, he had invited her here, and he had to take the lead in dealing with her. At last he did do something, he began telephoning around to her mother and sister. They promised to arrive, from Oklahoma, by plane the next day. Until then we had to hold on.

I lived at the Handlemans' except for my meals, and those I would eat early and in corners far away from Karen who would appear in the lodge at mealtimes. Herbert was at last showing her some attention and affection, and with the knowledge that she would be leaving tomorrow the place, which had begun to be generally disturbed, let her have her own way. She topped off the afternoon by parading naked in front of the lodge.

Karen had made me miserable. I grew afraid of her. I thought that after I left my house and moved into Marvin's she would follow me. The depths of it scared me. New depths to which I could fall.

The following day her mother and sister came. Herbert handled most of it. They took Karen off to talk and I hurriedly packed her old red Volkswagen with her stuff. It was hard because there was so much of it. Bows and arrows. Children's toys and a Coleman stove. Fishing tackle, some dolls, clothing (my clothing as well as hers for she had packed mine in with hers), books. Pieces of wood, Thermos bottles, galoshes. Summer wear and winter wear, sets of trout flies. I didn't want to touch any of it but it saved time if I packed it. I wanted her gone, I wanted her gone very much. The sister drove the Volkswagen and Karen went with her mother.

part two

✲ emptiness ✲

the incident with Karen had shaken my faith in Herbert. He had behaved very badly and incompetently, particularly in the beginning. How could he have been so paralyzed, I wondered. I spent several days by myself and he went up to the city. Life was starting to bog down. It was as if the light in a lantern-slide projector, showing the wonders of the world and imagination, had slowly begun to fade out. What had been adventure before, even threatening adventure, was becoming something else. I was beginning to find life more realistically; I was beginning to experience what was really happening in an unmeditated, unliterary fashion, and my reaction to this was to retreat from the experience, to turn down the volume, to close it out softly, unconsciously. As it became harder and harder for me to embellish with meta-

phor the actuality I was experiencing, I got more and more
depressed. At this point the depression was just beginning.
Something very mild, a vague and slight numbness.

I felt it was coming and I tried to break it. The girls were
there. I pursued them and I won. A seminarian who was a social worker, whom I met in the office and asked to make love.
We spent an hour together. A hippie girl, ex-nurse with only
one breast—we spent two nights together. An editorial assistant gone camping for the weekend: one night. And others, but
always the same: unromantic, uncomplicated, cold, and dull.

Then Nancy came along. She presented herself to my being
with sharpness enough at the beginning. I remember her sitting
down in front of me, across the table at the usual candlelight
supper. I had not seen her before. She was one of Fritz Perls'
students and they had just returned from traveling. It was Saturday night. Pardon the phrase: she took my breath away. A
jewel-like loveliness, short hair, quite thin, cheekbones, blue-
gray eyes, perfect features, medium height, wearing a blue-
gray man-tailored shirt, a lot of style, overtones of Garbo, both
Hepburns, little boy-girl, but forty-five, elegant, slow, refined
female movements. I was scared. But in the brief chitchat I
started, she seemed unthreatening, very kind.

It was weeks later that anything happened. After the Engle
week and after Karen. It was a Sunday afternoon; the weekend
seminarians were almost all departed, leaving me, to whom
they brought diversion and novelty, only my angry dullness.
November. The clouds hang low, gray-white, and the wind
though slight is cold. I meet her on the deck. She is different
from the seminar ladies who have departed—no errors of make-
up, no Susan Kalla gaucheries with curlers, no pedal-pushers'
lack of grace. She is different from the stylish hippie girls that
are left; no Joan Baez, she; there is no odor of the earth about
her. She should have been in Paris, not in Big Sur, I think.
There is something attractive, even in knowing she is Fritz
Perls' student. He is the dominant teacher at Esalen—the wise

old man. A frightening man to me, the very form and figure of an angry patriarch, Dürer's heads of the apostles, grizzled, wild-eyed, in the Munich Pinakotek.

She laughs at my jokes. She always said, thereafter, that she liked me because I was amusing. I could relieve her of her "boredom." A trifle precious, that, but acceptable against the grain of those massive walls and decks of redwood, unstained, unvarnished, uninlayed, naked, nude, that so depressed me in the unrelenting architecture of our barbarous retreat. We talked about one thing and another, and despite the cold, I began to warm. The fun of it.

She had traveled, we talked about Europe, Paris. She had lived in Paris. I had lived in Rome. I told her why I preferred Rome to Paris. But I was impressed. I hadn't lived in Paris. She told me she had a paper clock, something very elaborate to cut out and assemble, that she was saving against the days of absolute winter boredom. She told me of her husband, divorced, twenty years ago, of her two daughters, both beautiful. We laughed, and fenced, and flirted in ways that no two others in that place could have done. I began to warm. Clearly she liked me. She was awkward, not as fast as I was. But that was partly shyness. Beneath the shyness was the sense of inherent power that a beautiful woman knows she has.

I began to lapse into old extravagances: collect the props, set the stage, at last, life is going to be lived dramatically, we are to assume more interesting roles than this place usually allows. "I will get the wine." To the bar I go. "Not champagne"—too gross—"the best Rhine, one bottle, two glasses. Yes, uncork it, please." Enjoying the appearance of the wastrel that I presume I make I almost swagger through the dining room to gather up the woman, the beautiful older Parisian woman, and we climb to the house of the Old Man, Fritz's house, a circular place, like the housing of a dynamo, or the caves of Crete, or the huts of Africa, or the tombs of the Etruscans, or the stone churches of the thirteenth century and before, Aix-la-Chapelle, Ravenna,

Nancy, Theodora, Justinian, mosaic and stained glass, my imagination rushing here and there to crowd the scene with reminiscences, to enrich the life I am living.

We drink the wine and we talk and my excitement becomes more and more breathless. I revel in the connotations that endlessly rub me, rub my body, toes and calves and hair and cheeks; or connotations that I bring to rub me. I don't know at the time just how much I am manufacturing. I am proud, however, of my imagination, proud to know that for no one else in this waste can reality have such resonances, resonances which I heap one on the other until they have almost palpable thickness. No one here can do that but me. They have no background for it. Not even Herbert. They need forbidden and dangerous drugs to even get a taste of what I am experiencing, so I believe.

And I truly feel in love. We make sweet caresses, delicate love, her little-girl body under my hands, she doesn't know how to kiss, strange thing; I realize that she is a little afraid to kiss, afraid of love and of men. Maybe I can help her. I want her. I love her. I want all of her, all of her body to answer to mine. It doesn't do that, though; it is beautiful, precious, beloved, but it doesn't answer, there is a subtle stiffness.

Still, I am joyful. I have someone to greet in the lodge. To kiss. It is awkward: she is sixteen years' older; but she is girl-like and we are blessed; I can push aside the disparity that rises in my mind; and I act like every man in love acts. I am happy. Esalen and Big Sur be damned; I can even tolerate you. I am back where I need to be. In love with poetry.

A week passes in happiness and I write a poem. Extraordinary. I had written two poems in my life before, in high school, very discouraging Sandburgean affairs about the working classes. None since. But now, in the experimental air of Esalen, rejoicing in my new-found escape from Esalen, I write my third poem, first in fifteen years, inspired by Nancy:

You speak to me of crystal chandeliers;
The warm light drops its sounds in prisms sharp
Of heavy Belgian grapes that swell a threat
To end wood brown and sunlight common.

Lips sparkle teeth, yellow and glassy sharp,
And cool delights warm only sheets of fancy.
That fancied pleasure seems more real than real,
Can only make me wonder where I stand.

To know all this can chill the tiny pores
That sweat their liquids saline laced with dirt.
For my rich fancy cannot grit and crystal
In any but a poison grim combine.
Unless to rub out of the glass a shriek,
Which, since I love thee, is my own and
        thine.

I wasn't totally sure what I meant but I understood that it had something to do with my knowledge that I was doing what I was doing. I wanted the pleasures and richness and safety of imagined pleasures, the pleasure of poetry. And yet, Esalen dropped the glove—be real, face reality as it is, stop fantasizing. These boobs, by whom I was surrounded, would deny the tragic knowledge of two millenniums of great literary works. Though the central myth of love in the West was Tristan and Isolde, the disappointed but passionate lovers, separated from the flesh, Jim Bugle and Bill Schutz were maintaining that love was possible. Catherine seemed to speak as if she knew. Could they be right? Could the passions and the flesh combine, the idea and the reality? I had to admit that I had come here to try.

I never knew exactly why we separated. Maybe the things I have just said. Maybe because Nancy seemed, like me, too afraid of reality. Our actual ending was awkward, comic, and real in the extreme. I had felt my feelings for her fading. I was very upset about that and we were talking about it. I was having trouble talking about my feelings. She suggested that we play a free-association game. To my amazement I came up with the association that she reminded me of my Aunt Tillie. To my further amazement she suggested that I talk to my Aunt Tillie: a Fritzean Gestalt-therapy game where one tries to integrate the disowned parts of oneself by engaging them in dialogue. I did. I remembered Aunt Tillie. She was tough. The toughest lady on Clinton Street, full of tough merchants though it was, where my father and uncle had their stores, way back there on the Lower East Side of New York. She ran my uncle's store, flicking her cigarette, platinum-bleached hair. I wanted the part of me that was Aunt Tillie back—the tough lady who walked tough, her tight skirt snapping, who spoke tough, for whom only the actual was real. My childhood fears of Aunt Tillie were passed and I wanted her balls. And somehow to get her, I had to give up Nancy.

I felt much better, no longer guilty or heavy of heart as I had felt when I first told Nancy that I wasn't sure of my feelings for her. I needed to leave and she, beautiful spirit, made it easy. Like a gift, she gave me my freedom to explore further, to become a man if I could, though it would disappoint her and leave her alone. Perhaps she was partly relieved as I left her, alone, but relief or not she was generous to me as I pursued my foolish journey. I was always grateful. For she was ever my friend, my honest friend, and, in the dreadful months that followed, when I felt I was slipping and my mind was going, and that I would be institutionalized way out here, thousands of miles from my family, whom I didn't trust anyway; when I feared everyone; I knew that Nancy still loved me, as I loved her, and that she would take care of me.

When I left her, though, I found, despite my exhilaration, that I had nothing to do with myself. Emptiness again. It was good then that Herbert came to my relief with a change. He told me that a little apartment had become available near his place, at the back of Dennis's house. My own cabin was only a motel unit, part of a row of shabby cabins, and already full of bad memories. I told Joe eagerly that I wanted to move and he arranged it, glad to get rid of me.

I was very excited at first about my new place. When I woke up in the morning, I awoke to sky and sea and large old trees, sequoias and other kinds of pine, outside my window, the cliffs of Big Sur and water. But it wasn't an improvement. I knew that scene of rich purple from the sea and dark rich greens from the overarching trees was beautiful. I knew it with my head. I remembered the beauty of the Big Sur coast when I had first known it. I remembered feeling the lush and sublime serenity. Admiring the colors of the earth: green and red, yellow and flower blue. Almost grasping the peace. I remembered that. I knew that the view from my window, a large-paned window that would lift straight out with a rope and a pulley above the bed, was one of the best along that sublime coast. And I knew that my room was romantic with its window with a pulley, and its redwood woodwork, and its elevation over anything close by, as if you were on a ship, or a lonely promontory. And I knew that there were echoes, in that situation, of Scotland and of Amalfi and of Marlboro Country, all gloriously combined, as they are, in that coast line when viewed from that spot.

I knew all that, but I didn't feel it. So it was puzzling to wake up and come to this recognition. And I guess the central emotion of all those risings, week after week, was a feeling of loss. A feeling that, for me, the glory had faded from the most beautiful landscape I knew. And that was puzzling. Where had it gone? How could *I* have lost Big Sur?

Was it possible that Big Sur wasn't as beautiful as I remembered feeling and thinking? If so, I should go elsewhere, in search of beauty. But where? When I thought of other beautiful places that I knew and where I might go to spend a sabbatical, I was sure that they were no more beautiful, maybe less. It was a puzzler. So I woke up puzzled.

I dressed and went downstairs to my other room where the sink and the shower were. It had a cold linoleum-tile floor. Little black bugs, with hard bodies, not half an inch long, would have crawled in during the night, maybe a couple of dozen. They wouldn't threaten, they would curl up nearly into a ball if you touched them. I hated going downstairs, fearing I would tread on one of them with my feet, bared for the shower, and squash it.

In the shower, I would wash and wonder about what I would do that day. That didn't feel good. For there wasn't much for me to do. Nothing to look forward to, or to anticipate, or even to be anxious about. I was used to looking forward. I had felt my manhood gathering over the years around anticipation. Anticipate the exam, the task, the paper, class, the committee meeting. Prepare. Perpare the psyche. Feel the energy of preparation rising into the upper back from the lower, the shoulders getting stiff with prepared resistance, the throat tightening slightly as it holds back partly rehearsed speeches for the proper moment, the stomach feeling aglow with fear, and energy to meet the fear. But here again, there was something missing. Nothing to mobilize, either for or against. Energy not knowing how to come out. Me not knowing how, then, to feel alive if it weren't with anticipation. All my life I had avoided relaxing. Of course, I had told myself that I couldn't relax. I had never liked the beach for that reason. It always amazed me that people could like the beach. I always brought a book to the beach. But the beach is no place to try and read. So I would go home early. My father was always surprised at this for he remembered that, as a little boy, I had loved to go to the beach and when one year we rented a little cottage on Long Island for the summer I would be gone from the house all day, playing at the beach. It puzzled him.

So, when I automatically reviewed, in that shower with the little black bugs on the tile floor, cold, what I should prepare myself for that day, I found nothing. And that made me feel a little helpless. I didn't know how to be myself unless I was trying, and I had nothing to try here, not the way I had arranged my life. No tasks.

Rather than face that emptiness I resolved to focus on what was coming next. At least that was something. What was coming next was breakfast. I would walk to breakfast and eat it. The next hour or hour and a half were accounted for. I need not worry until then about not having anything to worry about. And so, since in fact it is beautiful where I lived, and since it is hard to resist a shower's energy and the warmth one rubs into the skin with a towel afterward, and since my hair was partly wet, my skin damp under the clothes, and the air a little cold, hurrying me forward, and since I had disposed of my emptiness for that moment, I stepped out of my little house not depressed, but with a little feeling of anticipation. The next hour and a half would have something to offer. I could make it through that and still feel alive. And I set out to breakfast with even a smidgen of hope and a sense of accomplishment at having conquered in the first crisis of the day.

My house was in a hollow on a plateau above the sea, bordered on either side by higher plateaus, cliffs. The southern cliff, no more than an eighth of a mile away, was where Esalen was. To reach it you have to head inland for a hundred and fifty yards. There, you cross the creek by the bridge where the creek starts to drop several hundred feet to the sea. Then you go seaward, up the road, to a fence that demarks Dennis Murphy's property, where I lived, from Esalen. There is a no-trespassing sign on the fence and you think you are protected on Dennis's property from the crowds of seminarians and the crowds of Esalen staff. It is a largish property, maybe eighty acres or so, and only about twelve people live on it, scattered here and there. It is private, it even has a hint of luxury about it, as if its inhabitants, at least those living around a very large and beautifully cared for lawn, were special. And I liked to think myself special and imagine that those on the other side of the property thought I was, partly by virtue of living at Dennis's. I liked living over at Dennis's. Though, again, I didn't like it as much as I knew I should.

Still, it was a comfort, usually, in the morning, when the crisis of the shower was over and I would stride, clean and newborn with the day, up the path to the river fall and then up once more, around the horseshoe to Esalen. I would feel pretty good. But once I crossed the fence, I would begin to feel differently. That part of Esalen was not cared for. A field had gone to weeds. The asphalt road gave out and became a narrow dirt path. The hideous house trailers that the staff lived in were redolent with reminiscences of *Tobacco Road,* and the motel units under construction at the end of the path were cheap-looking. I hated Esalen, every morning, when fresh from lawns and sea I had to face that ugliness. I was surprised to find that not everyone thought it was ugly. I wanted to cut down the large field of weeds that grew with the ragged purple flowers head high. But when I told Sandra, she told me that she loved them that way. It bothered me that she didn't feel the way I did.

I cross that waste, like stumbling as a child through a vacant lot in New York—that's what it made me think of, all the confusion. For me a vacant lot was a place in between. Between two buildings, lived in. Or, between two buildings that were not lived in, which were, in turn, between standing and being torn down. It was on a corner, or it was half a block and it was between being lived in once before, when there were buildings, and in the future, when there will be buildings again. Because it was in between, it was no man's land, or everyone's. It would be used as a dump and begin to have an almost organic quality. From level city it would throw up contours, rises, and falls. It could be played in but it was dangerous. There were places to break a leg. There were rats that might be scared up. There were ragged pieces of broken concrete to fall against. There were the sharp edges of tin cans, sometimes used in a fight, to open the skin and scar. There were watchmen, drunken goyim, usually lurking somewhere, totally unreliable, that came with threats and hurled anti-Semitic epithets at us. And, each morning, just at the level of consciousness, the thought would occur to me as I reached the top of the hill and looked across the overgrown field at Esalen and its brown buildings, the huge mountain looming beyond to frame it with grandeur, that I was crossing one of those dangerous childhood vacant lots, down on the Lower East Side, fraught with just such inconveniences and childish terrors.

When I reached the parking oval, which connects with the great highway and with the office, the site of official reception of seminarians from all over the world, who eagerly find their way to this place, I felt better. The oval is clear. They are trying to grow a lawn on it. Besides, it connects with urbanity, through the road, and through the office. This is the safer adult world, not the haunted world of childhood disorder. Here, cars come, to unload baggage, to unload passengers who enter the office, and fill out forms, and exchange money, and receive room keys. It is the rationalized world of commerce and institutions. I feel better now. My body edges itself a little taller. I prepare myself. I find myself preparing myself as might an actor when he is ready to go on stage. I can see, across the clearing, others making their way to breakfast. It is exciting. The familiar and the unfamiliar. Those whom I don't know, I eye with eager inquisitiveness. Who is this, then? A friend to be? A competitor? A future lover? What kind of body? What kind of face? Friendly? Aggressive? Are they more anything? More stylish, more intelligent, more good-looking, more energetic, more joyful, more anything?

The eager examination and the comparative thoughts rush through my brain. There is not much time you see. Not much time at Esalen. So, if I am to size up people, I have to do it fast, before I get in the lodge.

I imagine the thoughts of most of the people. They have come to Esalen as searchers. Searchers for wisdom and searchers for change, and probably searchers for both. They are all pilgrims, having come a long way. They can't get there by plane. They've driven at least fifty miles and the chances are they've driven a couple of hundred. They had read the catalogue and, like me, been intrigued and baffled by its procedures and promises. They couldn't help but approach such a place, whatever their ironic doubts about it all, with some measure of awe. They wondered which others were here, in that lodge, on the quest. And who would they be, those other pilgrims, and what would they offer and what would they try to take away?

I walk along one arm of the oval, passing the office with a glance to see that it is still closed. There is always disappointment in that. If the office were open, there would be another social place to go. Another human activity, besides what is happening in the lodge. An alternative. Perhaps an escape. With it closed I go toward a single destiny, a single drama, and that has not always been a good one. As I open the heavy redwood door of the lodge, I always feel the same feeling. It will get more and more intense as time goes on, as the months go on. But it is always the same. I feel it in my aching stomach. I experience it in more shallow breathing. In tensions in my shoulders and arms. All slightly tighter.

The life of the lodge is in progress. There is a steady hum of conversation. Occasionally a loud guffaw. People are greeting each other with embraces, smiles, hearty and gentle good mornings. The waitresses move through space, seeming to bustle and float at once, pouring coffee, bringing breakfast platters. The phonograph plays Vivaldi so as to keep the noise down to a manageable level. There is life here. And, apparently, there is community. Members of various seminars greet each other, ask about one another's health. Chat about the landscape. Members of the staff sit with one another. A group apart. The Residents form another group.

I must act quickly. I have got to scan the empty seats in the lodge and determine, without seeming to have a lot invested in the process, which seat is for me. I open the door and look around fast. It is important not to catch anyone's eye. If I do, then, he may wonder if I decide not to sit next to him. Being as incredibly self-conscious and self-obsessed a place as Esalen is, I enter the room acutely aware of my mood; moreover, I am aware that I am going through some larger psychic transformation in myself of which the mood is only a part. The choice of whom I sit next to is an extension of my growth program. Since I have neither work nor formal growth program, the mealtime appearances are decisive moments. If I sit with the people I am comfortable with, I would be comfortable. On the other hand, if I sit with the people whom I was less comfortable with, perhaps I would grow, extend myself, learn something new, acquire a new tolerance, more information, get into some area of humanity or myself that I am avoiding. I had to resolve this debate, for comfort or growth, in seconds, because after all, I couldn't stand around the dining room forever with all those awareness-trained eyes looking at me.

I believed that everyone would see I was uncertain, wavering, inconsistent, and, therefore, as I put it to myself, unmanly. I had come to Esalen equipped with all the trappings of manliness and, god damn it, I would not be unmanned. But there was the voice in me urging me to take chances and grow, and the other voice urging me to relax and simply enjoy myself. And the third voice urging me to hurry and not expose myself. And then a fourth voice comes in with the maxim that one grows by simply doing what one wants to do—as Fritz Perls puts it: by being where one is. That would mean that I would grow fastest by simply seeking my comfort. The fifth voice: but is your comfort what you *really* want to have? You want to have growth, don't you? And by contact with strangers and threatening situations? Sixth voice: that's just a mind-fuck. Seventh voice: no it isn't, he doesn't want that. Eighth voice: want what?

CHAPTER THIRTEEN

voices

in the early days of November, I would finally resolve my inner debate by searching out Herbert and safety. But the more I sat next to Herbert, the more I isolated myself from the Residents. Not just because I spent that time with him, but also because, so it seemed to me, the act of choosing Herbert was an act of rejecting them. I began to imagine increasingly that they would sense this. I had condemned their Program, condemned them for participating in it, condemned their leaders. Surely they must hate me, I thought. Some would still come up to me, particularly when Herbert was away, and urge me to join them again, but I saw through it. They're probably laying for me, I reasoned, waiting until they can get revenge or else they are feeling insecure and scared themselves about the Program and want me back to give approval to them. They did not agree with my saying that they were only trying to win my approval. They seemed hurt when I said it. That really bugged me—the unaware sheep make me look bad for rejecting their nice invitations! Finally, I began to suspect them of deliberately torturing me by their attentions—they must *know* I can't accept their invitations to rejoin their madness, why do they keep making them? Why do they insist on making me reject such apparently good-natured people? It only makes me look worse to everyone else.

I would glance uneasily at Fritz, to see if he were looking at me. I hated Fritz. I wished him dead. I had instinctively hated him the moment I first saw him. I hated his self-assurance, his lazy blue eyes constantly scanning the dining hall. I would joke with Herbert, in my Freudian way, about the necessity of "killing the father." As time went on it puzzled me that Fritz would not return my harsh stares. He never seemed to look at me. His blue eyes just swept over me and beyond. He even seemed to ignore my love affair with Nancy. He appeared not to be jealous. I began to wonder whether I was trying to impress him, rather than the other way around. Fuck him; *I* was the impressive one, not him.

Parts of my mind were still open to My surroundings. Sometimes I would sit down at the staff table. On my guard, of course. But, on the other hand, I was eager for human contact and I couldn't talk to the Residents. Unfortunately, nearly everything the staff talked about was something of which I knew nothing. They talked about work, of course. About what it was like, say, to work in the kitchen, how crowded things were, what kind of boss they had, and so on. To this talk I could only respond with silence. I was completely out of it. And I sensed a glee that they had that I was out of it. Not just me, but all the other paying guests. They were on the inside and the Residents and seminarians were not. There was a natu-

ral antagonism between those who served and those who
didn't. They talked about psychedelics. It was the autumn after
the great psychedelic summer: "If you come to San Francisco,
be sure to wear a flower in your hair." The refugees of the
Haight-Ashbury disaster were crowding into Big Sur and there
were literally hundreds of them around in those days. There
were learned discussions about drugs: pot, heroin, speed, LSD,
MDA, STP. Artificial drugs were compared with natural ones.
Mescalin and peyote were advocated and admired because
they were "natural." On the other hand, there was "nothing like
acid." Many people told me that acid would solve my problems. This got to be a hard one because the year was wearing
on. I was getting increasingly depressed and these hippies,
people with no accomplishments, no money, no security at all,
seemed sunny and resilient in bouncing out of their own down
periods. Perhaps here was an answer, I thought. Maybe I could
learn to be like them if I took acid. Why not be like Monkey?
He is always cheerful. Monkey walked with a bounce. He
smiled, he laughed, he talked of absolutes with the familiarity
of an archangel. "Man, we're all one; you dig, man; like we're
all one." "Man," staring up at the stars on a warm night, sitting
next to me on that porch bench, "man, imagine it's like this:
those stars and planets and the earth are all part of one large
body. And that body is a man. That's the way it is."

Such talk was not mere silliness to me. *I* had been taught, by
men who knew nothing about it, to admire similar lines: "No
man is an island," "We are all one man." Lines I no longer
remembered by Herbert and Vaughan and Saint John of the
Cross, and Coleridge and Wordsworth and Dante. These kids
are real mystics, I said to myself. "Bullshit," I heard a voice say.
"Look at them, they are bums, they have no accomplishments,
like you. They must be lying. Phonies."

"Maybe not," came the first voice. "Maybe they really have
found the way. Try it. Try acid."

"I'm afraid."

"Yeah. And they know it, *they* see you being afraid. Ridiculous, man."

"I'm not ridiculous," a voice insists.

"Prove it," sniggers the other.

I didn't. I couldn't.

Other voices on the staff. Again trying to make fun of me. Carol Stokes, the only Negro hippie in Big Sur, wiping down a dining-room table one morning: "The reason you look so miserable is 'cause you won't drop out and become a beatnik like the rest of us. Give it up, man. Sell your car, buy a truck and live in it. You're wasting your time with all this self-improvement crap here. Drop out." I heard it a lot, and I wondered. Let myself be a bum, do nothing, have no place in society? Impossible. Yet these people lived that way. A hundred dollars a month, no homes, no careers. And yet they lived, they were happy. Happier than me. "Maybe I should drop out," I thought. "There's an answer here. It's obvious, it works for these people. Take it." But I was too afraid. "Suppose they aren't really happy? Suppose they are just trying to take me in, pretending to be happy, like the stupid Residents? Besides, even if they are happy, is it good? Is what they are doing *good*? That's what's *really* important. Does it have objective value?"

I asked one of the dropped-out ones, "How can you just spend your time hitchhiking up and down the highway, Paul?"

"I dig it, man."

"Don't give me that easy crap. You're a bright guy. What are you doing about things, about the war in Vietnam? Don't you care about it?"

"Sure, I care about it. But right now I've got to be here, in Big Sur, that's what I've got to do."

So, for him, there was no objective truth, I thought. His girl friend had a different line: "The war is all right, man. Everything that is *is*. There's no evil, no good. Why do anything about it?" I heard that a lot. Maybe *that* was right. She seemed happy. To see things that way. But I couldn't believe it. I couldn't. Then Paul asked, as he was leaving, "What are *you* doing about Vietnam?"

"Nothing," I answered, silently.

As time went on I realized just how little I was doing about anything. And I didn't like that. I should be doing things, I should be doing things about the war, about famine, about poverty.

"But you're not. Fuck that. Fuck all that thinking about that stuff. What the hell does all that stuff matter—it just makes you miserable. Get with yourself and forget about doing good."

"Stuart," one of them asked one day: "Why don't you become a carpenter like Kit or Juan? You've got a lot of time and you're not doing anything else." "That's a good idea," I thought. "It's useful—no doubt about that. People respect craftsmen, particularly here."

"No, idiot, you're meant for greater things. After all your education and accomplishments? To become a carpenter! You're meant for more. Much more. And you know it."

I did. I thought I did. I must. But what things. What things?

The voices would wreathe me, circle around me, and enter through me, inside my head, busy, multiple, a long conversation that never seemed to end. And there were always the Residents. Maybe they were on the right track, maybe I should return to groups and body-awareness work and Gestalt therapy.

Herbert was getting increasingly cheerful it seemed to me, as I seemed to be declining. He was more and more certain that he was onto ultimate wisdom. He told me excitedly that his early mystical experience had just started things. "I think I've gone further than Jesus or Lao-tzu," he said.

"Herbert, pull yourself together."

"How would you know?" he said.

That silenced me—I didn't feel as though I knew much any more.

"Listen," he said, "what's bothering you? You look depressed."

"I don't know what to do with myself," I said and sighed.

"I'll tell you what to do. Do what I'm doing: give up being special. Give up being dependent on others *thinking* you are special. Give up looking for approval. Give up looking for status. Seem ordinary. Give up outside support."

"What good will that do?" I asked.

"Try it and see. Here, have another piece of salami."

"Thanks. But what should I do exactly? Where should I start?"

"Give up driving fast. Give up your fancy clothes. Those two things will help just fine."

And they did for a while. When I would take the car out now I stayed right in my lane and I followed the line that accumulated in front of me into town. I wore the hiking boots instead of my English ones and simple denim clothes. "Herbert is right," I thought, "give up being special, that's the clue. The trouble with the staff and the Residents is they don't know that. So they're always doing something weird, like taking acid, or wearing those fancy hippie outfits, or going to groups."

"Right," said Herbert with a big smile and a slap on my shoulder.

I was delighted with myself. By becoming ordinary I somehow became even more special than before—better than these others, at least. So much for my worries about dropping out or becoming a carpenter! I was changing fast. Faster than those in the Program: I *was* learning wisdom.

But I got discouraged again. The elation lasted only a few days and when I presented my depressed face to Herbert, he was disgusted. "How can you feel depressed?" he asked. "You must still be trying to be something you're not. After all I've taught you!"

"But I *feel* depressed." I could see he was getting angry at me. I was being a bad pupil in some way. I implored him to give me some more help.

"O.K. O.K. You've got to settle into yourself all alone. Go up to Fritz's house tonight. Sit on the deck, all alone, all night. Don't take any cigarettes. Fritz is away and no one is there. Remember, no comforts, nothing to distract yourself, no cigarettes, no coffee, no friends. Just you. That's what I did the night of my revelation."

So, having put on my pea coat, at about eleven o'clock at night, I went to Fritz's house. I took up my vigil on the wet deck high on the cliff overlooking the ocean. I sat in one captain's chair and put my feet up on another. And I waited.

It becomes difficult for me to keep awake, but I keep at it. I've never stayed up this long. Hours pass, dragging slowly along. I wonder what's supposed to happen. Herbert said that something would happen, some illumination. Nothing so far.

I sit and I'm getting tired and bored. It must be very late. My mind wanders. Suddenly, an image comes into my mind. A Monterey pine tree, hardly more than a shrub. There are no leaves on it. It is planted on the edge of a high cliff, not unlike the one on which I sit and it is naked to the blast.

This must be it, I think. It was a pretty intense image. I am that tree. Like that tree I exist. And, that is the truth, the whole truth. I exist, phenomenally exist. That's what Herbert was talking about all the time when he said get with yourself, stop striving. I exist. And existence, pure existence, is what we are faced with. There is no God, no cause or standard that can justify existence, just like Herbert said when he mocked the Residents for their "spiritual search." One simply exists, like a tree. I am filled with joy. I run down the hill from Fritz's, past the lodge, through the garden, around the horseshoe made by the falls, and home. I wake up Herbert to tell him. I am free from doubt. I am glad just to be, another object under heaven!

He is very pleased. "Go write," he says, "put it down." Good, I will follow his lead. What excitement. How profound. I've beaten the others, I'm way ahead of the other Residents, now, I thought. I'm having a real mysterical experience! I write:

> "I am a lone, smallish
> tree, on the cliff—plateau.
> Nothing else is like I *am*.

I have solitary, sure, perfect EXISENZ."

I realize I'm beginning to write in German but I feel it is right. I realize that I am misspelling the German word but the delirious excitement is all part of it, I am sure, part of such an experience. "All that one should—ought—can do is know." Just what Herbert says! "The man who has locked his circle can only further enhance his being by helping others to do the same." Yes, like Herbert, I must take what I have learned and help others. He will teach me how to do it.

I woke up the next morning feeling very smart and virtuous, eager to go out and help others. Herbert was very pleased with my progress—I had been too selfish before, he told me. After breakfast he has explained some more elements of his new philosophical system. I had only just begun, he told me. It was clear that he was proud to have me as a pupil at last. But I had to go on, he said. We had to tell others, bring them to sanity, and give them instructions. I told him I agreed completely. I would help bring in new people.

We were sitting conversing with quiet excitement on a large rock, facing the ocean and next to a path that skirted the lodge and went down to the baths.

Robert Portman was approaching, carrying a cheap rubber snorkel. "God," I said, "he's really doing it. You remember, he said he was going to experiment with sensory deprivation, explore his consciousness in the baths, under water." This was the Esalen occultism Herbert despised and that I found freaky and frightening. All this endless struggling to break through, to change, I thought, never satisfied with the way things are. Herbert nudged me. "Tell him, now that you know." I nod. I'll straighten him out. Very stiff, very stolid, rather joyless, marches Robert along, carrying his pathetic six-dollar snorkel down to the baths in search of the Absolute. I remain seated on my rock and advance to him only with words: "Robert, why are you going to the baths with your snorkel? Listen to me, I *know*. I have had a revelation like Herbert's and I can help you." Robert is a little startled. Herbert and I have not been his friends for a long time. He looks hard at me for a moment. "Stuart, if you were enlightened there wouldn't be that quaver in your voice and you wouldn't be swallowing so much, a sign of fear."

He picked up his snorkel and proceeded down the path, ignoring my feeble cry: "You're missing something, Robert.

"I pity that poor bastard," I said. But a part of me felt depressed, unrecognized. Maybe Portman did know more than I did. I wondered if Herbert would disapprove of me.

"Don't worry about it," he said. "That business about swallowing was just a mind-fuck. He'll come along; we've got to be patient."

My own sense of certainty about what I knew came and went but Herbert was always confident. "I've much more to learn," I said to myself. "I'll have to listen harder, spend more time with him. I *can* teach. I have things to teach. I just need Herbert's help for a while. After all, I did have that mystical experience."

CHAPTER FOURTEEN

❋ sinking ❋

as gurus, we specialized in women—they seemed more susceptible and, besides, more attractive. Some seminarians had just arrived for "A Workshop on Death." Can you believe it? I asked myself. They are trying to grow by thinking about death! The dozen of them had gathered on the lawn, grim-faced, sitting in the usual circle. One of them detaches herself and wanders away. Herbert and I are sitting on our rock, looking. She is middle-aged, with a faded face, lined, and pretty legs. I can't see the rest of her body because it's covered by a long loose terry robe, brown and orange. Herbert sees his chance. He leaves the rock and goes to talk with her. About twenty minutes later he returns alone. He explains: "She had a husband. He died in an automobile accident about three years ago, and she's hung up about it. We've got to make her realize she's all right. That she needn't feel guilt and that she should start life over, enjoy herself."

"But Herbert," I answer, "you constantly say there are no accidents. She must have had something to do with the death. She must be responsible, in part."

HERBERT: "Of course; she killed him; she drove him to it. But that's over. We can't let her feel guilty, it might make her kill other men. We should tell her she is truly good, truly exist-ent."

"I get it," I said, proud to understand the system, proud to have my question answered, proud of learning, proud of hav-ing faith in the teacher. I had been a very good student in school, just this way, nearly all A's in college. School had taught me faith: if I worked hard I would learn, understand, and be rewarded.

Herbert called her over. Introduced as the disciple and ap-prised of her psychic problem I told her that she needn't grieve any more, that time was past, she was a good person, a loving person. It was satisfying to be the good student again.

She flushed as the two of us assured her of her worth and told her she deserved to live and enjoy life. She wanted to be-lieve it, poor depressed lady, she wanted very much to believe it.

"Oh, but you don't know me; how can you be so sure?"

"We know a lot about you," Herbert said, "as for example that you are proud of your legs; you come on as prudish, a little bit, but you show a lot of leg."

I nodded, smiling. It was too much for her: her own desire to feel better, two younger men attending her, flirting even, our little piece of insight. She brightened. Looking up at the gray-ness overhead. "You're right. Enough of mourning and that silly workshop." She turned playful on the spot. I began to be-lieve in my powers—instant cure, I had really helped her. She taught creative writing at San Francisco State, she said. She was a published novelist and looking for a change in life. I was attracted.

But so was Herbert. He used his earlier success in helping her: "If you want to change, why don't you go to bed with me?"

"But I hardly know you."

"I gave you good advice before."

She giggled. She was really enjoying herself. "Or go to bed with me," I said.

"I don't know which of you I want." She beamed.

I could see Herbert really wanted her. So did I, by this point, but I didn't like competing with Herbert. It made me feel very lonely.

"You want Herb," I said.

"I do?"

"Yes," I said.

"O.K.," and she looked up with a girlish smile at him.

They walked off and, on the whole, I was pleased with myself. I had helped Margaret, been effective, and I had been a good disciple. But there were rebellious thoughts in me: I wanted to be a little better than Herbert, I wanted to take away the woman, walk across the property with everyone guessing what was going on. And I could see she was more attracted to me. Why should he get her? "Because he's the wiser one, dope." I still didn't feel at ease.

I drove up to Berkeley to visit my friends from the time I used to teach at the university. That was always a relief. Two graduate-student couples: Arthur and Daisy Pennington and Forest and Rebecca Pettle. I was sure that I threatened them by being at Esalen—it's so different from their history department life. They must resent me, they must want to put down what I'm learning. I'll just remain aware of that and *show* them I'm moving ahead, then they'll see how much I'm learning.

We are gathered at Arthur's house, he is a laconic Princeton graduate, now an indigent graduate student. I start an encounter group—openness and honesty will I teach. It started with Forest and Daisy yelling at each other. Forest, a fierce pint-sized New York Jew, was Arthur's best friend. Daisy was jealous of the time they spent together. Arthur sipped his drink. I turned it: "What have you to say, Arthur?" He mumbled something. "Arthur, let's play an encounter game. Ask each of us here if we know where we stand with you. You're evasive, unresponsive." Arthur went round the room and asked. And each agreed and said how angry he made them. Arthur explained how sorry he was. He was shy and maybe too reserved. He would try to change.

I managed the scene and was pleased with myself. The atmosphere of honesty had been productive. Everyone seemed pleased. I put my hand on Arthur's shoulder and he teared. Daisy hugged him. After a while, Forest grinned and said: "Let's go out and have a good time. We're almost late for our dinner reservations."

I jumped up gaily, relieved that we were finished, and walked over to Rebecca. I felt really good, jolly. "Hi, Becky," I said and I playfully tweaked one of her ample breasts.

She slapped my hand away. I was shocked. I had meant nothing; we were familiar enough so that there should be no offense; I was certainly not making a sexual gesture—I had never entertained sexual thoughts about the attractive Rebecca, she was Forest's wife and I just kept away from my friends' wives, kept them out of mind altogether. Why had she slapped my hand? "Don't treat me like some *thing*, Stuart."

"Rebecca, I didn't treat you like a thing."

"You did."

"Didn't."

The others come in, on her side. I am amazed again. Becky is furious. I have never seen her, a gentle girl, angry before. Old scores are coming up. It is not, as I had first thought, that she is

offended by my overfamiliarity: she is offended by my imper-
sonality, at the fact that I have been Forest's closest friend but
never close to her. I feel on the defensive here, I explain:
"Becky, I thought you were satisfied with our arrangement—I
am Forest's friend; I am nice to you; I don't get involved with
you. I don't want to complicate things, between me and Forest;
I don't know how to treat my friend's wife, so I stay away."

She only gets angrier, her voice nearly screams: "That's just
it, an arrangement; you don't treat me like a person."

The chorus grows, Forest nods his head, Arthur understands
her complaint; they say I have to learn to relate to women, to
be more real with people generally, to get off my high horse.
Becky ends it, still angry: "Look, Stuart, if you can't treat me
like a person, don't touch my breast, that's all." I am hurt by
their accusations.

It only lasts a moment. We go out and have dinner and
everything is cordial, but the next morning I decide to leave
Arthur's house early. "I had a good time, Arthur. Thanks for
everything." It was all right, I thought. Good companionship.
So what if they are critical of me a little bit. They don't have to
think I am perfect, do they? I feel scared again, though. I get
into my car.

I fight the feeling. I drive to a diner, get out, and find a
phone booth. Why not call Margaret? She had departed five
days before, but lived on the way back to Esalen, and she had
wanted me. That was exciting. It was a rainy day. One of those
drizzly romantic days I love. It would be good not to have to
return to Esalen right way. It would be good to go elsewhere.
Margaret was part of my old literary world. She was teaching
at State, we might know people in common. She could reassure
me in lots of ways. She probably had a nice house in the country, near Monterey; she must be well off. There would be moth-
ering. The comfort of substantial possessions. Like going to a
friend's house on college vacations—their family's life, its substantiality.

I called her. She wanted me to come. I would get there in time for a late lunch. She would have everything ready. I get back into the car with excitement. I turn on the radio and prepare to pass the hours in a leisurely drive through the rain. It's about midday and there is a suggestion of gold where the sun is trying to show through the drizzle. I feel better than when I left my friends.

As time goes on, however, I begin to get a little tired. As I near Margaret's house somehow it is less important and exciting than it was, not long ago, just a couple of hours ago, to screw Margaret, to be with another woman, to seek relief at another place. I want to sleep, maybe go back to Esalen, and just sleep.

I lose the house for a while, taking the wrong side road. But then I find it. Under big trees with thick wet leaves, the house is smaller than I imagined. And in a shabbier neighborhood. It was not unpleasant but it was not interesting. A little white affair, one and a half stories, cheap and neat and lower-middle class; it had a tiny lawn and a tree or two around it, but it was no romantic villa. I open the door to discover a plate of Dog Yummies on the floor, suggesting what I found: an ancient cocker spaniel, companion of the bosom to the disappointingly middle-aged looking lady who approached to take my coat.

The furniture was cheap. Too many pieces with that over-lacquered look: Goodwill rehabs of pieces, too many Mexican throws, Indian throws, inexpensive decoration, so much the furniture covering in every California student pad, everyone had been to Mexico—exoticism close and for a few dollars. There was a neatness about the place that contradicted the reminiscences of student life, a kind of scrubbed quality. I saw the principal book she had published, it had a peace symbol on the jacket, it was about radical politics: poor Margaret, caught somewhere between the glamour and energy of youth and her faded, closed-in middle age. Sweet lady, but with no feeling of security about her, no signs of conquest, only last year's novel.

There was no comfort for me in this: Margaret hadn't made it, there was no smell of triumph over life here, she was barely holding her own. She had looked much better at Esalen. There, the lines in her face had not mattered much. For there everything is romantic and everyone is glamorous—the coast lends its beauty and the mountains their grandeur, and all the people, besides, have the dignity of the quest they are on.

We sat down to lunch, some home-made gourmet soup, but served in ordinary china. Only the glasses are good—delicate; we had some passable *vin rosé*. We chat. About Herbert. About the comedy of her being confused about which of us she wanted. Then, the necessary filling in: she has lived here six months; she won't stay unless her contract is renewed; she teaches three times a week; she drives up there; she knows Professor X and I know him too. Forward, the wine works, the soup is good: she used to have a lover, not too long ago, they thought they might get married, but it hadn't worked out, he had been a bastard, treated her badly; she is, or pretends to be, a little bit shy in talking about the old lovers. It is good that, winning, she begins to look better to me, and I pursue, I am charming, I smile. I tease her about her reluctance. Life is returning. The juices flow, the body tingles, the mind focuses and enjoys. Reality once more, some pleasure. I flow to it. I become the hunter, she becomes the eternal girl, fleeing on that Grecian urn. Dessert is finished. Glow. More wine. It tastes better now. To the sofa. More flirtation. Who will make the first contact? It is exciting, sweet, anticipation. Still she talks about an old boy friend, she complains, she explains. I am sympathetic, and each of us peeps out from behind the conversation to see where our imaginary hands will make contact. I look at her legs, I am aware that she waits, just a second, to lower her gaze, for she should not be too aware that I am looking at her legs. We play well, I talk of Esalen, how crazy it is, how difficult it can be, how I like being with Herbert but, after all, isn't he a little crazy? She silently agrees with that; yes, she implies, I, Stuart, will be the better man. Her glance wanders, as though she is looking for a place to lie down, the sofa being too short. Or, do I imagine that? I press forward. I can't stand not knowing: I whisper: "Let's go to bed." The slightest fluster, hesitation— "Yes," she breathes. We walk to the bedroom.

A slight ripple of interference, jarring. She unlocks her hand from mine where I am lying down seeking to draw her to me and begins stacking records on the record player. Alas, too obvious this setting of the stage, too redolent of an act reiterated. Leave more room for specialness, don't show your practice. The rest is better, though. Her clothes I take from her. Her body is not what I have hoped. It has the ungainly form the nudes take in the early Dutch paintings: long trim legs suddenly swelling into roundness of belly and hip, hanging breasts, thin arms and neck, sensitivity, but none of that life-assurance of the athletic build, the Italian masters, and the Playmate of the Month. But the contact is good. And I am surprised. The touch is good though the sight isn't. Older women are marvelous that way, I remember. And I sink into the experience and the givingness of her, givingness that comes from knowing the whole chance is fading, now or never, the grave is coming; unlike the tennis-ball girls who still protect their perfect figures with the armor of rubberized resistance. Here it is sweet, wet, wet noises, open, open. We come together; our hands entwined, tightly, pinning one another's knuckles against the sheet. Rest. Then again, just once more, the records, occasionally, I can hear them this time. Still good. I fantasize as we embrace that I have found a lover, a friend, someone who will take care of me. I like it. I like her. We are warm.

And then it is over. I hear the music; Judy Collins; I look at Margaret, her skin appears rumpled like the bedclothes. There is, I would swear it, a slight smell of decay, as if her body resisted, so tired was it, the exertions it had just been forced to. Solitary lady, I somehow feel she wants to be alone now. I look around, returning from reality to reality—the cheap Mexican throws are still there. The day is darker. And, suddenly, Margaret and I have nothing more to say, or do. Strange. It was truly nice in bed, when we held each other. Better than most of the girls I have had that autumn. There was contact. Real. Suddenly gone.

We feel each other's distance. Not dislike, just certainty of distance. I begin to dress; she puts on a robe—the wrong color for her. I open it to stroke her long, full breasts marbled with blue veins, once more. There is a trace of gaiety. But it is time to go. It is getting dark, four-thirty. I have to get back to Esalen. She is disappointed and glad to see me leave, it is right, too bad. But she is a grown-up, I needn't worry about her, I can see that. Kiss good-by, something, mumbles about calling, seeing one another again, neither of us means it.

Back in the car. I drive through the night, catch the rush-hour traffic in Monterey, it's not bad. As I leave Carmel, the road narrows slightly. The wipers are thumping from side to side. It becomes lonely out there with the darkness and the wind. The houses are few. Not many lights. On the left, not much out of town, there is an expensive-looking farmhouse, russet and large, with many windows, prosperous. People have property there, something big that belongs to them, gentlemen farmers, probably. Even in this season, a few tourists are returning the other way, families, couples, and I can see them in their cars for a brief instant before their headlights compel me to turn away. It gets more and more desolate, and then the road turns upward, very slow now, rocks fallen on the road from the rain. I have to watch carefully. Now nothing, no one. Far far ahead the lighthouse beacon circles, brushing the road in its sweep. Winter and rain and no one but me. There is not much to look forward to. The wetness increases. The tiny village of Big Sur seems empty, no cars in front of the doors of the two motels as I sweep by. The damp gets into the car and into my woolen clothing. At last I turn off the darkened highway.

Esalen is wet. Mud in the parking lot. I walk toward the

lodge, open the door, light, noise, the slight smell of wet woolen clothing drying out on the wearers' bodies. I am not hungry. Herbert, tireless, is in the corner at a table plying the guru's trade with another lady, slightly younger than Margaret. He signals me not to disturb him. I eat, alone, avoiding the others, stuffing down some food, killing time. People begin to fade out of the lodge, I have my sixth cup of coffee, I take it with four teaspoons of sugar, the taste reminds me that I am alive. Even though I feel too full for comfort, I fancy that I am fading away. When I can take no more coffee, I get up and drive home, across to the other side of the property, through the wet.

I turn on the light. For a few moments, I can break the numbness with the ordinary and necessary activities. Undressing. Putting my clothes carefully over the chair. Going downstairs, brushing my teeth. The bedroom is cold, so I have to turn on the heater. The bed is cold so I have to get up and put on another blanket. I am tired. Thank God for these things to do, thank God I am tired so I don't have to think. It hasn't been a bad day. Not too much fear. It's over at last. When I turn out the light, there is some energy left. Don't let it go, don't let it push you around, don't let it turn into bad thoughts of your emptiness—the fact that there will be nothing to do tomorrow, the fact that you will live with your deadness. I reach my hand down toward my penis. It has had its exercise today. It isn't very responsive. But I smooth and stroke and jerk it into life. Ah, good, it is hard again. Life suffuses my body for a while. My mind races through the galleries of old snapshots taken by my eye and filed away for recall—hundreds of girls, girls from childhood, from college, from Berkeley, from Old Westbury. Old loves, some of these, bodies vividly remembered, experiences to relive. A kind of private richness. My world. And even, this morning's photograph, taken at $\frac{1}{100}$th of a second as I drove out of Berkeley: a seventeen year old with a short skirt and raincoat and boots. Just the knee and the muscle of the rising thigh to focus on. Margaret crosses my imaginary field of vision, my eyes are closed, but I dismiss her. Too real. I want something more Real than that. I find the picture, the still. That girl in Berkeley, she'll do. My hand moves faster. I feel big, above her. They are mine, my conquests, my slaves. My hand continues but the Berkeley girl is lost. I'm thinking about what Rebecca said. I'm getting away from the image. I must keep focused on the image for the moment when I come. It will be better that way. Back to the Berkeley girl. I'm starting to come, damn it, I'm coming, but I can't keep focused on that one image, that girl. There are others coming in. Some who don't like me. Margaret. There she is, I've got the Berkeley girl! Her picture flashes, millions of them a second. I'm coming, here I come, but I can't keep the focus. It comes, one second, then another, pure pleasure. The semen is still erupting when I start to return to myself. It's over. The energy and excitement are suddenly fading. And, I think, as I wipe my chest and legs with the sheet and turn over to a dry part of the bed, I didn't even get what I wanted out of jerking off. Something is wrong with me. Sleep.

In the morning, my escapes are finished, the only place I have to go to is the lodge. My late morning dialogues with Herbert plunge me further and further into his views which I half know are paranoid and deluded. At last, I go to the baths. It is another thing to do besides just sitting. Though I hate the baths, I go there from time to time, just to break the monotony, on the chance that something might happen. There is always the promise of seeing the bodies of the girls, and taking snapshots for masturbation. More importantly, there is always the chance that I might be able to enjoy the baths. The baths are special. Most of the things at Esalen are enjoyed by one group or another; the seminarians enjoy some things which the staff scorns; the staff enjoys other things which the seminarians scorn or are frightened of. The staff scorns encounter groups and the seminarians scorn outlandish costumes or vague occult-isms. I use this division to keep myself on top. I side with the scorns of both groups; both groups are foolish.

The baths are special though. Everyone seems to enjoy the baths. I saw that literally every kind of person used the baths: seminarians, staff, visitors, Big Sur locals, Residents, and also people of every age, including children. It was obvious that they found the baths extremely pleasurable. How often did I have to sit in the lodge, my body growing increasingly tense as the months went on, my anger at Esalen and my fear of it growing by turns, and listen to some seminarian, a reasonable looking middle-class type, maybe an engineer, come up from the baths, dehydrated from the heat, order a beer, sit down, look at me with a very relaxed, serene face, slightly sweating, big smile, and shake his head to say: "Boy, those baths are really something, aren't they? Haven't felt so relaxed in years."

And yet, I was as uncomfortable in the baths as I was else-where—even more so. In order for me to think of myself as even normal, not to say superior, I had to enjoy the baths. The fact that I didn't made me inferior. If I couldn't enjoy the baths, I was unrelaxed; if I couldn't relax, then I was not whole; if I wasn't whole, then I needed Esalen more than any-body, I would then have to do all the things I didn't want to do, there might be no end: baths, encounter groups, body work, even Engle's screams and tantrums. I would have to give up everything and do what they said.

Each trip to the baths was a test. I entered, stood on one foot to take off one shoe, then switched, took off my clothes. My neck would stiffen. I was trying to keep it from turning to look at the other bodies, and more importantly, to watch the other bodies looking at my body. I was worried what they would think of it. I was worried that they would see my hunger to see the girls. I was worried that they would think me tense. I was worried that they were observing me, for they must be doing that, I was such a special character, and such an enemy of the place, they must be watching my every move. I must be careful not to betray myself, somehow, I must get rid of that slight pain in my abdomen that kept me from breathing freely. Then, too, I could congratulate myself that I had a good-looking body. That was a comfort. That message passed back to the neck and down to the stomach: "Relax, see, your body is good. They can't get me there." But it didn't help. From the stomach and the neck came the answer, "But what about your legs, they're too skinny, and besides, your skin, it's got pimples, and the pores are too thick, and it's too white; maybe they're gonna see all that, and laugh at you for it, maybe you're showin' 'em that." I look up. I catch a pair of eyes, always. I scan elsewhere, the others aren't looking. Is this guy examining me? Is he piling up a dossier? Who is he, anyway? I've never seen him. Must be a new seminarian. What about the others? Maybe they looked at me when I was getting my shoes off. Damn it, how the fuck am I to keep track of what's going on? If I keep my guard up and look to see who's looking at me all the time, then they will know how tense I am. Besides, I'm not tense, damn it. I can relax and unwind like the rest.

I get into the tub slowly. I don't like the feel of the water— it's usually too hot. I sit on the edge with my feet in. I don't want to get in; but it's supposed to be good for me. Get into that hot water and you relax. All kinds of wonderful things happen. Trying to kill time until I can make up my mind, I scoop up some water with both my hands and place it on my face. I have a little acne, always have, and the doctor says it may never go away. They probably notice. Must make it obvious that I am a child. In some way, well, fuck 'em. If they want to think I'm a child, they'll learn better. I'll show them. The water with the sulfur in it will be good for my acne.

Eventually, I get into the tub, slip beneath the water. Part of my mind is racing, wondering what I am supposed to do, to feel, how I am best to get in touch with what is supposed to be a great experience, even though I am very uncomfortable. I look down, avoiding eyes. I hate my flesh, I hate its pimples and its sweat and its incessant itches. I itch more than other people. People are always telling me to stop itching, stop scratching; my father looking daggers at me as my little hand at age ten goes into my trouser pocket to scratch my balls. I hate having the air on me.

I look up, in front of me, the sky, the ocean far out, the line of sight doesn't take in the shore line. And, to the side, a boy sitting naked in a lotus position, eyes closed, facing forward. A girl doing some freaky Yoga posture on a table, her cunt points at me like an eye. Totally unself-conscious. They must be kidding. But I don't believe this, finally. They really are relaxed. And here I am, cowering in the tub, tense, getting in and out of the water, too hot. There is something really wrong with me, I think.

After a decent interval, when it wouldn't look like I had stayed too short a time, I got out of the tub and began to get dressed. I would always linger in thought at the railing for a few moments, not just to delay my departure for the benefit of others, but also to try and see, while I was still in the place and had the benefit of my clothes, if I could come to terms with it. How could that guy stretching his body on the bench feel so free, dirty, hippie-free?

By the time I throw my towel in the box and climb the few steps out of the bathhouse to the path leading upward, I am more confused than when I came, and it seems that the process will never stop. It just gets worse and worse. I head up the path, and all that I know to go to, to protect me, to keep me from going even more crazy, is Herbert.

"Go get me a cup of coffee," he said to me as I walked into the lodge, "very light, no sugar." I did as I was told and brought it to him. He was working on a new woman. "Cynthia —this is Stuart. Stuart can tell you that I know, right?" I nodded, hoping she wouldn't ask, embarrassed by his high-handed treatment of me, but hoping still to learn from him. His attention seemed focused on Cynthia, however. "Give me your right foot," he said. She blinked but I knew what he was going to do. "Give me your right foot!" He began massaging it with his thumbs, looking at me in triumph. He had explained it to me. This was the new method he had developed for first relaxing the seminarian who chanced his way. Then he would teach her and, naturally, fuck her. "Get me another cup of coffee, Stuart. Remember, no sugar." It seemed so ridiculous, I thought, guruing, massaging, even my serving him was ridiculous—just too incongruous. And I was more and more relegated to the role of menial assistant. But I went and got the coffee.

The next week, we spent less and less time together because Herbert would spend more time at home writing. When he came to the lodge, he was progressively harder and harder on me. "I told you to give up all gratification, all outside reinforcers, like me, but you still keep it up: the girls, thinking about becoming important, the whole bit. If you go on the way you're going you'll end up at fifty a Deputy Assistant Secretary of Health, Education, and Welfare." I didn't like the scorn but I tried to follow his advice. I stopped thinking about becoming important, I stopped chasing girls, for a while, but the only time I saw Herbert was when he came to the lodge to chase girls.

Then the weather cleared and there were two or three brilliant, sunny days. Herbert was more and more distant and less patient with me and others. He talked of leaving Esalen. The only time he let me be with him was at his house when he would read his endless manuscript novels to me, looking up in triumph after a scene he thought particularly good and saying, "That's some writing, heh?" "It's very good," I applaud, a little disappointed because I hadn't found in the passage the advice I needed. He was less and less willing to give me advice. He only wanted to work on his books. I stuffed my needs and my pride down and followed along as well as I could.

It was a few days before Thanksgiving and I had finally decided that I was just too lonely this way. I had found a seminarian named Janice, a thirtyish lady who smiled a lot. She seemed very interested in me. We were going to walk down to my house. I thought her more mature and healthy than most of the girls I had had. Feeling great about my new conquest, I couldn't resist checking her out with Herbert. He was sitting on the back porch in the cool bright sun. I told Janice to wait a moment and went up to him. "What do you think of her?" I beamed. "What do you care what I think?"

There was silence. I looked at him, half-puzzled, half-beseeching. He stared back with his big eyes. "Go do whatever you want. I'm through with you so stop bothering me. You're worthless anyway—see if you can become someone on your own."

The vehemence with which he said it. He wanted to get rid of me. And he betrays me. After I confide my weakness to him, he calls me worthless. "I'll kick you in the face," I mutter between my teeth. It's that childhood voice again and it embarrasses me but I mean it. He looks up at me, threateningly, the karate expert. "Fuck you," I said and walked away.

"At last it's over," I told Janice. "What?" she asked. "Never mind," I said. And as I strode off with her I got more and more confident. I put my arm around her. What a relief to be free at last. I'm on my own and doing just fine. I give Janice's shoulder a squeeze and begin to think just how I'm going to handle this seduction.

CHAPTER FIFTEEN

✠ sinking ✠

the next few days were spent in a mood of jubilation. I stopped speaking to Herbert and avoided him in the lodge. I knew he was watching me with his bulging eyes, his slightly nodded head, his black curls peeping over the crown. I would show him that I didn't care. Didn't care what he thought, didn't care about losing him, and didn't care that he was watching. I was having a good time, after all; the first day or two there was Janice. I am making it O.K. without you, Herbert. I am free. I am strong. Enough of my attempt to understand your "system."

There is joy in my step as I walk to and from the lodge for meals. I sniff the air with delight. I begin spending more time at Nepenthe. I drive the highway and I drive it as fast as I want to. Once more the four piercing eyes of my silver monster warn the coming motorist that something extraordinary is about to arrive in his space. Once more cars scatter from the path of the driving wheels of my chariot. Once more I look back and see the dust rising by the side of the road.

Then, I remember, the weather turned round. The bright, late autumn days turned into a California imitation of an Eastern November. Cold, rain, mist, and mud. Clothes and shoes are wet, no fast driving to do, nothing gay in the landscape, much less activity in the lodge. The exotic visitors from the road, hippies fleeing south from the Haight or north from Topanga, diminished in number. I began to feel very lonely. It was Thanksgiving Day.

All day long, except for an early breakfast, the lodge was bustling with activity and frequently closed to simply sitting. That was hard on me. The waitresses would open the lodge for lounging and then close it as the place went through the spasms of preparation for a gigantic Thanksgiving party, maybe two hundred people or more. Tables were set up in horseshoes so that as many people as possible could face each other. Garlands were placed on the tables. Then lifted as tablecloths were placed under them. Furious preparations were going on in the kitchen. Each place setting was given two glasses and extra waitresses were added for the occasion.

There was no place else to spend my time. Sometimes I would leave, because I couldn't stand it any longer. But I came back. I watched the preparations with a great mixture of feelings. I felt terribly left out. I had no relations with these people and their preparations. I would have nothing to be thankful for, a mournful guest at the feast. Such self-pity and real loneliness apart, I felt threatened. The other side, so to speak, was massing in force, was celebrating its ritual, almost as if having a full-dress parade. It was the first communal celebration since the wedding on the day I had arrived way back, it seemed six centuries ago, in September.

Though I was tempted to stay home, away from the party, I

went anyway. I would not be driven off, I would not let Herbert know I was down, or the staff. But the Stuart who entered the lodge late that afternoon, the sun already fallen, winter darkness already around us, a few waitresses finishing the preparations, was a different Stuart from the ones who had come before. He was terribly, terribly sad.

Somehow, I suppose, free of Herbert's support and insulation, the truth of how much I was missing was beginning to come home to me. People were coming, as the evening progressed, from all over it seemed, not only from the northern and sourthern reaches of Big Sur, but also from elsewhere. Seminarians, friends of the place, people I had seen before, others whom I had never seen, implying vast nets of associations out there, were rolling in, through the dark winter night, through the mud, exultant in opening the door, a rush by a familiar local to embrace the strange face. Suddenly it all began to seem very big. Esalen, the beloved place to them, larger than I had realized, so many place settings, so many strange faces, strange to me but familiar to others, Esalen, with a history before my time, a whole solid world, and me committed to oppose it. It was a sad and strange thing, something that made me feel very little, especially when, as the guests came in, I saw that there was forgiveness for all, even recalcitrant office girls who had been fired by the fierce Joe were welcome, at least for this evening: it was understood, somewhere, that all belonged.

All but me, I thought. My sense of my own isolation grew enormously in that late afternoon and also my sense of how freaky I had become: I had placed myself in a totally different position from all these people; I alone, except for Herbert, had elected to stay but had declared war against the place. I began to feel very small, kind of threatened, very queer, almost as if I had declared myself an enemy of mankind and of celebration. As I waited for the dinner to be served, my hands thrust into the pockets of my somber, dusty pea coat, wandering from room to room, to the fire and back, I must have looked sad. I seated myself in the gallery and watched the fire, conscious of the half dozen or so early arrivals sitting with me, and I began to cry. I was ashamed but I knew that hardly anyone would see me—looking at the fire as they were—there was a thoughtful Thanksgiving mood. I guess, partly, I was trying to signal for help, for a way back into the family, any family. A way out of loneliness. I guess these things. These are interpretations. At the time all I felt or was aware of was sadness, loneliness, and my contempt which I still clutched in an attempt to keep them off.

Once again it was Joe Harrison who surprised me. We were already seated at the dining table crammed together and mountains of food were beginning to be passed out, well served, the tables well laid, the guests facing each other, the waitresses serving the wine, all with great hilarity and ceremony. I had stopped the tears, I determined to keep my seat, not to show my sadness, not to yield in any way, to remain Stuart the Special One, the critic of Esalen, brave boy. But Joe must have known. He came up to me, this man whom I had tried to get fired with the others, and he said: "You don't look in such good shape. How's it going? We're going to have a little gathering at my house tonight. Duncan Jones, who's giving a seminar this week, will be there and a few of our friends. Why don't you come over?" I was momentarily caught off balance, and in that moment, I could not help but experience the reality of the situation; his generosity, his perceptiveness, his forgiveness; then I wrestled for an answer, my own mental picture of the gathering, intimate conversations, exposing myself to a group of people, their realizing how bad off I was, how miserable, how doubtful my worth. No, I couldn't face that. But I couldn't either play, for that moment, the accustomed role. I refused but I thanked him, both. I had not the self-deception left to deny Joe's generosity or to refuse admitting that I was saying no to the invitation because I knew I could not shine, because I was miserable and felt so in every way.

So I stayed in my place, and I ate the dinner, voluptuous food, many kinds, and free wine. I remember getting into a fierce intellectual discussion with some frequent and troubled-looking lady seminarian. I couldn't decide if we were flirting or not. I felt a little better for the contest of wits. Those moments of self-congratulation were the high point of my Thanksgiving.

Meanwhile, the merriment was going on around me. Esalen gets stirringly raucous and communal on such occasions, people really seemed together. While we were still eating, the dancing started in the next room. Rock and roll.

I finished, and walked in. The fireplace room had been transformed, the regular lights were out, it was filled with dancers, someone had brought a strobe light. I found that I didn't want to dance at Esalen. This night was no exception but it was special. For the first time I looked at the dancers crowded together with a deep, deep envy. I wanted to be with them. I really wanted to be with them. I watched the movements. Scrutinized the best carefully. Felt the strobe light blink-blink. Heard the music roaring out. Felt the energy. The delight. And I wanted to be with them. And I sat and smoked cigarettes. I wanted to dance but I couldn't dance. I sat there aching to join, but aching also with resistance. My body wouldn't dance. It didn't want to. I would not. I watched from the side for a long while as the seemingly better and freer people had their good time, and then I walked home alone. The elation I had about breaking up with Herbert was gone and I was sad, depressed. I began sleeping later and missing breakfast.

A few days later Herbert spread the word that he was going to leave Esalen. He asked Joe for a refund and though Esalen was in financial difficulties, as always in those days, Joe was too delighted at the prospect of Herbert's departure to quibble over a couple of thousand dollars. Herbert was very pleased with himself, partly for the new beginning, partly for having manipulated the management to the last; they were afraid of him, proving his power. There was a mood of bonhomie about him. In the dining room he waved me over. I was officially informed of his coup and his impending departure. I disliked his pride about overcoming Joe but with him going, it seemed all right to come closer together. He wouldn't be able to hurt me and it seemed proper to pay some tribute to our months of mutual support and protection. We talked a good deal. He told me he had been planning to leave, he was bored, he didn't want me to be dependent upon him when he left, that was why he had pushed me away. I believed about half of it. In a way, I thought, he is as confused as I am. Still, the feeling is nice, I rallied to the moment of parting friendship, I wanted him to have a nice good-by so I did some errands for him, helping him to pack his little foreign station wagon. Just before he left, I asked him for advice, almost in a jocular way, a valediction to our master-disciple relationship and to me both, in one last piece of advice. I thought we would smile over it, whatever he said, and the gesture, on both sides.

"Give me something to write on," he said. I handed him the only thing I had with me, as we stood by his loaded car, my checkbook. On the outside of the check register he wrote, "Be kind, always. Herbert." I was disappointed. I had expected, wanted, something warmer, something more personal, and more loving. It annoyed me. I had a funny thing about kindness. I wanted to be kind. But Esalen had forced me, I thought, to be unkind to many. I began thinking about that.

Herbert left on December 3. At last I was alone. I hated it. I tried to fight it and as I fought it, a desperation began to come upon me.

Annie, a tough teen-age girl, she's just gotten out of prison, she wears a dark blue turtle neck, I meet her at the bar, her hair is deep red, she falls down a lot, laughing loudly, very tough; she goes home with me. She fucks me. Very strong. I am baffled by her.

She's obviously no one, uneducated, crude. But she has been around, been in prison, brags about it, she's tough.

She makes a lot of noise. Joe fires her, then tries vainly to keep her off the property. We fuck a lot. She likes to fuck. She does it kind of professionally. As if her value is tied up in how well she fucks. Never met a girl like that. Girl gets points from how well she fucks. Amazing.

When I'm not being sad, I go find her. We make a lot of noise together. I yell and the hills echo; in front of the lodge, I scream: "Annie, fuck me!" She comes running. Jumps violently across my pelvis, her legs wrapping themselves around my waist, her arms around my neck laughing. She's like a twelve year old. Square shoulders. Stocky. And yet, some deep underlying sweetness. She walks in a very determined way. Tomboy. But big pro at fucking. Contradictions all over the place.

"No, Annie, you can't sleep here tonight. I like to have my privacy, my own place." "But Stuart, you fucked me last night. Don't you like me? I have no place to sleep." (She's trying to hustle me; move in; I'll never get rid of her; the loud mouth; she's so insensitive, so persistent, so pushy.) I start screaming— never screamed at a woman before like this—"Get out, Annie." She goes. I feel guilty.

Hilde, the opposite. Very beautiful face. Figure dumpy. Touch of *Vogue* model about her. Works at Nepenthe. She's older too, my age. Likes beautiful things. Speaks softly and elegantly. A refuge at last. Maybe a match at last.

I sit alone, at the desk. Herbert is gone a week. I am pretty depressed but I will try to write an essay, try to assure myself that I still have something left to say. I write long-hand. Seventeen pages, a whole morning. "On Boredom and the Modern Condition." Maybe I can still think. Maybe I can go back to

Old Westbury. Maybe I'm still O.K. But I don't believe what I am writing. The voices are there, all those Big Sur voices, all the voices of the human-potential movement blending, even Herbert's voice; it's a head trip, it isn't important what you've been doing, here we do something else, enlightenment is what counts, breaking through, breaking through to something, to something, but to what? Maybe it's crazy to write this. I stop. I get up from the desk. Walk around the small room. Throw things. No good. Walk outside.

I go to the lodge. Confused. No one to talk to. I sit with Ken Price. He asks me how I am. I say I'm unhappy, depressed, on a downer, whatever I say, however I put it. He has his work-gnarled hands around a coffee mug, quietly caressing it. Calm, he looks like a cowboy, wears a cowboy hat. Small man. Very deliberate speaker. He looks at me. Clear blue eyes. Starts explaining it all. Every person at Esalen will explain it all to you if you will listen. "Stuart, there are three things: the emotions, the mind, and the will. You've got emotions, you've got a good mind, but you have no will. You're paralyzed. Making yourself miserable. Make a decision. Any decision. Get off your ass."

I won't. I go away.

Can't stay this tormented all the time. I'll call up Hilde and go see her. She excites me. I go to the phone, outdoor pay phone, on the porch, outside the lodge. You dial first and then, when they answer, you put the dime in. Ring. Ring. Answer. I put in the dime. "Hello, Hilde, Stuart." It's night. About nine o'clock. Dinner is over. "I want to come over." The lodge door bangs open. Annie. Blue sweater, dungarees, no shoes, rain outside, runs yelling towards me. She won't let me call Hilde. Tries to hang up the phone. I tell Hilde I'll call her later. Run away from Annie into the night. In fifteen minutes, I go back. No sight of Annie. Ring, ring, dime, again Annie. Scream, argue with Annie, end up going to bed with her. She spends more and more time at my place.

More depression. More confusion. Fucking. Fucking. Joyless.

Annie wants me to enjoy. Gets mad that I am not enjoying. She is a joy giver, that's what she has to give. Why don't I tell her that she is giving me joy? Only joy is in the few pumps before the come. Otherwise, I am miserable.

Bright days. Wet days. She's oppressive. But she wants me. I let her in. She's very insistent. I haven't the strength to keep her out. For some reason I let her in. I feel more and more involved with her. Baffling. How come? What's the explanation. I don't like her. At least I don't think I like her. But she tells me that I like her. She tells me she loves me. She tells me I must love her. I do love her. She is so sure.

It's nice to have someone around who is so sure. She's as sure as Daniel. It's nice that someone is sure. And, who knows, maybe she is right? There is a beautiful hardness in her youth. The cold brown eyes. Maybe I do love her.

No, I don't. I can't spend my time on this, I've got to figure things out.

"O.K., you can stay, Annie, but you've got to find another place tomorrow." She reaches for my penis, her hot stubby fingers have learned gentleness, some relief there. I'll think about it in the morning.

I try to read. No, reading is useless. Can't do it. All the self-help, humanistic psychology, hip-religious books I brought with me: Rogers, Maslow, The I Ching. The answers I am looking for aren't in those books.

I've got to get out of here. I'll go to Berkeley. To visit friends. Annie: "Take me along." "No, Annie." "Takemealongtakeme-alongtakemealong!" Tears, shrieks like a child. "O.K., but be ready right away." She wraps a few miserable pieces of teen-age clothing in a large towel. Embarrassing. Not even a suit-case. How can I be with such a creature? Maybe I'm a snob. Shouldn't think such thoughts but she's just another dirty hippie.

Up to Berkeley, to the friends, they like Annie. A few days. Annie has to work. She has persuaded Joe to hire her back. I can't just put her on a bus. Can't abuse her that way. Who can't? Who says I can't? My shame. My guilt. Back to Esalen. Annie. People in the lodge? Voices. Voices. "Annie, help me," I ask. "Help me with my problems." "You don't have any problems, stop focusing on your problems, everything's O.K." "But Annie," say I, "I'm miserable. Don't you understand why? The things that are making me miserable, that I have been robbed of, all my doubts about my abilities, all my doubts about the validity of my world, all the voices." She doesn't understand. Doesn't think them important. Life is immediate for her. "Now. What's happening now?" she says.

My birthday is coming. Tomorrow I am thirty years old. Thirty is an important birthday. One of my old teachers, Edgar Cannon, told me that years ago, when he turned thirty. It is the day, he told me, when you realize you aren't immortal. I don't know. I don't know how I feel about mortality on birthday thirty. But I know I feel bad.

December 28 and the birthday. Herbert returns. Just for a visit. Wants to give me a party. Almost no one comes. But one girl. Another Annie. Leggy, blond, and wicked, a birthday present. Suddenly, just as we are about to go off, my Annie arrives. She had been in San Diego for Christmas with her family. She is back. I don't want her. I want the other Annie. Both names the same. Impossible. My Annie falls backward over the railing. Always falling. Hurting herself. I can't help but be sympathetic. I'll look bad otherwise. Herbert leaves. The blond Annie goes away. Parting looks.

I go to bed with my Annie. Joyless. I'm being pushed around. "Stop pushing me around, stop pushing me around." "Stop pushing me around," she mocks back at me. "What's wrong, can't you stand up for yourself?" she asks. Even this another trap. Everywhere a trap. And we fuck, and we fuck and I take care of her, feed her, give her a place to sleep, yell at her, buy her boots, she has no boots, give her things, scream at her, tell her to leave, she holds on, she knows what she wants. Four weeks have passed since Margaret.

CHAPTER SIXTEEN

✳ breaking out ✳

pain has crept into my belly, it is there all the time now when I wake up in the morning, anguish, ache, fear. As if the stomach were depressed and slow but the head alive with tremendous energy seeking direction, the body itself torn, the head tearing itself off the trunk, spinning, spinning into space, up toward the light, looking for some certainty, some solution, some decision; and then falling into darkness, the center of the earth, spinning everywhere, searching, asking.

I do something strange. I hear the Residents are going to work with Fritz Perls and, after days of hesitation, I decide to go. It was not easy to go. I have been afraid of Fritz, and I had been afraid of the Residents, I remembered the rat pack, I trusted none of them. I did it because it was a test of my courage. Also I had some feeling that Fritz was the best Esalen had and I ought to try him, a last test of the place, a hope that he could help me.

It is night. I know the session is to begin at nine o'clock. It is already a few minutes after nine. I climb the hill to his circular house, push open the big door, lots of shoes, I put mine down, I hear noise from the inner room. The Residents, twenty of them, are sitting against the continuous walls in a large circle of captain's chairs, there are spotlights, I blink on entering that circle, they all stare, I feel some satisfaction, in the midst of my own uncertainty, at startling them. And yet, I am frightened, awkward. Someone points me toward a chair. I look toward Fritz. I assume he's very interested in me. He seems unconcerned. We are here for a session of Gestalt therapy.

I sit in my chair, baffled by what is taking place, people get up one at a time and walk to an empty chair near Fritz. He smokes, asks them questions, asks them to do various things, they talk to an empty chair, switch seats, and talk back to their original chair. I get more frightened. The evening passes. Eleven o'clock, work over. All get their shoes and leave. I speak to no one. I tread carefully, I feel in danger here, I walk home.

The next day, Fritz gives brief occasional lectures. To get in touch with what is "real," he says, one must have self-awareness. From time to time, the others laugh as someone sits with Fritz in the "hot seat" but I see only misery, the misery of human striving and confusion; underneath all the surface social life, I am one who has dared go into myself and I have tested the limits of uncertainty. Bravely, I have looked into the heart of darkness, to see the emptiness, the death of all the gods, all certainties, all celebration gone into the void. There is some distraction from pain in this room, though I don't understand what they are doing. I wonder why I am here. At last, the last of two nights when Fritz will work with us, I get up. I walk to the chair. I must try it.

I get into the chair. He says nothing. Just smokes, stares

ahead. I make some joke, I'm a wit I am. Fritz smokes, then says, "You have come here to make jokes, show how bright you are, go ahead."

"I guess you want to be the bright one, huh Fritz?"

"Go ahead, be clever, it's all the same to me, I'm getting paid the same." Some of the group chuckles with him. I hate them, their final insult, laughing at me, don't they know what it took for me to come? I sense they do for most of them are very quiet and very intent. I don't know what I'm supposed to do.

Time passes. We sit. Fritz, at last, "What are you aware of?" I hesitate, it is painful to say it. "All that I am aware of is my own anguish." I wait, I have told the secret, told all here how much I am suffering.

Since there is no response from anyone, I dare to go on a bit; I hang forward in my chair, barely lifting my head, unable to look at the rest of them. "I don't know what to do. I've given up driving fast again. I get no pleasure from girls. I've lost everything. And I don't know what to do." I realize how pathetic I must sound, but I am going to tell the truth.

Fritz looks at me for the first time, just the slightest bit puzzled. "But what are you aware of in your body?"

Again, I hesitate. "The pain," I said. "The pain in the stomach."

"Are you sick?" he asks. "Appendicitis, ulcers, something?"

"No," I answer.

"You're a tragedy queen," he says. He pronounces it "qveen" with his German accent.

He sneers at my secret, at my life!

He goes on after a small silence, smoking: "You think yourself very special, very important, don't you?"

"No," I say. "Not important any more, no importance whatever."

"Yes, you do," he says. "A Byronic cloak streaming in the wind [he begins to smile in derision and amusement], standing on some promontory, staring into the darkness, a very special anguished soul out of romantic literature, *The Sorrows of Young Werther.*" He chuckles.

How dare he mock *me* with literary references. The barb is too special. He must have been studying me all the time. A few days before I had gone out on a promontory near my house, thought of casting myself over the cliff and on to the rocks of the beach. But he couldn't have seen me, no one did. I made sure of that. What does it matter, he has missed the main point —the reality, my pain. I protest.

"What is your name?" he asks.

"Stuart," I say, not believing that he doesn't know me.

"Close your eyes, Stuart. Go into yourself." I close them. A minute passes.

"What are you aware of?"

"I am aware of the pain, the dull and incessant confusion." I have the pain, damn him, I have it, it eats at me, doesn't he know, how can he make fun? He seems to be saying that it is a pose.

"Open your eyes. Look around the room. What do you see?" I look at the Residents, from face to face. I am shaking with fear as I raise my head. Downing the potential killer, Robert who has tortured me for taking his wife, Martha, who despises me, Bill the monster, even Nancy, the student, looking at me with clinical detachment. "I see," say I, "I see a group of enemies."

I notice a number of them shake their heads. Fritz only looks at his watch. "It's getting late." He turns to me. "Don't you see separate people out there? Do you see only a group? Are they all the same? Do you really know them?" He takes another puff before carefully poking out his cigarette in the ash tray. "You have only self-awareness. You care only for you. You have no *world* awareness." He looks up, tired, at the group. "That's enough for tonight."

I have only a few seconds to be stunned by the experience, as the session breaks up and people begin talking. I am angry at the way my pain has been dismissed. But I am also thinking: could it be I am so selfish, so wrong about the nature of things? Could it be that I am posing? Could it be that I have no awareness at all?

I get up to leave. But Bill stops me. The monster, and a few others, Bo and Nancy among them. He says: "Stuart, I'm glad you joined us. I always liked you. You're not like Herbert, you're not a bad guy, really; I always thought you didn't really want to be mean to us." Then, he embraces me. I begin to cry. It feels so good to hear nice things, good to be embraced, such a relief. Bill looks different than at the beginning of the Program. Softer, I never thought he could say such a thing. The others nod, they smile. Bo, warm but shy, reaches over to take me by the shoulder: "Come back to us." Then he leaves. It is all so contrary. Contrary to what I have been thinking.

In the morning I wake up with the same anguish as usual. But it's been added to. I now have doubts about whether I can even believe in the anguish I feel. No, no doubt there, I tell myself, I am miserable. I cry more often. I don't continue to speak to the Residents. Maybe they're not enemies but somehow I can't face them.

I go back to where I was before the Fritz group.

But I am starting to think of breaking away—maybe I'll go up to San Francisco, live there, and find something to do that will make me feel worthwhile. If I stay here, I'll kill myself, I think. Annie erupts into the room where I am lying in bed. I threw her out two days ago and with fiendish brilliance she has gone and successfully begged a bed in Nancy's house. "We're really becoming friends," she tells me with enthusiasm. Everyone around Esalen likes Annie, even my old lovers. In a way I feel more comfortable because she is so popular—her popularity can protect me from the critical hippies, from the Residents.

"I want to borrow the car, Stuart." I can't believe what she is asking. She knows how I feel about that car, even though I drive slowly now. I wash it and polish it and the little spots where gravel has chipped the paint are like holes in my own body. I *know* that's absurd but that's the way I feel. And now this female hobo wants to borrow my five-thousand-dollar car. Almost all I have in the world.

"I want to show you you can trust me, Stuart."

"NO."

"You know Harriet, the girl with the little boy who lives down the coast, she's been waiting two hours for a lift. The kid's driving her crazy."

I think of refusing—spitting on the hippie Harriet and her hippie infant. I am angry. But Annie has me boxed in—I can't look that cruel and selfish when she is being so giving to others.

"O.K., Annie. But don't scratch it."

"Gee, thanks, Stuart. Harriet will be grateful."

I lie down and take a nap.

It is four o'clock when I wake up, they left at noon. I hear gravel hitting the fenders below my window, the motor is choked off. Door bangs. She comes running, "Stuart, I scratched the car."

How can she do this to me? How can she? She knows. She borrows. She promises. And she scratches. I am furious. "How did it happen?" She looks miserable, penitent. "Harriet made me drive her home, up the dirt roads, all the way into the woods. I asked her if it would be all right and she said yes. It's all her fault."

"Why did you do it?" I insist. She hangs her head. "I smoked some grass and just wanted to do what she asked." Damn it, damn her: she knows I despise her concern with popularity. She knows I despise her bombing out her mind with pot. Everything. All at once. Car scratched. Trust betrayed. Pot smoked. Popularity sought. Annie always the popular one, just in case I don't work out I suppose. *She* will survive. "Let me see the car." I look. Twig marks, long subtle scratches on both sides. Damn her. Only one thing to do. Enough stifling myself lately, hanging back from doing what I feel. I'll act Esalen style, Big Sur style, do my thing. Be real. I force myself: I punch her in the stomach. Wham! It is just punishment. She should approve, herself. She believes in hitting, Self-expression. But I didn't do it hard enough. She has an athlete's stomach, hard as a weight lifter's. I can see she expects it, wants it, amazing people who live here. "Come here," yell I, and blam, I hit her as hard as I can, full fist. She doubles over, clutching her stomach she goes into the bathroom.

I listen to her vomiting.

I have never hit a girl. How can I do such a thing? Partly I did it because they told me to, those Esalen voices. Annie is your agent. She tells me she loves me, but she is one of you. Catching me in this trap. I apologize to her, I pet her, say how sorry I am, explain how shocked I am at what I have done.

I've got to get out of this place.

Annie sleeps at my house again that night. She is very happy. The next day I go over to the lodge to get my mail. The first printed copy of my book arrives, *The Picaresque Novel*, a handsome jacket. I turn the pages. It's only a small thing, and I wrote the first draft six years before. But people on the porch are impressed, and I feel its slim weight thinking, sure, I did something before. I can do it again. I'll go up to San Francisco, maybe I can return to literary studies or, who knows, I used to have good ideas, I'll call George Leonard, maybe he'll give me a job with *Look*, I could be a journalist. I don't know, but I will know more if I get out of here.

I'm going. I can get most of my stuff in the car. All my clothes. Those beautiful suits and jackets, handmade, Brooks Brothers, never worn in Big Sur. I stuff them carefully in the back of the Corvette. I'm getting out. Going to the city.

Annie once more, "Take me, take me." Big argument. "You don't like the city. Why do you want to go?" She pleads. She cries. "I'll think about it, Annie, let me have a couple of minutes to think about it."

"I'll pack while you're thinking."

Once more the towel—it's even *my* towel, to wrap her junk.

"You can't come," I say at last.

She is so disappointed. The very face of woe, tears streaming from her eyes, her face red, the cheeks nearly raw, ugly, contorted, the way a child cries, with every bone and fiber.

"All right, you can come," I say. I've very little energy—just enough left after all these months to make my escape. I can't waste it on her. "Hurry, let's go."

"I can't, I forgot, I've got to get someone to take my shift at the restaurant." She's a waitress now, my dear Annie, so she's going to delay me even more. A powerful woman this, a power, something to be afraid of. But I take her. After all, besides all the other reasons, how can a man in my condition refuse such apparently resolute devotion. That's what clicks it: a little voice, he speaks in cricket tones among the other somber debaters, the Roman Senate of my mind, urging: "Be smart, you might need her, never know, it's something, take it, even if it hurts." Another Senator rises: "It might work out." Yet another: "Try." And still another: "You can always get rid of her." I husband my failing energy and resolution waiting for her to return. It gets dark. At last, jubilant, she rushes in. I am grim-faced as we descend to the car, slam the doors. On engine. On lights. It has begun to rain very hard—a cold winter storm and I am afraid of the long ride. Almost immediately, Annie falls asleep smiling.

We manage to get past Monterey to the point where the road diverges. Route 1 continues toward San Francisco along the sea, the other route goes inland and is safer, wider, and better lit. The sea road is dangerous in bad weather. I wonder for twenty minutes as we approach the intersection which road to take: the way of adventure or of safety. The wind whistles through spaces between the windows and their rubber fastenings, it is pouring and very dark. Safety or adventure, safety or adventure. I have never taken the coast road. I swing off onto it as lightning cracks around me. And as I stare through the windshield I wonder only: HAVE I DONE THE RIGHT THING: HAVE I DONE THE RIGHT THING? A hundred and fifty miles and five long hours later: GIVE ME A SIGN, O LORD! WAS IT RIGHT TO TAKE THE COAST ROAD? WHICH IS THE WAY? WHICH IS THE WAY TO DO ANYTHING?

CHAPTER SEVENTEEN

✠ escape ✠

at the time, I felt no comic distance, only rage that I experienced as incessant anxiety. In the stomach, in the chest, which felt collapsed, in tiredness, wanting only sleep, rest. We get to San Francisco, at last. I have been there before, but only briefly. I hardly know the city. I get a map in an all-night service station and try to deal with the maze that strange traffic engineers have laid out for me, one-way streets that are not on the map, dead ends that run straight into the sides of hills. I manage to make it, late at night, to a cheap motel. I've got little money and I've got Annie to support now, too.

In the morning I call George Leonard. He will have dinner with us that night—meet him at Johnny Kans, famous restaurant, another big *Look* magazine expense-account dinner. That's an encouragement.

But now I have to find an apartment for two. I go to a miserable rental agency where for ten dollars, which I can ill afford to speculate with, they give me boxes full of rental listings and, the first visit, make two phone calls for me. The whole dreary business of finding a place in a strange town, a throwback to the grim days of graduate school, little money to support me in looking, wanting a nice place, a place that has some air, some interest to it, some charm. The frustration of not being able to afford atmosphere, not really wanting much, three rooms maybe, but with something—a view, a fireplace, a garden, something humanizing in this city so full of beautiful places to live, and not quite having enough money; debating about spending more of the small store; rushing here and there to get change for the telephone, the rental agency won't give it; I don't know the neighborhoods, they ask me where I want to live, don't know; two minutes they spend telling me about neighborhoods, then they tire, others are waiting; I flip dully through the stacks of cards, not knowing what would be a promising address, turning to other captives of the agency, similarly miserable-looking people, for advice—sorry, they are new in town too; at last, into the car, search for a phone, sorry it's taken; no, the landlord is out, could you come at six o'clock; then the business of endlessly crisscrossing the strange town, from one address to another, not having the surplus energy to do all that I am doing and also organize my searches by district, back and forth, and Annie no help.

"Read me the map, Annie." "I can't," says she, "I don't know how." "Get change, Annie." "I can't." A whine, a cry, she is afraid of the city, she has never lived in a city, only part of one summer on Haight Street, a disaster when she freaked out, screaming, through the summer night among the flower children. I am sympathetic but she is worse than useless. To my surprise, humble but interesting old apartments in decaying neighborhoods, the kind I would have been glad to rent, are not good enough for her. She is, besides everything else, spoiled. Her parents live in the country, near a river, big house. This tramp wants green grass, trees, clean streets. She makes the search more difficult. It starts to rain, driving becomes more perilous. "Stuart, let's go back to Big Sur, we have a nice place to live there, I don't like it here." I blow up, beaten; "Annie, you wanted to come, you knew at the time that you didn't like the city. It has been hard for me to come, why don't you help, at least not complain, be cheerful if that's all you can do." She's not one to be accused of impotence. Besides, she is not inhuman, she wants to help. "What can I do?" she asks. "I need support now, Annie, no further demands." She asks me to stop the car, then tells me to get out. "Get on my back," she says. She weighs no more than a hundred and twenty pounds, I weigh a hundred and sixty—she will give me a piggyback ride. It is funny, funny to change the level of reality from worry about bourgeois comfort to the play of children, funny that she is so strong, but not all that funny to me, for I still must find a place, for both of us, I think to myself, as she lopes down the street with me clinging to her back. In fact, I feel only the weaker that this strong girl, despite her whinings, can carry me around like a child.

Dinner with George was a bust. After an hour of good drink and Chinese food I asked him for a job at *Look*. "You mean you want to do a story?" he asked back.

I dropped the subject—I had no stories in me. It was all I could do to put one foot in front of the other. I thanked him for another lovely meal and drove back with Annie to our motel. She kept encouraging me to go back to Big Sur with her, "where the air is clean."

The next three days I continued to look for an apartment, as if I would do what I had set out to do, even though my will was failing. I roused myself again and again and Annie and I returned to Dorothy's Rents to see the old ladies who run the

place, the largest center for desperate people in San Francisco
trying to find a roof. I figured if I charmed the old ladies, they
would give me special listings, the few good ones among so
many. But though my charm had worked in the renting offices
of many colleges and universities, it didn't seem to work here—
these were not college-educated secretaries susceptible to the
bright young man, but symbols of doom, symbols of failure to
find; their hair is dyed blue-gray and they all wear glasses connected to beaded chains around their necks, and their dresses
look like they have been left over from the thirties; their make-
up is wrong, stark—purple lips, pink-dusted cheeks, caked in
the crevices; they sit at old desks; all very nervous, they move
with starts as if they feel the weight of expectation, the weight
of demand, that the younger people, in their twenties and thirties, many couples, put on them. Find me a house, find me a
house. And there is the scent of secret sexuality in these young
couples, the old ladies know that the young ones will fuck once
they have found a house, they know that. And that must be
why, the old ladies who move with such stiffness and such jerky
motions, that must be why they can't be charmed, why they
make phone calls to prospective places behind closed doors,
not letting you see or hear, why they lie to you, telling you that
the address of a particular listing is in a nice district when, if
you go, you find it next to a gigantic and gloomy reservoir of
natural gas, gray, steel; and besides the sexuality, they must
resent the fact that nature and poverty have conspired to lock
them in here, at DOROTHY'S RENTS, VAN NESS AVENUE, San Francisco, where their job is to encourage people to think they will
find an apartment and to sign them up and collect their ten
dollars and their job is then to discourage people from bothering them too much so that they can sign up new hopefuls as
they come in; yes, I think as I shuffle those wretched cards back
and forth, these uncharitable ladies must resent that, too, must
resent having to lie; and they must resent, besides, the pathetic
and wavelike force that rises across the desk from the hundreds

of daily lower-income hopefuls who want large apartments, with views and fireplaces, and gardens, all for one hundred dollars a month because San Francisco is a city of taste and people of vast numbers know what is nice and they want me, they want me, Grace, with my pinked cheeks, and purple lipstick and legs fallen away to sticks themselves, with my rattling beads like the chain of Scrooge's partner, they want me to help them. I hate those people looking for apartments.

My own desperation and dismay does not prevent me from beginning to have some sense of the neighborhoods of the city, to know where I want to live, but nothing that I can afford shows up. I resent the meals we are eating out, the innumerable dimes I am spending on telephone calls to landlords, even the gas the Corvette is using. I would like to be rescued. I want very much to be rescued. Annie whines, complains, gets hungry, needs to be fed. She gets more miserable in the city with each passing day. Every burden makes a difference to me, even the Corvette's being hard to steer at low speeds so that my shoulders begin to ache from pulling on the wheel; my left foot aches from pushing the clutch in and out.

We stop, evening, in the rain, and eat overpriced franks at the Doggie Diner on Van Ness Avenue. I am annoyed extremely that I cannot afford Tommy's Joynt, five blocks up the street, where the atmosphere is gay and the sandwiches tasty. Instead, and somehow it is Annie's fault, *I* must frequent this fluorescent desolation, the white lights making everyone look sallow, blemished: there are a bunch of teen-agers playing the juke box; will they jump me? The white tile, the white lights, the blue tile floors make the place seem like a gigantic bathroom, and I eat the sweet meat of my foot-long hot dog slowly, watching hungry and healthy Annie munch hers down untroubled by perceptions or fantasies like mine. There is so little I can share with her. For her a Doggie Diner is a Doggie Diner

—there are nicer places but it's groovy enough, the hot dog is what counts.

She has had contempt before for my pretensions and my evasions and my insecurities. They are sissy things to her. She comes from a family of ten children and she has seven brothers. She can beat them all up. She is a creature of struggle, of the sibling rivalry, of the pseudosexual wrestling matches with brothers. She is not without sympathy, though she is largely without understanding of me, but there is a part of her, at this time, that cannot keep from making fun. It is one of her weapons, like her pratfalls, to demonstrate, beyond a shadow of a doubt, that the real is flesh and strength and things that can be touched—not the illusions and shadows of the mind, God forbid. That's middle-class shit; she knows and she will oppose it everywhere for she had fled from her parents' home because of it. She began leaving home at fifteen and lost her virginity to her brother that same year, a lovely boy, a poet, delicate of feature. At sixteen she was arrested for driving down the Bayshore Freeway, on the back of a motorcycle, stoned on acid, and wearing only the top of her bikini. The lawyer, she relates, was smart, he got her off with a plea of temporary insanity. She cut all her classes and was put back in high school. She hung out in Hollywood and had been to orgies where a famous Hollywood lawyer having stoned everyone on his drugs proceeded to beat her with a whip. When the next man had come to screw her on that occasion, he had to fuck her up the ass, she told me, because her back with its stripes was too sore to lie upon. She had kept house for twenty or thirty or more at Fantasy Meadow, one of the first communes, and watched it burn down. She had posed for nudie magazines eating the pussy of another girl. The nudies liked her red pubic hair. She had been arrested for possession in New Jersey, caught with the largest haul of marijuana in the history of the State, and held for two months in State Prison. She had lived with innumerable men and regretted only, though she would say this half-jokingly, that she had never ridden with the Hell's Angels. And she was only nineteen when I met her.

I was fascinated as I learned these things but deeply suspicious. What did she see in the likes of me? And indeed I had good reason to be suspicious. For she constantly laughed at my squeamishness, my caution, my scaredness. We finish our miserable supper, the taste of brown-red meat, onions, ketchup still in the mouth, and go to search out our last apartment. It is at the foot of Nob Hill. We drive there in the dark. A pleasant surprise, a pretty house. Annie is pleased, I am delighted. We ring the bell. A breakthrough at last. The man comes, reluctantly: "Sorry, it's taken, I didn't have a chance to take down the sign."

We walk toward the car. I slump with misery. She, on the other hand, does the best with this discouraging situation, she fights back: "Stuart, I've got to pee, I'm going to do it in the street [wicked smile], watch." And she goes toward the stoop of a brownstone and in that little corner between stoop and building, she squats in the shadow cast by the street lamp, pulls down her pants. I hear and then see the trickle.

The hippie is attacking me, attacking respectability—civilization, even. She pisses on me.

But I am too tired to fight her. She would defeat me anyway —make me look cruel. I will let her stay a short while longer because part of me knows, in some dim way, that she has been sent to be my teacher, to rub my nose in life, so to speak. "Get in the car, Annie." She comes running, a smile of triumph on her face. She has had her revenge on San Francisco.

✳ the still point ✳

when i awoke the next morning, Annie was whistling as she patted herself dry after her shower. She was probably thinking that I was too discouraged to go on looking for an apartment in San Francisco. She was right. I lay in bed listening to her, sure she would be certain we would now go back to Big Sur, and I decided to go to Berkeley. Not to spite her; my mind was on other things. I'll go to my friends in Berkeley. They'll help me. I've got some energy left and I'll cross the Bay. I'll see the old colleagues, take a room, use the library, study, and write.

It is sunny, thank God. At last the rain has stopped. A favorable omen. I am looking for good omens. We check out of the motel and take the Freeway to the Bay Bridge. It is exciting to cross. The longest bridge in the world, I guess, five miles or so, a delicious treat for a quarter, to be suspended so clearly, between places, to be in limbo. Twenty minutes later we are in Berkeley. Annie says, looking through the glass of the windshield, "Berkeley has the prettiest girls." Not true, of course. Just like pretentious Annie not to know the scholarly habit of taking her ignorance into account, so I think, eager to stop her opening gambit, her infernal pretentiousness, her stupid claims. Why can't she allow herself a little doubt, like me? Rome and New York have prettier girls. Annie is only talking, possibly about the West Coast. I start to feel anxious again. I go to Arthur's. I don't call, I know I have a bed there, they are poor but they have always welcomed me. Arthur is a good friend and a good fellow. I can endure his quietness and I can use some of that warm dying now, that sweet smell of unwashed laundry—he and his wife are not too clean; it will be good.

We pull up in the driveway of the old wooden house, ugly, white paint turned yellowish, lawns long since paved over with concrete; the landlord got tired of the weeds that the students who live in his apartments let grow: lazy bastards, let the house decay, what do I care? You can feel the resignation as soon as you see this house, all those student houses in Berkeley. And I look forward to the sweetness of decay permitted: I want that rest; no responsibility; suspension; a little bit of death to calm the pain.

Their door is locked, however. They are not there. When they aren't home I always raise a window just off the front stoop and swing myself inside, hopping over the chair that nearly blocks me. It is upsetting, now, to find that window locked too.

I left a note in the door. "Let's get some lunch," I said to Annie and we went and ate a hamburger and drank beer and then we drove around town looking for Arthur but I couldn't find him. And as the sunny afternoon wore on I found the anxiety and paralysis which I had left, temporarily, at Esalen, returning in a massive way, beginning to infect, like a poison, my every limb and part so that they tightened and felt weak, as if fear held them. It had been a different kind of misery in San Francisco, a dejection, mostly. This, though, was more like the old thing, an obscure fear, unspecified, as if my being itself were in danger, as if my body were being drained somehow of its substantiality and I were becoming more and more shadowy, flesh and blood replaced by mere feeling. It was starting as we drove around.

At three o'clock, the little white paper was missing. I stopped the car, backed up to the house and drove onto the sidewalk in front of it. Knock, knock. Long time. Knock, knock again, steps at last. Opening door. Not Arthur—Arthur's wife, Daisy, pleasant, but she isn't Arthur, and I know she doesn't thoroughly like me, or, for that matter, anyone, so far as I can make out. I am disappointed to see her face, fearful of her censures. But she is pleasant. "Sorry, Stuart, you can't stay here this time. We've got some people here." "O.K., Daisy, maybe we'll see you later. We've got to find a place to stay." I wave cheerily and lower myself back into the car.

I knew it. I knew it. I knew it the moment I saw the window locked. Even this little pleasure, this little help, was going to be denied me.

Forest. The other friend. I can stay with him. We drove over, just a few blocks, to his house. He was home. Little Forest, small and blond and handsome, and opinionated. He was home and preoccupied, for there were many details to arrange. He was driving to New York soon, in four days, on Sunday, to start teaching at N.Y.U. I had helped him get the job. Rebecca would be left behind to finish out the quarter; he was nervous about leaving her and he had much to do before he left. I asked him if we could stay there. He pained me: "I'll have to ask Becky when she gets home."

Why couldn't he do better? Why couldn't he see through the pain and simply say "yes"? Why these marital games? I longed to shout, "Forest, I need it!" But I was not much of a screamer and I was afraid they would call the men in white coats or simply, that they would throw me out, threatened by such antics. I knew that one doesn't scream, not among friends, we friends don't scream, we know the limits of what we can expect from each other, we are mature, aren't we, middle-class-American-adult-friends and we know that friends are for fun and that friends are for having a nice time and that your spouse is the only one you rely on, if you've got one, and otherwise, you play it cool and if some disaster happens, like sickness or old age or madness, well, the agency or the insurance or the police will take care of it, and we friends, we will come visit you, once in a while, maybe, so let's be friends and let us talk about love, by all means, and let us call one another when we are lonely or depressed, but that is pretty much the end of it, isn't it, for we all have our separate lives to lead, and our ways to make, and it is a struggle, and privacy is important, and don't bother me too much or I'll drop you, you're too much of a burden, Friend.

So I didn't scream; I took the proffered drink, grateful for what I got, and waited for Rebecca to come home. As the drink took its effect I even began to feel a little better. Despite the failures I had had in Berkeley, I was, in some sense, on home ground here.

But there was another side—things had changed. I gradually registered that fact as the afternoon wore on and we waited for Rebecca to come home. Forest was busy. Mountains of note-cards, piles and piles of books, papers, offprints thrown together to help him prepare for his history doctoral examinations. There were ranks of blue volumes, *The Oxford History of Europe* above his desk, reference troops, neat and at the ready. His typewriter, an old black manual, office size, was squarely stationed to one side. In the corners, in the john even, were recent magazines: *Esquire, Playboy, Commentary*—it suggested that when the ardors of scholarly studentsmanship were finished, there was time and energy and interest to read current things, to keep up, to keep alive, to keep in the swim, to move forward. All my fantasies of working in the library again, taking up my career as a literary professor, being the professional intellectual—all dissolved. Of course, Rebecca let Annie and me use the upstairs room though she seemed a little bored about the whole thing, she was busy and had other things to do.

Annie left the next day. I put her in a car with a seminarian driving to Big Sur; it was Friday afternoon and she had to be back to wait on tables. I was deeply glad to get rid of her, and yet I eyed the driver, a hapless young psychologist, with jealousy, even clutched her to me. I didn't know what the hell I wanted.

Forest, I asked Forest what I should do. I didn't tell him what I was really feeling: I wanted to move in with him and Rebecca.

Forest is very down to earth, a realist, he prided himself, little man, on how well he could manage the world, no one could get around him, he knew: "Look, you've only got two choices, the rest of this stuff about living in San Francisco or Berkeley is all nonsense. You belong in one of two places: Big Sur or Old Westbury, so either go to one or the other; the rest is unrealistic. Look," he said, "drive with me to New York—you have to go there anyway in three weeks for that conference. You'll visit Old Westbury, see your friend Edgar, have a ball with him, we'll go fast in my car, the Jaguar, just the two of us, we'll talk. You'll feel better, you'll decide what to do."

I began then to split in two, not two personalities, not Jekyll and Hyde, nothing that dramatic but I became obsessed with this particular choice; stay in Berkeley, go with Forest. Not much of a choice but for me, it was a matter of life and death. It was as if the whole experience, all those months, were focusing here, for some crazy reason, in this choice. I began debating this decision the second Forest told it to me. He was leaving in two days.

"I should go back to Old Westbury."

"I should stay in Berkeley and try to pull myself together."

"Go with Forest."

"Delay. Delay. Above everything, Delay. Don't do anything. Just stop. Delay. You don't know what to do. Think it over more."

I drive around town during that day. Toward evening, I return to Forest's. He and Becky are busy. He reads on. She reads on. I stare into space. Thinking, thinking like a moron trying to read advanced equations, I am practically squinting with attention, thinking, bang-bang go the answers, the contrary answers. I go to bed. Sleep, that'll help. Sleep. Dreams. I wake up. I wake up debating whether I should go to New York or stay here—everything is heavy-laden with significance, import. This simple decision, my life depends upon it, narrower and narrower.

I go downstairs. Smile good morning. Everyone else is normal. I will try. It's, above all, it's so embarrassing, so shameful to be like this. I can't let them see how bad it is, can't crack. Eat breakfast. Just like going to the lodge. And so it continues through the afternoon and evening.

The night passes slowly. I am asleep but I don't really sleep. My mind keeps working on its problem driven by the anxiety in the stomach, turning over alternatives and imagining them, seeing dangers on every hand, and trying to avoid them all but having to make some decision. It was wrong to leave Esalen, it was a sign of weakness. It was wrong, by the same token, to stay at Esalen—I was doing myself no good there, I wasn't getting any place. It was wrong to take off to New York three weeks before I had to, it was wasting time and I couldn't allow myself to do that. They, the others, those for example who had sent me from Old Westbury to Esalen, wanted results and maybe, in three more weeks, I would have something to show. Everyone wanted results. I deserved some comfort though, didn't I, I wasn't worthless, I was a human being, wasn't I? To go to the East, to be with my friend Forest; maybe I would enjoy the drive.

It was all happening somehow slower than I have written. There was a part of me that wanted not to move in any direction, that wanted to sink deeper and deeper into the pain, into the nothingness, until I could bear it no longer and I would, simply and mysteriously, die or I would be driven outside to smash my plastic car, Fiberglas fragments cutting like steel, into a telephone pole.

That night all else disappeared: Becky and Annie and Forest and most of me. I was coming to the still point of my turning world. It was all slowing down, it had slowed down for months, all of me had slowed down, slower and slower moving, less and less motion, becoming aware of less and less, engaged less and less. As Dante describes the place where Satan is, the very center of hell, the still point of the turning world, in his cosmology the simple center of the round globe itself, and Dante, to my great surprise when I attempted to be a student of his *Inferno*, had said that at the center, the bottom of hell, there was not fire but ice; Satan was frozen at the center, that did not move, around which all revolved, in ice. And in those two days, in my own silly way, my unheroic way, I seemed to have finally reached that point. To have come, without a Vergil, uncomprehending, a blunderer, a ridiculous figure, not even very evil, to the end of all motion.

But it was not a rest to which I had come. Within the ice in which I was frozen, there was ceaseless torment—a stillness and yet not a stillness, only a diminution, a being so shrunken that one doubt could occupy it completely: should I go or shouldn't I, all the night through. And the added torment that came from my awareness, no anger articulated, that there was, outside of my still point endlessly revolving around itself, not only the whole world, but worlds, spheres and angels and paradise and heaven. My torment came from knowing that, knowing how miserable I had become. And it came from not knowing how else to be, for it was necessary, absolutely necessary, a matter of life and death, somehow, that I spend my time considering the alternatives even when I was asleep.

I awoke still thinking. With two hours to go until Forest was scheduled to leave, to drive off across the whole United States, I was slowing down time, hoping and wanting more time, watching the clock, aware of how long had elapsed between the time that Becky had pushed down the plunger on the chrome toaster, the seconds sliding into one another, and the moment, which I hoped to delay, when the toaster came to life with a pop; aware of how much rubbery time stretched between her going to the refrigerator and clunking down on its handle, and the heavy door opening, and her stooping inside, to emerge, then, with the orange juice, and unscrewing the top from the bottle, as I partly watched from my seat at the table, and then bringing the bottle to the glasses, and tipping the bottle, and then the juice pouring out, and everything happening, so much filling up the moments, as I waited there, desperate, trying harder and harder to make up my mind and part of my mind working to fight down any show of emotion, how could I betray my anguish over what was, so obviously, a mere bagatelle, nothing, a simple matter, one that a normal person, like Forest and Becky, for example, would decide in no time, fighting the feeling of how unnormal I was becoming, fighting to keep down the madness, at least keep it away from others and moving, after breakfast, in my slacks and rich-brown woolen sweater, through the house in a gentle way, seemingly a serene way, from room to room, as Forest bustled to prepare the car, to tighten the straps on the last suitcase, to check this bundle, that bag, to pile his elegant and showy wardrobe into the deepest closet for later shipment, to get his tool box, in case there were repairs on the way. Very excited he, nervous about leaving, but looking forward to that long drive in his own red, brute machine, time passing slowly and fast at once, for me, panicky that time was running out, that Forest had decided that I would not come, vital Forest, with whom I had so much in common, the clothes, the cars, the fast driving, the art, the pretensions to style, the longing after some social transcendence, he too a New York Jew, and pleased with himself that he would make the journey alone, the long great drive.

"Forest, I'll go!"

He looked at me with an ironic smile but he took me.

We drive southward, Highway 17, the Freeway, past Oakland, past Hayward, past San Jose, to merge with 101, the great north-south route, marred with endless diners and cheap fruit stands. The same route I had driven many times before to Esalen.

I remember that we had to stop in Gilroy, anonymous place strung out along the highway, to get gasoline and that as the gas was being poured, I got out of the car and I began doing breathing exercises, breathing in and holding my breath up to a count of ten, and over again, ten times, and the purpose was, if possible, to use this method of deep breathing I had learned from an Esalen staff member to get rid of my anxiety, and I told this to Forest, who looked at me as if I were nuts; and through my ache I hoped, too, that Forest would be impressed, my last gesture it would seem in that direction, that he would be impressed and think that I had learned some things at Esalen which were mysterious and significant and which made me better than or at least as good as him. It was the last act of comparison, the last con job, for, after that, I settled into the ride, enjoying his driving me, and my not having to do anything, and enjoying the lack of responsibility. We were off, and no one could ask me to be productive or important or responsible, not even myself, for the next five days.

part three

✠✠

CHAPTER NINETEEN

✳ going home ✳

i had not the confidence to drive
the coast road that night, so I was glad that Forest wanted to
drive. He had looked forward to the endless meditation of the
trip, our mini-epic journey across the country, and we had
sandwiches, and cigarettes, and the glow of the dials and the
gauges, snug in our little cockpit heading toward Route 66.

The road wound down in the darkness, southward, the ocean
barely to be seen from the sheared cliff hundreds of feet below,
not going fast because of the rain, studying the pavement for
changes in camber, potholes, small landslides, just enough potential danger to make it interesting and attention necessary.
We didn't speak. At San Luis Obispo, we stopped to study the
map, turning on the interior light, and then heading eastward,
at last, to pick up, over the mountains, a freeway, and less ad-

venture there, but a sense of the great energy of the country as we passed heavy-laden truck trailers, even this late at night, one o'clock, speeding to bring people their needs, industry singing in the whirr of their tires, the continuous blasts of their exhausts, and then silence, just the two of us, in our fastest of cars, until we passed the next many-wheeled monster of the road. I began to enjoy myself, to let the adventure penetrate me, and to become fully aware that for a few days my incessant worries could be postponed.

We entered Bakersfield, our first city, garish with neon, complexes of cheap motels, a mobile society, and stopping at a diner, ate excellent brown chili, served by a plain waitress, the best chili I have ever eaten, with the usual saltines, and plenty of coffee to keep us awake, for we were going to drive through the night, late into the next day, and to sleep during the sunlit hours. The comfort for five days to come of perpetual night and my loving to eat at those roadside places, enjoying the cheap food and the companionship of the working-class faces, drivers, stunned by the late hour and their endless task, and the diners like hostels, refuge stations in the Alps, cameraderie unspoken, and then back into the car, and onward, me dozing, then waking; we smoke, the burn of cigarette glow in the night, and fewer and fewer cars as we crossed into Arizona. And more darkness and more driving and stopping, at last, almost a dozen hours after we started, tired, at a good motel, Holiday Inn, waking up the night girl at the desk, and collapsing into bed, asleep, just as the rest of the world was dawning into morning twilight, we two intrepids, travelers. And to wake, at three in the afternoon, and to shower, and depart, lugging suitcases back to the car, shaved and ready, to a large breakfast, at five o'clock in the afternoon, the faint sun behind us, already sinking in the west, the clouds still hanging on, and endless flatland, desert, the painted colors I had heard about since childhood, looked at in my plastic View-Master, and night again, and dinner of hamburgers and coffee, and more miles, keeping it up, keeping up a steady seventy miles per hour, maybe a little more, alert for police, increasingly alone.

That second night we began talking. It was already late, eleven o'clock or more; Forest had taken the first shift, I had felt able to take the second, and now he was driving again. The road ahead, four lanes, was clear and straight as a rail, across the desert, and there was snow on the ground on both sides, a few days old, lending to our visits a sense of peace without threat. At first we talked about Forest, his feelings about leaving Rebecca, leaving Berkeley and California, going back to his home city, taking his first teaching job. He had regrets but he was confident. I had never seen him so settled, certain and manly. In the past, I had always taken Forest with many private reservations: he was an enthusiast, and what he said had to be partly discounted as the unconsidered passions of the moment.

But this night, he seemed different and so, when he spoke, I listened more carefully than before. We talked about many things and I listened, mostly. I didn't feel I had much to say. The one thing I clearly remember is a brief discussion of politics. Several months before Forest had participated in an anti-draft protest in San Francisco, one of the first violent demonstrations of the movement. He had been put in jail, released, tried, and sentenced to five days for helping to overturn a bus in the middle of an intersection. It was his first serious political act and at the beginning it had something of the character of a practical joke to him. But as I listened to him talk now about the war, the country, politics, I felt a new seriousness. He knew a lot about the background of the war and he had thought a lot about politics. "What are you doing, Stuart? The country is going to hell, maybe the whole world, and what are you doing?" It was an irritating, even a self-righteous remark, and certainly not an extraordinary one. In the days before Esalen I would have simply counterattacked: "What are you doing that's so useful?" But this time I was prepared at least to think before I spoke and it occurred to me that, as best he could, Forest had been doing something and that he was worthy of honor for it. I stared ahead in silence and he let the subject drop. In some way I didn't quite understand, this part of our talk made a difference to me.

The rest of the time my consciousness remained entranced by the peace of the road, the attention needed to drive, the sweet warm food of the diners, the relief from worry that the trip allowed. We continued, night after night. In Missouri we drove for several hundred miles on wet pavement and Forest would intentionally slide the car, smiling at his own skill, through the long sweeping curves of the empty highway, as if we were on a road race in Europe. The moon was out and the highway glistened back its frost. Mile after mile and minute after minute, each of us paying the closest attention to the road, and feeling in our backs the nudging of the seats as they told us that the car was moving sideways, controlled but constantly on the edge of slipping away. An exquisite silence.

There were a dozen such vivid scenes, each of them helping me, lifting me from the center, not enormously but enough to give me back some feeling of life. When we entered Pennsylvania and connected with the Turnpike, road of my college days which I had traveled dozens of times back and forth between New York and Oberlin, I was enjoying the return to that road, and I was helping with the driving, struck by how slow this superhighway of my adolescence now seemed compared with the great contemporary freeways, and enjoying the dark green of the pines beside the road as I nudged the speedometer up to seventy-five and eighty and even ninety miles an hour. And when they stopped me with their radar speed trap, at three o'clock that cold night, I was not even annoyed, but I enjoyed being out there, talking with the state policemen, playing the games with policemen that you play when they catch you for speeding, arguing, being apologetic, playing sheepish, and at last when there seemed no appeal, agreeing to be cooperative. And off again, back to our car from the little trailer just beside the Turnpike fence where a lady judge had taken my confession of guilt in a cheery spirit and wished us a "nice drive."

I called Edgar Cannon from a Howard Johnson's on the Turnpike. I remembered when these decaying restaurants of gray stone and plate glass had been built, years before, and I could guess just how good or bad the canned clam chowder and the plastic hot dogs would be. Familiar territory.

I called Edgar collect. That was the way our relationship was. He had been my Freshman English teacher, a man of dazzling brilliance and great learning; as a young man he had been a fellowship collector, a Princeton graduate, a St. Paul's graduate, and a Yale graduate. I saw him walk into my first provincial college classroom, out there in the wastes of Ohio, me surrounded by frosted doughnuts and clothes in the sport-shop window of the most wooden taste and men still wearing crew cuts and none of the girls, except a few, with long hair like they had in Greenwich Village, none of the girls with arty long earrings, and everyone so Midwestern nice to each other and all of them going to church, incessantly, the girls dressed like women of fifty. He was thin, about one hundred and sixty pounds, six feet one or so, and wearing a tweed jacket, and a tweed coat, and a blue button-down shirt, the first I had ever seen, and he carried in his hand a heavy black typewriter case, with the stickers on it from the University of Utrecht and the Dutch Fulbright Commission, and his cordovan shoes, and he even talked to himself, out loud, saying funny things, and I loved him at once. Then to discover, in those eager days when I was sixteen, fresh from Grand and Broome Streets, and so new to so many things, that he liked me and that he knew Latin and Greek and Anglo-Saxon, whatever were all those languages, for languages I presumed they were, and he also knew French, and German, and some Italian; and he knew about philoso-

phers, names I had never or hardly heard such as Plato and
Aristotle, and Epictetus and Plotinus, and Bruno and Pascal,
and Kierkegaard and John Wisdom and Wittgenstein, and
Spinoza and Camus and Hegel and Fichte and all those exotic
names from all over, names that seemed to my hearing as if I
had heard them before, all my life, names heavy in their sound-
ings with the power of intellect. And besides all this he knew
all about literature, literatures, from all over, magic stuff to
which I came then as an ignorant barbarian, untaught, only
having lately learned that literature was the repository of whatever redemption a person with some chic might hope to earn,
and Edgar knew about that stuff, and he had known about it,
so it seemed, forever, for his parents had gone to college, and
their parents, and they read books at home, and he being a
gifted child, one of America's special children, had heard about
The Song of Roland when he was young: "Stuart, you don't
know who Roland was? Roland, Orlando?" "No, Edgar, I just
heard about him last week from you; how long have you
known about him?" I ask, half-defensively, for I had been a
good high-school student and I knew a thing or two. And he
answers, with no trace of trying to crush, every appearance of
absolute candor, one born to these privileges, he answers: "I
guess I've always known. I can't remember," he puzzles over
the enormity of the difference between us, "when I haven't
known." He, himself, collected Gothic miniatures, precious
things and he knew about Europe, and he knew about taste,
and he knew about the high academic life of America, and of
what they thought and said and ate and wore at Princeton and
Yale and all those fabled places where I had not been accepted
because they had all the bright Jewish boys they knew what to
do with, already. He shocked me with his scorn for the other
Oberlin faculty, provincial mediocrities he described them,
much beneath him, too bad, but that was the case, timid in
every way, even intellectually, fit only to teach Freshman English, no "superscholars" they as he was, one of the most learned

men around, particularly for a young one, bored, bored with his colleagues, their marriages, their lack of wit and brio, their pious middle-class securities and timidities, their faculty-novel life. Not such for him, he would carouse into the middle of the night, with a few selected fellows, most of them students, for the students were brighter than the faculty, he said, and he bitterly resented the system for making him teach three sections of Freshman English and one of Sophomore Lit for his first teaching job. He resented that, he didn't know how to do it and he deserved graduate students. So he did. He was right to resent whatever had placed him in Oberlin rather than at some major university, and he was right in knowing how mediocre his colleagues were, and, despite all that and all he gave me, I realize in this writing that though he had material to work with, though I had started before, he gave unremitting encouragement to my snobbism and taught me the paths into which it should flow.

I loved him, then and for many years after, and I gave absolute credence to nearly everything he said; he was truly my teacher and I fed on his words. He it was who had told me that one could not be educated without learning foreign languages and so I had learned them, half a dozen, fighting them all the way, feeling that while it was the right thing and the honorable thing to do, I had not really made the decision. And he had told me to get very good grades and be Phi Beta Kappa in my Junior year, and I had done that. And he had had a Fulbright, so I fixed things, made the proper gestures and got the proper points, and I got a Fulbright. And he had gone to the Yale graduate school, and so I went to the Yale graduate school. And I took the teachers he proposed, and I imitated the sound of his voice and the intonation of his sarcastic remarks and the energy of his great heart and his endless yearning after perfection and transcendence, things weren't good enough for him and he was obsessed with the problem of mortality and the need to recover the splendor of earliest youth, and all this and more I listened to, for I loved him and I thought him the best man I had ever met.

But that had been years ago, and when Forest dropped me off in the early morning, at Edgar's apartment, waving a tired farewell, things were different. I knew how different they were that very morning for we sat in the prosperous apartment on East 72nd Street and drank and talked until after the sun came up and I remember being acutely aware that although Edgar was no longer the poor instructor at Oberlin, and that although he had achieved some eminence in his field, and although his fifth book was about to be published, and he had a substantial salary, and he lived alone in his comfortable apartment, surrounded by elegantly bound books on the most difficult subjects, and he never had to teach Freshman English any more but had all the graduate students he could desire, and all of that, the fact was that he was a disappointed man: he had failed. And I, curiously, was in somewhat the same situation. We sat there in that apartment, so much more elegant than the hole in the corner he had rented for seventy dollars a month years before on Lorraine Avenue in Oberlin, Ohio, in our shirt sleeves, or was it in our undershirts? He had his glass and I had mine and there was a certain mellowness and a certain melancholy about the occasion, for it was as if life had beaten both of us: we had succeeded and yet we both felt troubled and bankrupt, empty. And the feeling between us was warm, don't misunderstand me, for I was not thinking about repudiating Edgar in any way, I still loved him, loved him for all he had meant to me, God knows, absorbed a large part of him into me, but something, nevertheless, was gone—I was grown-up, too, we were equals now; equals in our measured misery, and it put a whole new cast on things, on our relationship, and on things besides; it was as if I had grown up and here we both were, and instead of asking Edgar for advice about my life, as I had been used to, I realized that he could not very well understand what my experience at Esalen had been and I found myself giving him advice, and the general tenor of my counsel was to urge him to give up the endless fantasies of existences above his present and possible ones and to stop searching after childish joy, the splendor in the grass, Wordsworth, Dylan Thomas, and Vaughan, and that he simply try to make do with what he had, get married, or other things along such practical lines. Before, I had admired his fire, his idealistic rejection of what he had taught me to call "a trivial mode of existence"; I used to imitate his admiration for tragic heroes whom he described as men and women incapable of accepting the crude and corrupt realities of the world with which they were confronted; they were too good for reality; I had imitated his fits of temper, his impatience with stupidity or lack of imagination; I used to admire his great eating and drinking, nearly Gothic consumption, his suffering, in short. But now, this time around, at least, it all just wasn't working for either of us and though I was glad to be there, I felt sorry for him.

❉ turning round ❉

we spent the next few days quietly, sitting around the apartment and talking about one thing and another, catching up on the lives and careers of our mutual friends, some of them old schoolmates of mine, all of that cozy gossip that makes so tasty the reunions of old friends. We ate out a lot, going to various restaurants that Edgar had discovered. Extremely generous, he treated me to big dinners and it was restorative in the extreme to be taken care of so; he was always a giver, was Edgar, and he helped me a lot with his gifts, his Southern (for he was from Virginia) hospitality.

I settled into this comfort and cordiality for nearly a week, but at the end of that time I had to acknowledge to myself that there was nothing more to talk about with Edgar and no new restaurants. I tried some of the usual expedients, weary even in the act of trying. I called old girl friends and visited them, some of the ladies who had given me such solace in years before: Phyllis, Eunice. We hardly touched hands, it had all turned cold like the January snow, everything between me and them astonishingly different. For some obscure reason, which I did not understand, I could not ask them for reassurance anymore.

I took the train out to Old Westbury, but it too had changed. I had expected, in a vague way, that I would find what I was looking for at the college, that they would give me a place of honor because I was, after all, a professor, and that they would give me a warm place to be so that I could pull myself together. Everyone was very busy, however, and though they greeted me warmly, they were too occupied to give me the attention I wanted: students had to be admitted, catalogues written, architectural plans gone over. There wasn't, however, anything immediate for *me* to do—I had been away too long. Harry Galtzer took me into his office and asked me how I was. I began to weep, then sobbing, the pain in my stomach, not daring to say how bad it was, wanting sympathy.

One of them, Tom Walinsky, surprised me, nice man, he surprised me by seeming unmoved, almost as if he were saying that what I was suffering was good for me, as if he was glad to see me so humbled, toward whom I had had such contempt, a glorified social worker.

I was too down to protest. Five o'clock came and I took the train back to New York, eager to get back to the safety of Edgar's place. When I got there at seven o'clock, he was on his way to bed, depressed as usual, my mentor.

I fixed myself a hamburger for supper and then made myself a drink. It was very quiet, only the sound of Edgar's snoring from the bedroom. I tried to relax. I leaned back in the corner of the sofa and put my stockinged feet on the edge of the coffee table. I glanced at the softly colored beige walls and the rug with its faint brown tint, the shaded lamps, *objets,* books from floor to ceiling in their wooden cases, a sense of spaciousness, the picture window looks out at the great city, over the roof-tops of the Upper East Side, toward midtown, the Empire State building. Depression and ache turned to a pleasant mel-ancholy—at least I was protected here, I could stay here, Edgar would let me, I could stay here forever.

And then the ache returned. This isn't your place, it is Edgar's, you didn't earn it, you don't deserve it.

Even with the ache, the tears starting to come, I knew that after all the months of aches and tears and evasions and confu-sion, this was the time. I had to make a decision. I had to de-cide what to do with myself. In just four days I would have to go to my conference in Washington and what would I do after that?

How to make a decision? Fritz and a million others at Esalen had told me that one was supposed to avoid programing, sup-posed to avoid decisions and flow with the Tao, take things as they were. "You have to *do something* to get yourself back to-gether." Maybe Herbert's list, I thought. Herbert had told me that when he had been about my age and in a big life crisis, just divorced, confused, a failure, he had stepped to his desk, sat down, and written a list of resolutions: to stop smoking, to go out with women, to go to the gym, to go into therapy, and so forth; and he had followed the resolutions and they had worked.

"It's too mechanistic."

"Try it anyway."

Bits and pieces of advice, voices again, whirling beginning, threatening to overwhelm me. I forced myself to be quiet and to listen without answering.

"Stuart, you've got to make a decision."

Ken Price had said that during the worst of times; he was right, I must hold on to that one.

Crazy image: I found myself imagining the Bryers ice-cream signs in the candy stores of my childhood. They advertise ten or fifteen flavors but as these change all the time there are spaces where you can slide in this week's selections. I didn't want to lose what Ken had said, so I started from the top and I placed it in the slot, prominently, "Stuart, you've got to make a decision."

And that was frightening, a frightening thing to do, for now I had to know what to decide, I needed to search backward, sitting on my sofa, through all that I had learned, the million voices at Esalen, the voices of my girls, and the voices of my friends, and the voices of my parents, and the voices that were in my head to begin with, and I would have to offend some of these voices in deciding because I couldn't listen to all of them, and I needed courage to take the leap, and I needed support, and I needed to think that I would do the right thing when I decided. I remembered that Bill Schutz, a man who had the most right among all of them to think that I was bad, to think, to take the present instance, that, for example, I would make a bad decision, had said to me that night, almost two months before, at Fritz's, "Stuart, you're not a bad guy, you're a good guy." And I seized that remark, so important from one whom I had offended, and I took it and printed it clearly too, I slid it into place, clearly in my mind, because a thousand irrelevancies and doubts were circling around as if, just on the edge of firelight, I could see the flashing eyes, and I had to keep my attention to the basic things, for that was the only way to keep them off, they were whimpering and screaming for attention, their weird red bodies, tails and tridents, and forked hooves, and wicked smiles, fur and fangs and talons, smirks and sniffles and hyena laughter, the tempters of Saint Anthony, I thought, in the twilight and dark regions of my mind. My only task had to be, having found the fire with its clear light, to read what had to be read, read my own holy scripture, the first chapter, then the second, and pay attention only to them, and if I could do that, and keep paying attention, I would make out the third chapter and the fourth and the next, and as I did that, if I had the nerve and the will and the Grace, then hopefully the fire would get larger, in the middle of my mind, and it would light up things, it would light up the shadows and I could live.

I bore down, my body must have tensed just the slightest, sitting there in that living room, the skyscrapers visible in the darkness, patterns of light and towers and needles shooting skyward, and you couldn't have seen much change as I did this, and I bore down and *made* things clear: yes, that's right: *Make a decision.* And, *You're a good guy.* And, *When you're in real trouble, it's O.K. to make a list.* And I had three, I had those three cards, neatly printed up there, in the firelight, and I pulled my mouth tight with determination, getting up cautiously so as not to jar those three realizations, and I walked, almost at a crouch so as not to jar things, to the dining-room table, and I found a pencil, and I found something to write on; it was, if you will believe me, the back of my Esalen brochure, and I sat down, with my pencil, looked at the white space, and began to try to find the basic principles on which to build my new universe.

What did I want? What did I really want, I asked myself, clearly and globally, first things only. And the answer was only a minute in coming, even though I was surprised with it: "I want to be good." I was surprised but I wrote it at the top of the paper: "I want to be good." Then, I took the pencil and I underlined it to make sure that it stayed, that I stayed clear and that this was the first principle, the one I had decided on, and I didn't let myself stop to think about it, for if I had, then I might have debated it, too much, and all would have been darkness again. I held that line, the basic line that had come up from the deep, like the part of the stern of a wrecked boat that bobs to the surface and carries the name of the vessel that has gone down. And I remembered fragments of other people's advice and the marks they had made on me: Herbert's parting words which he had written in my checkbook: "Be kind, always." And the delight I had taken in hearing Herbert, despite his actual meanness and paranoia, preach love for humanity and goodness. And there was Bill's comment at Fritz's house again. And just the night before, in a philosophical discussion, Edgar had said: "People all want to do the right thing." And Fritz had said that I was only aware of myself, selfish, a tragedy queen, a gloom caster, depressed, bringing everyone down. And I had tried, tried before, to be good, yes, it was very important, but I hadn't tried enough, and here were all these people telling me I was right to try and some telling me I could try more and that I could make it, that I was good already so why hold back?

That was where I would begin. Underneath the basic desire, the decision, one I could barely understand in its entirety, a little mad, so global a principle it was, underneath the line I had drawn under the decision to be good, I made my first mark: "1."

I have been going around, casting gloom, being depressed, making no contribution to the world, it is hard to stop, hard to be gay; I feel as if I have no contribution to make. But there is one thing I can do, can force myself, even if it isn't natural, make a decision and do it—

"1. Instead of bringing people down with a depressed look, I will smile." That was it, the first part of the program: "I will smile."

That first pathetic and small resolve, the actual number "1" in the program marked the end of one time and the beginning of another. For I could do that much. I could smile. I could certainly do it. And since I could in fact do it, I could decide to do it. And having made an actual decision, one actual decision to change the way I had been, I was on my way.

Of course, I felt foolish, it was all so absurdly mock-heroic, and that thought itself was a temptation: the smirking devils with their irony were still circling around. Irony could be a killer at this point. I fought it down. I felt determined and even a little inspired. I didn't distract myself though, I kept to my work. I wrote down "2." And I pondered, though just for a moment, what else I could do to be good.

"Be nice to your family." Another surprise, but there it was: Edgar a Southerner, it was his influence, he was a stickler for filial piety, and though I had always hated and feared and resented my family, there it was: "Be nice to your family." I thought, right after I wrote, of an evening with Herbert where we had talked about my mother and I had complained that this woman had tried to keep me from life, overprotected me, misunderstood me and Herbert had simply said: "Reverse it." And I had thought then, difficult though to give up the circle of wound, resentment, retaliation, I had thought of the good she had given me: humor and warmth and care. At the time the thoughts had vanished, buried in depression. But now they came back. Perhaps there were things to discover. Certainly I owed something besides the Fifth Commandment, "Honor thy Father and thy Mother," remembered from Hebrew school. I so much wanted to, I felt so guilty not to, I owed them. I owed them. I didn't know how but I would try.

I had to keep the process going. I wrote "3." Already my body, insubstantial and dead before, was coming back to life. I could feel the energy begin to tingle, faintly, within, and for the first time in many months, the hectic and maddening activity inside my head was finding some echo below it, something was happening, and as it happened, the old fear would come rippling through me, cold and painful, deadening that new energy, fear almost formless, without any particular name. So it was important for me to keep on with it. I pushed my pencil through the arcs to make the 3 darker. I waited. I grew anxious. I pressed my toes against the floor as if to stand and let myself take another step, make another decision, raising myself slightly with the effort of allowing something, anything real, to break through the paralysis of fear:

"3. Do a good deed a day."

Even at the time I felt the doltishness of that one—the pathetic idiotic quality. Where was the sophisticate, the young man of letters, the young playboy? Where was he gone? Turned into this simple-minded machine, imitator of Herbert Retter; I couldn't do this, I couldn't let myself do this, look so simple, be so cretinesque—obviously, as I had read, the serious things in life do not take place in such a fashion, there is glory to them and there is squalor, Ribera's brown Spanish saints, the ecstatic eyes and the sense of earth and dirt about them. I had neither glory nor squalor. I was sitting at a table in a comfortable upper-middle-class Manhattan apartment, clutching a pencil, at age thirty, my drink sweating on the coffee table in the living room, and I was writing, "Do a good deed a day." It was hard to do, but I did it because it seemed, after so much searching for the golden door that would lead me out of the suffering into which I had fallen, this was where I had come to: "Do a good deed a day." The sophisticate had reverted to the Boy Scout Manual.

"So be it," I said aloud.

It started to come easily now. They had said that I was out of touch with people, that I was arrogant, they didn't trust me. I would return to Esalen and instead of being aloof and special, I would follow Herbert Retter's advice rather than his example: I would become like everyone else. I would lose myself in the group. All that I had been taught not to do, all the precious individualism that our Western authors preached to me, all the insistence, from my first Freshman class in college onward: have your opinions, think for yourself, don't be one of the herd, all of that, I would let that slide, just let it slide away for the moment. Was my individuality real anyway? Betty Fuller had said that I wasn't an individual but a composite.

"4. Go back to Esalen and go to groups."

They had told me that I wasn't in my body. I remembered Bernie's hand on my shoulder, "You find this very difficult, don't you? Maybe we could do some work privately sometime."

I didn't know what they were talking about, but O.K., I would give it up, I would give in, become like one of them for a while, I would work on my body, I would go to at least two workshops having to do with sensory awareness or whatever other cockamamie name they had! Maybe I wouldn't get too much out of it: maybe I would only realize again how different I was from the others for whom it seemed so easy; so that I wouldn't excel; better yet, I would humble myself: it was about time.

"5. Go to sensory-awareness workshops."

"6. Go to a political demonstration once a week." I was less sure about this one but I wanted to do something. It was right to do something.

I smiled to myself as I looked at my list. It felt good, and I knew, by this point, that I would go through with the thing and that I could even see the irony as I was doing it. But there was one more item. A darker one. The girls. The endless girls. Becky had told me that I treated her like a thing, Rebecca, my best friend's wife. And Robert Portman with his "sociopath" word. And Phyllis, a former student, who had said four nights ago that I had used her. All true. I had known it. No one had to tell me. It was beginning to occur to me, that whatever else happened, I must stop the lying to myself and the lying to the girls. I didn't know how but somehow, I must treat women as people, learn to do that.

"7. Learn to treat women as people."

That was the last item on the program. Almost immediately I was swept by a new fear, fear of not being able to take those steps. I gritted my teeth and let my mind rush around trying to find the assurance that I would keep moving. An act. Something I could do that night. The last item on the list was the most dismaying when I looked at it: how the hell could I learn to treat women as people? After all, there was no school to go to for this sort of thing.

I must do something, though. Obviously there is not much I can accomplish this single night. Yes, there is a key. I must be

more modest. I must be more modest in my demands on myself. I can't learn how to treat women as people this one night.
But there must be something I can do. Simple things that
would move the process along.

There was no girl around to do a good deed for.

Annie, I could write to Annie. I had let her, too long, torture
me and torture herself with me. She was suffering. I was suffering. I knew she was dependent upon me. It would hurt her, she
would scream and groan for me not to leave her. But it was, the
whole relationship, destructive. I must explain this to her, show
her that she was only hurting herself. I must withdraw myself
from the relationship for her sake. I must do this, it was the
good thing to do.

So I wrote her a long letter, in which I tried to explain these
things to her, painful though it was and because I knew they
would hurt her and I did want to be good. And I wrote to
another girl, a seventeen-year-old girl I had met at Esalen who
had developed a crush on me and had written me and, instead
of, as in the old days, enjoying her crush and wasting her time
leading her on, I wrote her and told her to find a boy friend her
own age. And I apologized. Apologized for not taking her seriously. And I wrote to another person, an old rich lady whom I
had asked to give me money to help support me at Esalen and
who had refused. And I told her that she had been right to
refuse, that I had been spoiled, that I wanted the money for my
own protecting indulgences—the comfort of the trips to
Nepenthe for drinks when the anguish at Esalen got unbearable—and that she was right not to give me the money and
right to save it for the people whom she gave money to and
who really needed it, like the Negroes in Roxbury.

And it was hard writing those letters. I didn't like doing it
and they took a long time to write. It wasn't just the wincing
pain of confessing myself, of telling the small and wretched
sins. That hurt, it is true. But it was a sense I had as I wrote of
not knowing exactly what I was doing. A feeling that maybe I

was overdoing it, even being a little patronizing, suddenly knowing what was good for others—that wasn't what I was trying to say and yet that's the way it sounded. There was arrogance there, the very thing I was trying to get away from. I didn't know what to do about it. I wrote the letters slowly. Recopied them with corrections, trying to change a phrase here and there so that, whatever it was that was wrong with them, they would be all right. But they never came out quite that way. Instead of helping those people the letters were mostly helping me but I had to send them anyway, even if the letters weren't perfect, because there was more good than bad in them. They were on the right track and I had to keep going now. I knew that. I will send them. I got Edgar's roll of stamps, stuck them quickly on the envelopes, and nearly ran, in my stockinged feet, out into the hall where I pushed them into the mail slot.

Relief. This far I had gone, doubt or no doubt. I walked back into the apartment, my feet touching the wooden floor, and I looked out toward the city. I smiled to myself. There was something absurd in it all. But it was late, I had begun and it was time to go to bed. For the first time in a very long while, I didn't flee from life to bed; I felt I deserved some rest.

The next day was like the first day of a new life. When I woke before Edgar did, rather than wait around for breakfast, or in my depression, make myself something by myself, only enough strength of will to take care of my own poor self, I reached outward. I had to think about it and I had to force myself. I decided and determined that I wouldn't eat until Edgar got up. It wasn't that I felt like waiting: I didn't; I wanted to eat, to slump into my self-protection and self-obsession. I forced myself to think about what was the good thing to do. And the good thing was to wait. It was a little gift. When Edgar wandered into the kitchen I looked at him with shining eyes.

I would falter during the morning, sinking back again into the depression and the voices and the darkness. And then I remembered and I rallied myself.

Later that day on my way to Old Westbury, I left the apartment, my first battlefield, and rang the elevator button. I waited for the elevator to come bearing with it the first part of the world outside of the apartment that I would face. I was used lately to hiding myself. To looking down at the floor and carrying tears in my eyes when I saw people, especially strangers. Their apparent energy, their life, their accepting the world as it seemed without my incessant questioning about what was the right thing, had depressed me. How could they live such lively lives while I, who was clearly a superior person, was suffering so, out of virtue, not knowing what to do, no one path absolutely right? The elevator door opened: a young, rather plastic couple, she with carefully teased hair, he with a very expensive brown leather portfolio, obviously earning a lot of money, probably in advertising, with their toy poodle, and the short irascible elevator man, a neurotic Italian with a short temper who had yelled at me and Forest the night we arrived. Instead of looking down and tearing, with mingled contempt and self-contempt, I looked them each in the face and smiled. The elevator man scowled, the woman looked straight ahead, and the man simply said, "Good morning." No matter. I could give. I could give. Not as happy as they. Suffering. But I could give something. And as I gave they began to look different to me, just a little, somehow. I could imagine them suffering or having suffered, perhaps like me. I could feel pity for them. Not a patronizing pity, exactly, though there was some of that, for I could see the pathos of how their lives were small and bounded; but also and more importantly, a more generalized pity, a pity for the humanity of them all, and of me, each of us. A sense of something shared began to come over me. Just a taste. I had never quite felt it before.

CHAPTER TWENTY-ONE

✠ reconciliations ✠

the following afternoon, I went to see my mother for the first time in a year and a half. I hated her. I found her the symbol of everything in my childhood that I hated: all that was lost when I was banished as the child of divorced parents from my father and his male strength and his good income, money that could have allowed me to hold my head high as the others in the summer camp to which I went, where it was so important that your parents have money. And she had been overprotective, always, afraid for her own safety, the clank and crash of double locks on the doors, the endless advice, even in my adult years, as I exited from the house, of "Don't go with nobody strange." "Don't walk down dark streets." The admonitory finger shaken in poor stage replica of some warning fury, all belied by her obvious weakness, no avenging spirit she, getting older by the year, feeling sorry for herself: "Stuart, be careful, come home early, call me." The endless instructions, every winter, when I would make a brief Christmastime appearance for form's sake: "Stuart, no scarf? Buy yourself a scarf. You know you have sinus. Let me buy you a scarf." I writhe within at this: I am not sick. I have never had sinus trouble, even though my mother had dragged me to an uptown specialist, week after week, to have metal rods with swabs dipped in chemicals poked up my nostrils. I have never been sick. I wasn't weak. The other kids would laugh at me with my scarf. But, she is my mother, so how can I, after all, express this rage—that is bad; how can I tell her that I think she is trying to kill me? I feel her clutches. And then, too often, I burst out, and yell at her, and I slam the door, as I rush away, for breath, for life, and she immediately opens it, and relentless, screams after me, "Stuart, watch yourself. Don't walk down dark streets." I am twenty-five and a Doctor of Philosophy at the time.

When I come home to New York on holidays, I always stay with some girl friend and never with my parents. My mother asks me, at each brief visit to her, to go with her to a restaurant. It is clear she wants to show me off, to show me off to the other women, the other deserted and desolated chicken-soup dispensing furies of the abandoned Lower East Side—desperate and impotent generation, left behind by the tide that had brought them and others all the way across the cold Atlantic, all the way from landlocked Poland and Russia, and had washed the others as far as Forest Hills and Great Neck, but not these, these were left behind, the failures, as I thought them, judging them by the values they themselves had taught me. She wanted to show me off to these, to celebrate me to these. I would not participate in this. I would flee from them as far as I could. I couldn't afford it, Ladies. Can't afford the chance of being drawn back down, stuck, on the Lower East Side, a failure, grumbling about how the neighborhood is going to the dogs, being taken over by new immigrants. I hate your prejudices, your parochialism, your tribal celebrations: the son home from college, let there be feasting in the Temple of the Almighty, Hosannah; and let the Lilies be Scattered and Danish Put Out for the Son, home from college. They, most of all, wouldn't recognize my independence or understand my style of life. They were oblivious to it, didn't care, the stupid ones, they just didn't give credence to America and its values, it simply didn't exist. For them, their tribe was all, all there was. Any concession to them, however trivial it might appear, was a risk. A great risk.

It was in a high state of anxiety that I rang her doorbell that afternoon, for I had resolved to be good beforehand, and to be good to my parents, in particular, and I was going to do that, but it was fraught with peril. She opened the door and kissed me on the cheek and immediately asked me if I was hungry and wanted something to eat. It was starting, the manipulation. I felt the anger rise in me. But, instead of saying "No," for I wasn't hungry, I said "Yes." I ate whatever she gave me. After all, this is what she wanted. And what, really, did it cost me to do this much? I reasoned. It was hard to do. I had to keep my wits about me, my mind focused on my program, she had a million ways of sucking you in, making you furious. For after I had consented to eat, after I had sat down in her parlor and was eating, whatever it was, she asks, jokingly: "The food? Lousy, huh?" I am being manipulated for a compliment, and I am also being further sucked in, further into her territory. I catch myself in the act of trying to decide whether or not to say anything or to scream THE UNTHINKABLE, THE THING A JEWISH BOY SHOULD NEVER SAY: "Yes, you old bitch, it's lousy." I catch myself, because, after all, I have my program, and what does it cost me to say, "No, Mom, it's good." What does it cost me? Funny thing, after that temptation. She doesn't try anything like that again for a long time. I began to believe that maybe if I give her the little courtesies, the little recognitions she wants that maybe she will not try to control me any more.

But my motives are more than tactical: I am not doing what I am doing to survive. I am really trying to reverse it. "Reverse it," Herbert's phrase. I am trying to see if I can be good to her, because when all is said and done, I want to be good to her. I want her to feel good, and to perceive me as good, and I want to perceive myself as good, and I want her to get something good from me. I realize, at last, that I have done pretty well, when you come right down to it, and she must have had a hand in preparing my successes as well as my failures. So, I offer to take her to a restaurant, even though I just ate, to let myself be seen by the women, to let myself endure the shame and the danger of being seen with this weak woman on the Lower East Side, to go, even, to a Jewish restaurant, to go to Ratner's with the poor mother, from whom I derive no glory.

And so, she puts on her coat, and her scarf, and her gloves, not without asking me why I haven't got a scarf and gloves, and what my father will give me for Christmas, with a little look, such a look, that says, what she has said in words so often about my father whom she divorced: "If you are nice to your father, he will be good to you." But on this occasion, I am less conscious of all her offenses, and all my fears and resentments, I am concentrating on doing the right thing. So, for the first time in years, despite all her entreaties in earlier days, I offer her my arm, and I begin to see her not as an overwhelming monster whom I have to hate if I am to survive but as an old lady, living alone with her neurasthenia, year after year, in that fading neighborhood, and I can be big enough, I am big enough, if not to save her, if not to take her on as a charge, for I am not big enough for that, yet I am big enough to do something, and I offer her my arm. We take the bus to the foot of Delancey Street, under the Williamsburg Bridge, where bad boys hung out when I was a child, we talk about the weather, it is cold, and we go to Ratner's. And we eat. And we are very nice to each other. And I even let her take me to a store, a tasteless store, not my kind at all, and let her buy me a scarf, with her five dollars, let her buy it for me, let her put that yoke around me, for she wants to do it, and it is, I realize, just barely, for I am still afraid, one brief flash, that by letting her buy me the scarf she will get a lot of pleasure, and besides, most important, the revelation flashes by the frightened child, he can only catch a glimpse, it is kind of beautiful that she still cares about my health, still wants me to be warm.

As I leave her at the bus stop (she insists, though I am more than willing to walk her home, another concession), and as I make my way to the cast-iron green entrance to the subway, I am touched. My mother, despite everything, really loves me, I could never see that before. I was too busy defending my life: I thought I had to.

I am struck by this revelation, but I do not dwell on it. The depression is still with me. Even if she loves me, I am still nobody, failing, dying on my own. It takes most of my energy to keep to my program of self-rescue, to remember to keep smiling at people I inadvertently jostle on the subway, not to drag down, not to drag them down. And besides, that night, I am going to meet the other and more formidable half of the family: my father, his wife, my sister, my brother-in-law, nephew, and niece. Other kids might only have to endure one torturous set of scenes while they were abused by their families, picked over, criticized, laughed at, but I had to endure two sets, because my parents were divorced. So, what I went through with my mother that afternoon, I would have to go through with my father and the rest of the clan that evening.

I approach the meeting place with my resolutions. We always meet in restaurants. Not always, really, for sometimes we meet at my sister's home or sometimes we meet at my father's apartment. But generally, we meet in restaurants. I guess it goes back to the time after my parents were divorced when my father would come to take me and my sister out for an evening and we would go to some fancy restaurant where, gradually, the headwaiter would come to know us, and then we would go to Broadway for a movie and a stage show—Cavanagh's and then the Roxy, or the Capitol. Once, when for a year around the age of twelve I decided to turn myself into an Orthodox Jew, I insisted that everyone eat at Lou G. Siegel's, the uptown kosher restaurant. Or, it may be that we ate at restaurants because my father couldn't get away from the fucking store early and it would be unseemly to eat dinner at a late hour at home —something like that, something to do with the store. Anyway, we always met in restaurants, a kind of neutral territory, where factions gather: there is me, a faction of one, and my sister and brother-in-law, they are another faction because Seymour is not a blood relative, and there is my father and Byrdie, his wife, yet another faction because she is not my mother, and the two grandchildren, my niece and nephew. It's funny, yet it seems right, to meet in restaurants. This family has no home, Mom and Dad aren't there together, the family doesn't really exist. Mother and Father eat in separate places. I was strange enough already, couldn't you have had the decency to give me the cover of a family?

That was only the beginning. Then we would gather, as we were gathering tonight, the phony family (part of me wanted so much to be normal like the families on the radio), and we would display to the whole world, so to speak, just how wretched we were. Everybody talking at once. Bad jokes. Idiotic discussions, *ad nauseam*, year in and year out, between my brother-in-law, an insurance broker, about rates and premiums and deductibles, and side arguments between my father and Byrdie about which was the date the premium was due, April 10 or May 10, and the most learned debate ensuing about why it must, of necessity, be one or the other. And everyone embarrassingly talking louder than they should, and people looking at us. And I, not knowing what to say.

That was the worst part. I didn't know what to say. I was, after all, the guest of honor at these occasional gatherings. I always felt that they were given for me with the deliberate intention of keeping me in the family, I knew my sister thought that way. It must be so. No one, surely, could enjoy them. And I could feel the net encircling me. I should remain like them, at least stay in touch, and, so the theory went, I supposed, at some later date, I would come to my senses, stop pretending to be an upper-crust goy, and come back to the family, to its ways, to Jewry, probably even take a job in the store, tell bad jokes, talk too loudly, and generally be boring and crude. Never, never, never would they give me recognition in my own right. Never could they do that. I would watch them try: "Well, Stu, what's new?" one of them would ask. And what was I to say? "Well, what's new is that I am losing my mind because I can't decide whether the right style of life would be that of a hippie or the one I presently have, that of an establishment intellectual." Or, "What's new is that I have been observing you all talking together about trivia and I am totally bored." They had me. I was speechless. I had the choice between saying what I thought, in which case they would simply laugh at me, criticize me, or make me feel guilty. Or, I could lie and try to talk about insurance, or cars. That would be one of the frequent questions: "How's the car?" As if it were a person. But I saw through that question, I saw the real intention. The real intention was to show that I had made a mistake. That, in buying a foreign car (a Volkswagen, years before) rather than a "normal" car, I had been taken in—just like an intellectual to be taken in—and I had bought something fragile and foolish. A schmuck. They had told me that when I was younger: "Book-learning isn't everything." I freely translated: "You are wasting your life, be like us."

My strategy at these meetings had evolved over the years. I went, of course. I went, because I was still financially dependent, in part, on my father. I didn't want to lose the insurance (in a way I too was an expert on insurance) of his support. Deep down, I knew how fragile I was, I might need him. And I went because I was supposed to and guilt told me to go. When I was younger, I used to argue: my point of view against theirs. They talked about "beatniks": I defended the "outsider." I was the active snob. Then, as time went on, I grew simply more aloof. I dressed better and better. My manners, to others, at least, grew more and more polished. So, I would sit there, among the barbarians and simply hold my tongue. Pray for it to be over. Leave early, saying I had much to do that was important.

That night I determined to do things differently. We gathered in the Steak Joint, vulgar, overdecorated, overpriced, a place for a performance rather than a meal. We had met there before. I came first. It gave me time to brace myself, to mentally review my resolutions and set myself toward doing something different this time. Then, came my sister and niece and nephew. My brother-in-law has left them off and is busy trying to find a parking space. I assist everyone in getting his coat checked. Then we stand around. The first question, for which I have been preparing, trying to rehearse an answer though I didn't know what it was to be, trying hard to keep my mind clear and focused. The first question is: "Have you been waiting long?" My sister asks the question, affectionately.

Now what kind of an idiotic question is that?—so I would have begun angrily to reason to myself in the old days. How long could I have been waiting, a few minutes? So what? And what is one supposed to answer? Am I, learned and sophisticated Stuart, supposed to treat such a question seriously? It says nothing. We discuss nothing of importance, like literature, or philosophy, or music, the things I know about and am good at. No, we avoid all of that stuff, so as to trap me on this ground of trivia, ground that all my academic training, all my intellectual cultivation has taught me to despise.

This time instead of flying into a rage which I don't dare to express, because I am afraid of these people, I need them, though I don't even know why, instead of mumbling some answer, so as to give them no answer, to irritate them with passive resistance, to look the other way, to light a cigarette, to brace myself for the next question and its implicit attack, I make an effort, and I take the question straight: "No, I've only been waiting about five minutes." And I try not to and I succeed in not wincing when my sister says, with no intention of profundity: "Well, that's not long." We move into the dining room. I have resolved, and I am going to do it.

My brother-in-law arrives, and heaves himself into a chair, with a hearty smile, and gives me his hand, he has always patronized me for some reason, always called me "Stewella," the bilingual diminutive form of my name that my mother used when I was a child and, naturally, still uses from time to time. I have hated his patronizing me. Why should he do it? I have my accomplishments and he has his. Why should he patronize? Defensiveness? It still hurts, even if he is being defensive. Or perhaps it is because, as he seems to hint, that I am not manly enough for him, not enough of a regular guy, interested in money and sports and insurance and business. And that hurts, I must admit, because I have always liked Seymour and his manliness and have wished he would take me straight, instead of sometimes straight and sometimes with sarcasm. So he sits down and he asks the inevitable question, one of those questions that used to drive me crazy to try to find an answer to: "Well, Stewella, what's the good word?" Now there is a question. My uncle, Uncle Sam, Aunt Tillie's husband, used to ask me that question every time I would see him: "What's the good word?" when I was a kid. And it had baffled me. My mind would begin to search, at age eleven, for a particular word, like a password: Money, Car, Store, Matzoth-Ball Soup, "The

Charge of the Light Brigade." Then, as I grew older, I discerned the intention of the question was to ask for news. But it didn't say that, did it? Suppose I answered: "Well, I just got a scholarship to college," or, "I read an interesting book." That wasn't a good word, was it? It was baffling. So baffling, that I had once told my father about this particular aspect of my problem and he had instructed me what to answer. "You answer with, 'Not much, what's the good word with you?' You turn it around," he would say. "No big deal, just inquire after the other person."

I was shocked at this instruction. Clearly, my father was right—the question was not to be taken seriously. It was simply a conversational gambit. A way to get things started. And clearly, Sam used it because he was preoccupied, and it was handy to have something to open with, year in and year out, preoccupied as he was with something that seemed to lie near his feet, as he sat, eternally, by the cash register of his store, staring at the floor, and playing with the Scotch Tape dispenser. And, even in those years, I forgave Sam most of the embarrassment of silence he caused me because I realized, in some vague and intuitive way, that he was shy, as shy as I was, and that he was suffering his own suffering, in some way, and he didn't really want to talk to me, that was true, but he did, you know what I mean, and this counter, this token phrase, was the best he could muster. But I had not been successful, even in those days, after I had talked to my father, with his instructions, for when I tried it on Sam: "I don't know, Sam, what's the good word with you?" I got no place, for he simply said, "Not much." And then would draw off another three inches of Scotch Tape, somehow glad to see me, a kind of twinkle in his eye, and look down at the floor.

So when Seymour asked his question, my mind raced and in line with the resolution, I did the best I could, and the best I could was to try again the reply that my father had urged me to use to this same question, years before: "Not much, Seymour, what's the good word with you?" And I found that though I had been right, as a child, and it was an impossible question, for even the voluble Seymour in answer to my father-directed reply could only respond lamely, looking aside, his head turning slightly as if to pull back and then leave the field free for starting over, "Not much." But the difference was that Seymour didn't let it stop there. He came back with something else, another track of rail laid into the social wilderness, some other inquiry or other statement, and I realized, another brief flash of light in my emerging education, that the routinized and meaningless exchange about the good word had done something, it had broken the ice, and while it might not lead to the deepest sort of interchange between persons, the love, which I guess I really wanted, it might lead to something somewhat more close to love than mere silence. There was a plausibility about all this, for the first time. They were reaching out toward me, and I had reached back. I was still depressed, still scared to know that I hadn't any excuse for living in the world, my ego crushed at Esalen, and my mind would wander, and I wasn't getting what I wanted, but my program was working somewhat, for I saw, now, that they were reaching out by these questions, reaching out, and that was something, and maybe, I had been too impatient with them, all these years, maybe they were trying to love me, and maybe I was pretty strange to their eyes after all, and now, I was trying, for what it was worth (it might not be worth much), only an experiment, to reach back a little, humbly, in their terms.

Eventually, my father and Byrdie arrived and the usual free-for-all began. I think it fair to say that despite the variety of other attitudes and postures to which I have alluded—rage, snobbism, contempt, the critical eye, exasperation at vulgarity, all of it—the main thing that I experienced on these occasions was a feeling of quiet intimidation, a vast shyness and embarrassment. They all talk at once. They poke at each other, so it seems to me, giving each other endless advice. Beware of telling them too much, they'll jump right on you. They jump on each other. No one ever seems to be exactly right. The inquisition and scrutiny extend to the slightest details, especially to the slightest details: "Where did you park, Dad?" my sister asks my father. "In the gas station, on the corner." How to reproduce the split second of silence that follows, for it is only silence, but in that space you can almost hear the minds of everyone working, calculating whether this was the best of all possible places to park, whether it was safe, for example, or too expensive, or whether it was convenient. Silence, on this occasion for, after all, parking on the corner is pretty good. Can't do too much better than that. But beware of parking two blocks away! Without much being said it will be made to seem that you are some kind of schlemiel, a real asshole, for not having found a parking place closer. Of course, there is an allowance made for bad luck, mere chance, but look, after all, dozens of other people found parking closer.

I guess what I wanted most from my family was unconditional acceptance. For some reason, I thought I was entitled to it. And I was desperately and continually disappointed, because they seemed so critical, not just of me, but of each other. Little was unconditionally approved. It all got mixed up in my head. This critical attitude. Once upon a time, at dinner at my father's house, we were watching television and a toothpaste commercial came on. Now, as I remember the incident, I started the criticism, you might say. Stuart: "You know, Dad, you've always used Colgate toothpaste; you should use Crest, because you don't get so many cavities." Dad: "Where did you hear that?" S: "The American Dental Association says so." Dad: "They probably bought them off."

I begin to argue, surely, I reason, life cannot be that corrupt, one needn't be that much on guard. My father insists. "It's all a racket." At which point, as if to trounce me forever, Byrdie: "Let me tell you something, Stuart, you remember the

TV quiz programs where the shoemaker answered all the questions about opera and won $64,000?" I am puzzled but answer, "Yes." B: "Well, your father was the only one at the time to see that they were fixed." Dad: "Of course. How could a shoemaker know so much about opera?"

You know the way it had been structured, at least as far as I saw it, was that I was the idealist, the youngster, the book-worm, and they were the realists, all of them, even my niece who so conformed to their expectations, though she never said anything, exuded a patient tolerance for my stupid excesses, my gullibility. Life, it seemed, was a struggle, a series of snares, and one must be on the look-out—never give freely; never give affection freely. That was the way I saw the situation. I wanted them to be truly understanding and proud of what I had done. It pissed me off to achieve what I had and then have to explain to my parents what I had done and why it was important. I remember when I was elected to Phi Beta Kappa, I had called my father, knowing that he would be excited. He said: "What does that mean?" Not out of malice, he just didn't know what it meant. They made fun of my long hair, of my friends ("Remember Ronald, the one with the beard?"). Freaks. My friends. One freakier than the last. I loved my friends. The same with my girl friends. I remember taking Marcia, the girl to whom I had just in warmth and sweetness lost my virginity, beautiful and precious time, into the store to meet my father, and then, later I asked him what he thought of her, and he said she was "dirty." Dirty! She had dirty tennis sneakers!

And it got so complicated. Because I resented them so, but I wanted their approval. Wanted them to see me as I saw myself. And instead we were engaged, so it seemed to me, in a kind of cultural warfare. At least, I saw it as warfare. And here we were, one more time, in the restaurant as usual, pretending to be a family, and no one letting anyone else say anything, everyone interrupting, demanding attention, uncivilized, insensitive, definitely not like the families on the radio. And my nephew, Gregg, looking silently away, in extreme boredom, or something more, hurt, as I had looked when I had been a young child. And my niece generally quiet but occasionally entering into some conversation, dragged in by her parents, who somehow didn't find much good with her either. It was true that she was getting good grades but, Seymour quickly added, addressing my father in complaint: "She spends all her time studying, a regular bookworm. She never goes out. And when she does go out, she goes out with bums." "Drop-outs," my sister adds, laughing a little at what she thinks is friendly satire. My niece, of course, is called on to defend herself and with the inadequate eloquence of the teen-ager merely exclaims, reproachfully: "Aw, Ma." Sally: "Well, it's true," fiercer this time. "Look at Joey. He's dropped out of school. He doesn't do anything. His parents support him."

What always appalled me in these exchanges, what I can't understand, what makes me feel like the all-time freak, is that it is clear that people are not really trying to hurt each other. And it seemed pretty clear that they really didn't hurt each other. There is a different attitude than mine toward all this verbal violence, this much is clear because the violence is so casual, unthinking. It leaves me wondering. How can people be this way? Maybe it doesn't hurt them.

But these thoughts were not uppermost in my mind on this particular occasion. They were the background for what was really going on. The depression I had brought from Esalen, that feeling of worthlessness was still with me, I was aware of keeping back tears all through dinner. There was a special hurt for me in feeling so bad and realizing, now that they were all here in the flesh, that there was no way I could communicate these feelings to my own family. And then, struggling to surface above all this, my resolve, a resolve born of faith, not of understanding, that whether I understood my family and my relations with them better or not, I would be good. I would forget the endless account books, the ledgers of rights and wrongs, the detailed entries of every hurt and slight they had visited upon me since my earliest days, the calculations of just what quantity of meanness was contained in the remark: "Well, Stewella, what's the good word?" The fine scrutiny of my life against theirs, double-entry bookkeeping, to see where the real sums were added up, of clothes, of taste, of table manners, or morals, or culture, or decency. I would forget the yellow ledger sheets with their thin blue lines, all that I had added up since our operations had begun, on my birthday.

I had my resolve. I push aside my decision made years and years ago, never, never, under any circumstances, to play their meaningless games, their false and phony games, especially the game of asking those dumb questions. Everyone is talking and eating and drinking. Jumbo shrimp cocktails have yielded to massive steaks and huge baked potatoes. And I turn to Elise, my fifteen-year-old niece, and I try to think of what I am supposed to say to this girl, according to the rules. Something about school. And what can I do that might be helpful to her? I don't really care for her, you understand, don't even know her, but they have called me selfish, those voices back at Esalen, and I know they are right. And I will do something about it. And I turn to Elise, and I say: "You must be starting to think about college, Elise. Let me know if I can help you in some way, give you advice, give you pointers, I don't know but maybe I can be of use." It was the first time in fifteen years that I reached from my world into hers, voluntarily. She thanked me, shyly. The party went on around us. Neither of us, too shy, could say more. But I could feel, though my back was tense with trying not to look around, I could feel the table responding to this event. Not in a dramatic way, of course, that would have been out of place. But it seemed as if a hush had fallen over the din for just a second or two.

The next couple of days were like this one, though less and less rewarding. I kept trying to stay awake, to do the right thing, to stick to my list, but not much was happening. I was simply moving where before I had been still, I thought to myself. Meanwhile, the day of my departure from New York to Washington was nearly upon me, and I was faced with the prospect of going back to Esalen, a resolution which I had taken, but a prospect which frightened me extremely.

My father and I arranged to meet for lunch at Lüchow's Restaurant. He always liked for us to get together each vacation by ourselves to talk. I usually didn't. I did it because he insisted. It always seemed to me that there was an inquisitorial quality about these luncheons. As if my progress in life was being reviewed by the highest committee. Things I had said during the family dinner would be brought up for elucidation through further testimony, casual words dropped during brief visits in the store would be the subject of expanded discussion.

I waited for him outside. A gray day on Fourteenth Street, cold, about thirty degrees. It was supposed to be for one-thirty. He was late. Nothing new. I resented it, of course, but I waited. I was too timid to go inside. I feared that I would miss him so I would stand for two or three minutes or so outside and then look in at the restaurant entrance, to see if he had somehow slipped by me, then dash out and look in at the bar entrance to see if he was there. So little had I come to trust myself that although the spot where I was standing was in between the two entrances, no more than five feet from each, I couldn't be sure, I had to check, as if my father possessed magical powers, powers of the Parent I had known in childhood, and could somehow slip by me. When he arrived, at last, half an hour after the appointed time, I was brave about the whole thing: I gave him a smile, I would not withhold that, I was through punishing him. He asked me why I had not waited inside. I evaded the question, how to explain to your father, who expects you to be doing well, that you are afraid to sit inside; embarrassed to meet the glances of the prosperous-looking business types. But I continued to smile, and I asked him how he was, something I wouldn't have done in the old days.

We sat down. He was cheerful and hearty, as always, and took the menu from the waiter with the pleased look of antici-pation of a man who enjoys his eating and drinking. We or-dered and then settled down to our talk. A talk of many things.

After a while, he asked, "What are your plans?" I had been dreading the question, it was the hard question for me, the one I had a hard time even thinking about, myself. I told him that I was not sure, I might go back to Esalen for a while or stay here.

"Son, I don't want to tell you what to do, but I think you should go back." I was surprised, surprised that he would have an opinion, not to speak of so strong an opinion. "It's done you a world of good."

I remember that the room suddenly felt stuffy, and the dark furniture and the black tuxedos of the waiters reeled slightly before me. "I don't know if you're aware of it, but you've changed immensely. It's hard for me to know how to put it, but you're becoming a person. I think it's wonderful."

I thought, as he spoke in praise of the way I was and of my going back to Esalen, of how hard it had been, how I had suffered, and how I wanted his comfort. And I thought of how long it had been, a whole lifetime, that I had waited for him to approve of something I was doing in such a total fashion. No trace of criticism. Not giving advice, even. He was, quite sim-ply, pleased. I thought, all at the same time, of how I had measured myself for change at Esalen, change, the big crite-rion, the measure of success, and how I had feared, to the very day I left there, that I had not really changed, and now, step-ping forward to bear witness, the man who knew me longest, my own father, said I had changed. And I thought of my pro-gram, and how it had made me behave differently to the fam-ily, my parents, Elise. And I thought that even though I wasn't "myself," so to speak, even though I was still depressed and afraid, and even though I did not know where I was going, with my famous resolutions, and with the notion of returning to Esalen, the fact had to be, simply was, that I was doing something right. And an intimacy with my father I had never felt before, a simultaneous feeling of being at once the son, dependent, petted, and grateful for the helping word, and also the equal who had suffered his way to understanding and won something, and the superior who knew that going back to Esalen was no easy thing. All these feelings and impressions, so rich, so richly interwoven, that the air itself seemed to get thick and warm and to form itself around us, held together in that space, surrounded by dark woods, mirrors, and crystal, pocketing us together, a father and a son, two men, for the first time, two men who had earned the right to be together because they had both suffered in order to grow up, in that intimacy, over the remains of my elegant lunch and down the front of my face, and onto my vest, the warm and salty tears, while my father only watched, and I reached out my hand, across the table, for him, and he took it. We had, starting that moment, both of us, begun to forgive each other for a thousand mutual hurts.

We talked on and on. Something modest but new had begun. I felt myself taller for it all, after the tears; more of a man. We embraced, on the cold street afterward, parting in the dingy winter afternoon. Much would happen later, we would spend some days together first to clear accounts—to go over all the hurts, real and fancied, all the resentments—that was eight months in the future. But this was the beginning and the generosity of his approval gave me courage to continue the journey I was on.

I left the next day for Washington, bound for California, afterward, and as I flew down on the Eastern Shuttle, looking out the window at the earth, I thought of all that had happened in the last few days, and I finally admitted to myself that a new sense of things was beginning to come over me. It hadn't come all of a sudden. It came in flashes; it came in steps; it gathered into a pool, and it was not on some particular day that it happened. I wasn't even exactly sure what it was. Partly a sense that reality could be born again. The sense, when seeing my mother, that she was not the enemy, the fierce large female person of my childhood, who could still rob me of my very manhood. Rather, an old woman, who had cared for me. Edgar Cannon, not merely teacher, and father figure, and a man who gave me things, but out there, object of possible transactions, a man to whom I could give, a brother. The sense that I got when to satisfy the resolve that I do a good deed a day I gave to a beggar. A few days before, when I walked back a block to give a dollar to a beggar we had passed by on Madison Avenue, Edgar had remarked: "He's probably richer than both of us." And I knew he was right, but I found a voice saying aloud, my voice: "Yes, but he is begging for all of us." I laughed at it: Stuart the sudden philosopher, voices speaking through me. Something starting to happen, what, what was it, when I held my father's hand and cried? In these acts, and others like them, so difficult for me as I was then, and so modest in their worth, I found myself softened. Softened against the world and myself. I didn't understand what was happening to me but it seemed very important—glimpses of the highest knowledge and pleasure I had ever known.

CHAPTER TWENTY-TWO

⁂ another beginning ⁂

in washington, I stayed with my friend Hugh Stein, who worked for the Bureau of the Budget. He had been a research sociologist and then, about two years before our meeting, he had started on a new career, just at the same time that I was leaving literary studies to try to find something that seemed more meaningful than doing empty acts of criticism. He had heard about a paper I had written on the tyranny of college grading systems and had looked me up. We shared many things in common, griping about the educational establishment, talking of the need for more excitement in education, more honesty, more joy, and eroticism. Talking about ourselves. Believing, when we had broken from our academic strait jackets that there was an energy abroad in the whole world, a new age was coming, the kids would bring it in, with acid and rock, helped by places like Esalen and by encounter groups, McLuhan, Buckminster Fuller, computers, automation —Utopian visions of 1965. Each of us had wanted the same things: more life, more money, more power. And we had learned new things and exulted together, assuring one another that we were right and the "Establishment" wrong.

And slowly our feeling changed. We began to realize they had co-opted us. Glumly we began to describe our jobs, his at the Bureau of the Budget, mine at Livingston and Old Westbury, the same way: "radical-in-residence."

All this had drawn us even closer together though I had never loved Hugh, my professional comrade, the way I had my other friends. He was too plonking, too square, I thought, with his suburban house, and having been a student politician before it made sense, and smoking his pipe and generally being a good guy. I had paraded my clothes, cars, and women before him and his wife, implying how dowdy and pathetic was his rebellion against the forces of respectability.

The night I came, though, sitting in their living room, I was silent. Dread was building in me about returning to Esalen and the conference which would start the following day. Even being with Hugh served to recall triumphs that seemed no longer available. He too sat silent and thoughtful. He had also spent a large part of the fall at Esalen, as a seminarian, and with similarly disorienting results. Two very different kinds of people; once again we were drawn together by what we shared.

"You know, Stuart," he said, "I think there is something religious about what we are going through."

"How do you mean?"

"I'm not sure, exactly, but I think what we are after is religious in some way."

"Are you sure that isn't your acid experience, Hugh—just chemistry?"

"No, I'm not sure. I wish I knew."

"Who ever thought," I said, "we'd end up talking about religion rather than computers or encounter groups?"

We smiled, we sat some more, and then we went to bed. We both seemed depressed.

The conference was on "Our" topic: The Future. In earlier days, I would have shone, a man with answers. Stein, too. We would have circulated, soaked up panels, asked bright questions, had loud and impressive dialogues in the lobby so that girls could hear, nodded our certainties of disagreement to one another, when a more famous speaker fell into error. Hugh looked disgusted. I felt the futility of all this airy speculation when what seemed real was my incessantly returning confusion, my pathetic resolutions, and those occasional new glimmerings of feelings. How could people talk of Utopias and "problems," "solutions," "programs," when Stein and I, who had tried to live the future, were suffering?

"Let's go to a bookshop," he said.

Aimless and endless meanderings in the dusty stacks of the used-book store. I found myself almost afraid to buy. Waiting somehow for the right book. What was the good book for me?

The Crisis in Psychiatry and Religion, by a man with the unlikely and unstylish name of O. Hobart Mowrer. I saw it on the shelf. Not anything I would have bought in the old days, but something was pushing me toward these two fields. I reached for it. On the back, it said that the core idea of the book had to do with guilt. I turned to the main essay, and I read the first couple of pages, ending with this paragraph:

> As the title of this paper implies, it will be our plan to consider, first, the possibility that in psychopathology guilt is *real* rather than illusory ("delusional"); then we shall explore the correlative proposition that the aim of communication and self-disclosure in the therapeutic situation is not mere understanding and insight (in the Freudian sense of those terms) but a changed, repentant view of

oneself; and finally we shall examine evidence for believing that, however necessary they may be, contrition and
confession are not alone enough to restore psychic and
moral equilibrium and must be followed by meaningful,
active forms of atonement or restitution.

I pushed aside my automatic reaction to the stuffy academic
style, the mannered performance of scholarship, so out of place
in a discussion of topics like guilt and redemption. I attended,
rather, to the point of the passage; it made an astonishing kind
of sense. I had not thought much about guilt when it occurred
to me that I wanted to be good. I had never thought about
atonement or restitution when I had decided to be good to my
mother and take her to that long-promised restaurant and I had
let her take my arm.

Years of psychotherapy, years of psychotherapy before coming to Esalen, where I had dragged myself, three times a week,
to what someone once called "the paid friend." Dragged myself
to justify myself. To beg, from the silent therapist, the peace of
his agreeing with me, the sense that I was right in what I
thought: "Help me! Help me, Doc! My parents are trying to
get me, the world is absurd, people are phonies, my talents are
not being rewarded." Sitting in those chairs in those offices, in
Cleveland, and then in New Haven, and then in Oakland, and
then in Berkeley, talking, talking, telling my woe, and never a
word, from those silent "doctors"—never a word to tell me that
I was wrong or right. Years in which I dragged my resentments
into little rooms, voiced them, left lighter; they would return,
and I would return, and I never daring to see, never being told
that I felt bad because I thought myself bad and that some of
this, at least, was no illusion.

It didn't sink in at once. But that paragraph seemed as if it
had been written for me. I worked on it, wondering how to put
it into further effect, how to make it work for me at Esalen.
"Confession." Old-fashioned words. Very old-fashioned words.
"Expiation." "Atonement." "Restitution." Religious words. And,

to my amazement, they seemed the best words to describe what was happening to me. I *knew* a lot about the religious; endless religious poems I had studied. But I had read the later Donne for his "wit," and Milton for his "rhetoric," and Spenser for his "fantasy," and so with all the others: Jacopone da Todi, Angelus Silesius, dozens more in French and Italian and German. I had read them for everything but their religion. I *knew* a lot about religion. But to find religious ideas relevant to me, cynical Stuart the New Critic! I mused on the thing.

It was as if I were being transposed. The ground upon which I lived, I had thought I knew well. The assumptions on which I had made my way around the earth, I thought I understood: secular, psychotherapeutic, materialistic, in short, modern. And now, my experience was transposing me, placing me somewhere else, and to understand it, the common-sense agreements of contemporary life would not entirely work; rather I would have to leave my world and move instead to Dante's, the world of old books and older systems of thought. Incredible. I, suddenly involved with Spenser's magic, with the speculations of medieval theologians, Dante's mystic rose, Donne's cries to God, men dead for centuries. Distinctly unmodern men. Men whose universe had not only an earth, but a heaven, too. A two-story universe, William James had called it. Next thing I might be believing in Angels, and God, and the *primum mobile,* I laughed to myself. A reverse Copernican revolution. Instead of looking up at the stars, I might have to look down, down from the spheres onto our little earth. I tried it, just in imagination. It was exciting. It fit some of the new ways I had been feeling. A little frightening. How far out would I find myself at the end?

The next afternoon Hugh and I went to be on our panel. I had accepted way back in October even though by then I hadn't wanted to go to any conferences, none. They had offered to pay my way, and I had thought then, as before, that

every conference attended was a step up the ladder of consultant careerism, and every conference where I was asked to participate on a panel moved me closer to bigger jobs, bigger fees,
bigger audiences, bigger influences, my name, at last, long-
hoped-for, in *Time* magazine. So, I had agreed to come and be
a member, along with Hugh Stein, my twin in the resident radical racket, and Harris Wofford, my square boss, well washed
and breezy, intellectually befuddled, a man with secular ambi-
tion and spiritual aspiration, I had thought him, but not sufficiently radical. There were others, students, one radical and
one square, and two other adults. A large panel, addressing
itself to the topic: "The Future of Education." The audience
was a hundred and fifty eager editors of the nation's college
newspapers—quite an important crowd, if you think about it.

With Hugh, I reluctantly found the largish room in which we
were supposed to deliver ourselves of wisdom. We pushed
open the tall leather doors: high ceiling, even lighting, a ros-
trum with a long table draped in green, seven chairs for the
panelists, seven microphones.

It was a strange thing. I felt when I entered the room as if
we were worn-out vaudevillians, we knew the scene, and we
had done the number before, in front of audiences smaller and
larger, younger and older, more or less radical. I had preached
the word, impressed them with my vision, with my information: that was a very good part, the information. Because I
would say something, make some prediction, like that people
would become more oriented toward their nonvisual senses—
as McLuhan contended. And then people in the audience, feeling threatened, would challenge me in the question period:
and I would tell them that it was already happening. And I
would reveal wonders of which they were then ignorant: The
Fillmore Auditorium, Esalen Institute, the real meaning of tex-
tured stockings, and so forth. And I would do this with confidence, like a magician, and so would Hugh, for we were among

the first adults to have heard of such wonders. Presto: the future, Ladies and Gentlemen.

But it was different for me this time, and for Hugh, too—confused and depressed and shaken as we were. We didn't really want to come. They were all there—our friends and acquaintances, professional student radicals, professional educational reformers, professional mediators between the old and the new, all of us familiar to one another, idealists, yes, and a new tribe of hustlers at the same time, I thought. Despite our depression and confusion, Hugh and I felt a little superior, for we weren't as fat as the others this time.

At last, the audience, coming in during all this musing, settles itself and the chairman seats us at the table and we look at the audience, and the audience looks back at us, and we all wait. The chairman announces that we will begin with a few remarks by Dr. Stein and then simply go down the panel, Mr. Wofford, Dr. Miller, and the others, in that order. All the eyes turn toward Hugh, who is seated at the right end of the table. His head hangs forward as if to signal that he is deep in dejected thought. Everyone waits. Then Hugh raises his head, his brown eyes look up at the audience, scanning, he extends his face forward on his neck a few inches, reaching for the microphone. His amplified voice makes a startling noise in the quiet room. "I have nothing to say."

You couldn't help but feel a lot of things. I did. The first flash was one of shock and surprise, and then admiration, for it was quite a stunt, after all, to be the first member of a panel of experts testifying to a sizable audience on an important topic and then to announce you had nothing to say. And I felt, also, a little envy that Stein had beaten me to it, simply by virtue of being the man at the right end of the table, for I had decided, as we had all taken our seats in front of the microphones, that I could say nothing, in good conscience. But my main feeling was the sadness of it. The sadness that Stein and I had nothing to say. He was saying by his silence that he doubted that the new education, the education that we had said would save us all, would in fact help. Mostly, it had depressed us and taken away more than it had given.

Harris was next. Despite Hugh's provocative opening, which gave promise that this panel might be different from other panels, Harris did his usual thing, a tiresome and rhetorical speech combining an appeal that mankind return to the "Socratic dialogue" and there find the end of its problems, with a public-relations job describing how "exciting" this new school would be that "we," he motioned toward me, were putting together at Old Westbury.

When it was my turn, I said what I had decided. I agreed with Hugh. I reported that I had nothing to say, I was confused and depressed by the prospects of education. About a dozen words. Despite the nearly dadaist silence of two of its members, the panel continued for a while, but in a half-hearted way. At the end, the audience sat baffled. Discouraged. Pissed and disappointed, they sat. Hugh got up to leave at the beginning of the question period.

I was tempted to follow. It was what I felt like doing. But I stayed. I just couldn't leave like that. It was too dramatic. Though I had resigned as an up and coming "expert," right there, before the educational community, admitted emptiness, dropped off another ladder, I didn't feel that it was right to leave. There would have been something angry about leaving, something aggressive and destructive. And, in a way, something too superior, about leaving; superior to the panel, to the idea of panels, to the audience, to the occasion, to the crisis in education, all that. The old Stuart would have left, the Stuart before the list of resolutions—but now I couldn't. If I had no bold speculations to give, I should give whatever I had.

Most of the questions were being addressed to Harris, and though I disliked Harris and thought him shallow, I stayed and helped him answer the many about the program at Old Westbury. The suspicion crossed my mind that I was doing this so as not to offend my boss too much, to leave open the door to returning to the College. That may have been part of it. But as I answered the questions, things became clearer. Before, when I had said I had "nothing" to say, I meant nothing very important, original, exciting to say. There were, however, things to say, much smaller things. Things as small as answering the question of a young man about how he might get an application form to Old Westbury. I could answer that one. Give that much. It was time to stop being so damn important.

When the panel came to an end, I was just a little proud of myself. Harris, energetic, tirelessly forming his new college, told me he couldn't spend much time with me, he had to fly back. The conference swarmed through the lobby; placards, and beards, mini-skirts, the rushing of messengers, literature being passed out, buttons protesting, identifying, life. Stein was dour, wrapped in the bitter heroism of defeat, a silent integrity. Tomorrow, I thought, I was going back to Esalen having done some right things, having had some marvelous but brief experiences, fulfilling my contract to myself, trying hard to burst the boundaries of my failure, but still a failure, or feeling like one, the old fear, that I had acquired at Esalen, again in the bottom of my stomach, still there, despite my being nice to parents, to my audience, to Harris, to strangers. It was still there.

part four

✠✠

✻ new life ✻

and it was still there when
I arrived at the heliport in Berkeley, and Arthur Pennington
picked me up, and we drove to Becky's and collected the rest of
my clothes and my car and I headed, once more, down the
highway, to Esalen. It remained with me all the long four hours
of my slow drive. A bright, warm Sunday with creeping tourist
traffic on the Coast Road. I was so fearful that I had kept from
myself, almost successfully kept from myself, even the questions that were most closely eating at me: What would they
think of me? How would they greet me? What would I find
to sustain me in the place where I had met so much pain?

But after I parked my car and got out, my anxiety dissolved
for a moment because the place seemed so different. It was much
quieter. The swarms of hippie hangers-on were gone. I didn't

see a single seminarian as I walked through the parking lot toward the office. On the front porch was Betty Fuller, big fat Betty, whom I had despised for her weight, for her schoolmarmish good cheer, for the very fact that despite my disliking her she had always seemed to like me. I was wary. "Hello, Betty."

"Hi, Stuart," she shouted. "I'm really glad to see you."

"You are?"

"Sure, I am."

I forced myself to believe her for the moment.

"Why is the place so quiet?" I asked.

"Haven't you heard? We're closed. There is no money. They've fired the manager and Joe and borrowed money to get things going again but it'll be a couple of weeks before there are any seminars. Jim Stiner is the new manager and Robert Portman and Joseph Prouty are helping him. The rest of the Residents are doing the work of the place because they had to lay off the staff, so we've all been making beds, serving meals, tending the grounds, without pay."

The news startled me. It was a new place that I was coming back to. In many ways that was not a comfortable thing. I had come back to be in workshops and now there were none. The place had been taken over by the Residents it seemed, and they were the ones I had most offended. I wondered what I would do, the fear in my stomach returned.

"I really am glad to see you," Betty said again.

"Thank you, Betty, it's nice of you to say so."

"I mean it, you dope. What has been happening to you? I heard you were in the East."

I make myself continue the conversation. "Yes."

"Tell me about it. What did you do? Did you see your family?"

And we sat on the porch bench, and faced one another, and I took her attentions for what they seemed. I put away the fears that she would be out to destroy me, like all the others. I didn't know exactly what I was doing, or what I had come back for but I was clear about a few things: that I had mistreated everyone here and that I had been self-obsessed and that I owed them something. The best I could do, just now, was to reach out. And once I decided that, things became very easy. There was something about Betty that encouraged confidences, a sense that she was really interested in what I had to say. I found myself telling Betty all that had happened in New York, of my list of resolutions, of the success with my father, of my daring to think that I wasn't a bad guy, and my deciding to come back, to take my chances, to try and become something new.

She was touched but she must have seen my lingering apprehensiveness. "Now, don't change too much," she said with a smile. "I always loved the way you could tell people to go fuck themselves. You know, I get so sick of being a good girl. But it's just marvelous that you've decided to give Esalen another try. This isn't the easiest place to live, you know. I guess all of us have had our difficulties."

"Really?" I asked in wonderment.

"Sure. Do you think you're so special?" She grinned. "Come and let me give you a hug for being back."

As she was releasing me from her fierce grasp, Robert and Joseph came up. They were talking about the business; Robert had a loose-leaf notebook and he and Joseph were studying every aspect of the operation to see where money could be saved. They seemed very busy.

"Hi, Stuart."

"Hello, Robert, Joseph."

We looked at each other in silence. Remembered hostility wavered in the air. Then Joseph examined me sharply. And he grinned with amusement at the momentarily tense situation. He saw how much had changed. "Have you come back to stay?" he asked me.

"I hope so," I said.

"Welcome back," he said, and he gave me a hand shake and turned away to his new business, satisfied that we were finished. Robert was slower, studying me for another minute, his eyes wide, as if to take in everything. I made myself look back at him without fear or anger. Then he smiled, too. "Welcome back, Stuart. I wish you luck." And the two of them walked off. I heard phrases like "chart of accounts," and "centralized buying." Betty waved me a good-by, she had an errand.

They were all glad to see me, at least they didn't object. I had worried that they wouldn't let me back in or that they would attack me. It was wonderful, this casual welcome, after all my abuse of them. And the same was repeated with other Residents all that day.

The question, the following day, was what to do next? My resolve to go to workshops was thwarted for the moment. Even the Residents were not meeting regularly as before. I was relieved when someone told me Annie was away visiting her parents, but I felt out of things. People kept to themselves or worked on crews doing various jobs around the place.

I hadn't counted on manual labor. As a child, I had learned to hate work. My father had worked in his store immigrant hours, six days a week, twelve hours a day. On Sundays, he would work only eight hours. Sunday night was a big night. It would be about the only time I would see him, except in the store when he was too busy to pay attention to me. We all wondered why he worked so long. Was it really necessary? I thought him trapped in running up and down the stairs of that two-story shop, moving boxes around, waiting on customers, unpacking shipments, rolling the awning up and down, dragging out the trash, watching the customers to see they didn't steal, arguing, begging his saleswomen to work on the days he needed them, enduring the shrill curses of enraged lady customers who had some complaint, but never having the time to lead a normal life, to enjoy home and family, to read, to have hobbies. It seemed to me, with my interests in books and dreaming, a living suicide.

I would never work so—manual work or commercial work. I would not get trapped. My mother urged me not to get trapped like him. I was too delicate, she implied, too good for that drudgery. And I learned to agree, avoiding work after school. My college summers I did everything I could, while my friends worked in steel mills and on construction gangs to earn money for college, to persuade my father to send me to summer school. And when I did work two summers, as an office boy and a waiter, forced to it by my father's telling me it was good for my character, I would become stupid and I would suffer and I couldn't learn the most elementary tasks. I was meant for better things.

But at Esalen, all were working. I lay on my bed after lunch and wondered what to do. The others probably liked it but I didn't. Maybe that's good though, I said to myself. It could be a way of expiation, a way of paying back for all the insults and anger I had spread around. And, even if I didn't like it, it was a way of giving up my specialness, my pride. I decided to try it.

So I got up and went to the office. Sandra was there. "So, you're back," she said. "Going to hang out some more?"

I took the slight sneer without replying to it. "No." I smiled to her. "I want to go to work. Are you the person who gives out the assignments?"

She flipped through the file. "All we need, Stuart, is a cabin girl, someone to make beds and clean rooms. Do you want to be a cabin girl?" she asked archly.

I hesitated, they would laugh I was sure at the great Stuart making beds and cleaning toilets, and not even getting paid.

"I'll take it," I said.

"Well, I see there are some changes. Go to Mary Jane at the laundry room in half an hour."

Mary Jane I knew from before. She was an ex-social worker who had come to Esalen, dropped out, and joined the staff. A fat cheerful girl with a big smile who would get into fits of depression. She was the head cabin girl.

I left Sandra without asking where the laundry room was. For some reason, I felt too ashamed to ask. I blundered around for the whole half hour and finally found the room by catching a glimpse of Mary Jane going into it. I told her I was volunteering to help make beds.

"Good," was all she said. I was relieved because I hadn't really known if she would welcome me: toward the end, in December, I had stopped speaking to the staff and they had gotten pretty tired of what they took to be arrogance. Mary Jane was a little distant now but she was pleasant enough.

"Stretch your arms out in front of you," she said, and she piled me up with sheets and pillow cases. Another girl, one whom I had never seen, joined us. Also a hippie type. We went to the first cabin and they showed me how to make up the bed in team fashion. We would strip off the old sheets. Then one of them would get on one side of the bed, I on the other; we would spread the new sheet out flat, then both place ourselves at the foot of the bed, and work upward tucking it in. Then the top sheet, again working from the bottom. The blanket too. All very methodical and quick. The beds would get made very fast. I concerned myself only with following directions, fought my shyness and fear of these people, and tried to concentrate on doing things right.

To my amazement, I began to have a good time. Conversation became easy. They gave me tips on how to tuck in a corner or fluff a pillow, we began talking about our backgrounds. Mary Jane it turned out was from Brooklyn. They spoke about the doings of Zack Durham, a famous Big Sur local, and I asked about where they lived, how they managed to survive on their measly wages. We even laughed about the way I had been when I first came: "Those English boots," Mary Jane chuckled.

My body warmed with the work. After a bit the two of them stopped to have a cigarette. I had one too, smoking and looking with them at the ocean. Then we moved onward, cabin after cabin, all afternoon, alternating conversation with silence, my back beginning to ache slightly, from all the bending and stooping. There was much less talk as the afternoon wore on. Then, at last it was over. "Let's go get a beer," said Mary Jane. "I'll buy," I said, and we trooped to the lodge.

After we had finished our beers, the girls went to the baths. I sat at the dining-room table looking at the sun on the ocean and let my sense of the thing collect. It had been a kind of miracle. Not a great smashing thing, of course, more a muted affair, something subtle and yet definite: here I had sought to do penance, to humble even to humiliate myself, and what had happened? After a few minutes of discomfort, I had found myself blessed. My fear of two of the staff had evaporated, I had enjoyed the conversation and the physical work. Most important was a sense of comradeship, a kind of quiet communion in work which I had read about somewhere before. I began smiling to myself. Something was going on. Something was happening to me and it evaded any easy explanation. I seemed to be inhabiting a new kind of world where blessings descended regularly. My mind searched for quotations. Where was it written that one might put forth a little effort in the service of the good and find joy flooding in? Where was it? I had never read the New Testament but that felt like the right book to look for. I wanted to get some guidance, to keep this experience going. I got up from the table and left the dining room, the door swinging shut after me, to see if there was a Bible in the office.

The office was closed; it was after hours and another strange girl was making the cash register, eager to finish and get away from her work. But I knocked, and reluctantly, in the dimness of approaching evening, she put aside her additions and got up and walked to the door. She let me in and I told her what I was looking for. "I think there's one around the back office somewhere," she said. And she went back to bending over her accounts. I looked around. On top of the desk. Opening cabinets. Searching in old wooden file drawers.

At last I found it. A black, leather-bound volume, with gold stamping. I had never held a Bible in my hands, a proper *goyishe* Bible with both Testaments. There was a certain apostasy in it, but I was already launched and though I felt the black volume in its weight on my hands as a foreign object, like black rock from an alien planet, there was warmth growing in my body, a radiance I had begun to feel, now and then, during the last few weeks. The weeks had been full. Each act a sort of suicide, a leap over the cliff of what I was used to and into the unknown. The miracle of working in the cabins was on me.

I had closed my eyes, enjoying the strange feelings. I opened them, blinked, looked around. Then I looked at the Bible. On the cover, stamped there, in gold letters, was the name of the owner: "Carter Hamilton."

"Fantastic." "Fantastic," I said to myself. "An incredible coincidence." Carter Hamilton had done gardening over at Dennis Murphy's place way back in October. A tallish, blond-haired and softly bearded youth, nineteen, with that peculiar touch of innocence about him as he worked, dungaree-dressed with his hoe under the bright sun, that makes one have to use the word "youth." One day, Herbert had told me that Carter was in trouble with his draft board back in New Orleans. He would have to go back there to see them and needed money for the journey. Herbert told me to give Carter some money if he came to ask. Herbert had given him twenty-five dollars.

A few mornings later, about nine o'clock, when I was eager to get breakfast before they stopped serving, and the sun was out, and my house was still cool from the night and the shade of the overarching pine trees, and you could see the dew

sparkle on the lawn, Carter knocked and entered and I knew
that he was there to ask me for money. And there had been a
certain pathos in it, that this pleasant-looking yellow-haired fellow, so young, would have to leave the sunny landscape, itself
full of yellow, where it seemed, perhaps leaning on his hoe, that
he belonged. He must go now on a succession of Greyhound
buses to a faraway city, to draft boards, and the chance of
death. And all this moved me to give him twenty dollars, even
though I didn't know him and I wondered if he were telling the
truth, wondered about his protestations that he would send the
money back, wondered why I was giving away my money to
anyone, particularly this stranger, and also a bit of resentment
because Herbert had made it hard for me to say no, and so had
Carter by just coming up like that. In the end, after he had
taken the twenty and gone off, I felt I had been hustled, and
tried not to think about it, because it was only twenty dollars,
wasn't it? But it bothered me anyway.

Of course, I had never heard from him.

Until this evening. And there it was, the Bible thrust into my
hands, when I needed it.

A mere coincidence, of course, but I had another feeling
about it. I felt I was entering a new order of reality. Reality was
still the same, yet all different: suffused with warmth, intan-
gible relations between things. It was, I thought to myself, another little miracle, akin to that feeling of brotherhood I was
starting to know—with the cabin girls, the people in the elevator, my parents, even. Something you couldn't see, violating
notions of separateness. Uncanny relations, as if New Orleans
and Carter had returned me a book through space-time, all the
way to Big Sur. The book had been left here way back in October. But it seemed as if it had been left with purpose for me.
Another way of looking at things, wasn't it? As though the earth
were alive, charged with meaning, and energy, and purpose,
and even time didn't interfere.

Again, I had heard such talk as I was talking to myself, holding the book in that darkening room. I had heard it from teachers, when they first explained pantheism to me. And I had read it in Plotinus with his talk of God being light and radiating through the universe. Or the Pseudo-Dionysius, the Areopagite, who had enumerated the attributes of God: loving, simultaneous, omnipresent; in the Indian formula, too: tat tvam asi, thou art that. And here I was, seemingly experiencing the thing. Carter and the Bible and The Debt and the Draft Board. Incredible. Was God involved in such things? God in twenty dollars and the draft board in New Orleans? Could it be that those attributes of simultaneity and omnipresence and goodness—divine qualities which I was feeling as the evening closed around the building like a mantle—belonged in my world?

I snapped myself from the reverie. It was delightful to feel the shiver of electric energy as the universe seemed to pulsate through me, but it was silly, wasn't it, and madness, to think such thoughts, to dissolve space and time so casually, even though it seemed good and sane to feel that the world was blessed? I didn't want to lose that feeling. But the dissolution was frightening. I shook it off, though a part of me remained in that new territory, anyway.

It was already quite dark as I took the book, and the girl let me out into the night air. I began to walk slowly across the property to my house, the moon not yet risen, the path before me obscure, and I was filled, as I looked back on the day, with a sense of joy that brought me to tears as I walked. The stars were only beginning to come up, and, for some reason, there at Esalen, back in that magic landscape of Big Sur, a presence that had haunted my childhood, informed so many nights when I was seven and eight years old, seemed to come back to me. The old God of childhood, that paternal deity, all-powerful, master of all events, final resort in trouble, a gigantic male presence that brooded over me, in the heavens, especially in the black heavens of nighttime. I had never entirely lost touch with Him, through all these years, for in my moments of special anguish or danger, all else failing, even though I knew better, I would call on Him. And that night in Big Sur, the ocean vast, with light still at the western edge, and a few stars blue-white, here and there, I looked at the immense sky and felt his return. I felt his warmth, his breath overreaching the earth was on my shoulders and on my neck when I bent my head toward the ground. Or something at once more gigantic even than Him and less precise. I walked along the dark path, down toward the Hot Springs creek, my Bible in my hand, and felt the large and pleasing warm tears brimming in my eyes. How little I had deserved. And how much suddenly, for no sufficient reason, had I been given. Strange mixture of the Hebrew God of my childhood, that stern promulgator of rules which had to be exactly obeyed, and something else which was new, another intimation of Deity. Jews don't kneel; it is forbidden, but it seemed right to kneel, and my knees rested gratefully on the cold path. I was filled with a sense of my smallness. A mighty power was present to me, but it was full of love and I felt that if I merely did the humble thing, the little thing, without phoniness or selfishness, it would give me such Grace as would bring me again to tears of thanks.

CHAPTER TWENTY-FOUR

✠ becoming a servant ✠

i didn't have much time until dinner that night but I went home, with my Bible, and I began reading the New Testament. I read with a kind of carefulness, that I had never accorded any volume before—determined to ponder each word's significance. But the opening pages of Matthew were hard for me to find revelation in: "The book of the genealogy of Jesus Christ, the son of David, the son of Abraham. Abraham was the father of Isaac, and Isaac the father of Jacob, and Jacob the father of Judah and his brothers, and Judah the father of Perez," and on and on for over a column of densely printed ancestors. It didn't mean much to me. Nor for that matter did the next column with its account of the birth of Christ, and Herod's search, and the flight to Egypt, and the long-awaited return. I read with care, in the dim light that shone down from above my bed, disappointed, knowing that dinner was already being served, but feeling a little anxious that I had found no guidance here, until, at last, I came to the baptism:

> Then Jesus came from Galilee to the Jordan to John, to be baptized by him. John would have prevented him, saying, "I need to be baptized by you, and do you come to me?"
>
> But Jesus answered him, "Let it be so now; for thus it is fitting for us to fulfil all righteousness." Then he consented. And when Jesus was baptized, he went up immediately from the water, and behold, the heavens were opened and he saw the Spirit of God descending like a dove, and alighting on him; and lo, a voice from heaven, saying, "This is my beloved Son, with whom I am well pleased."

Its meaning shone forth to me. Christ, the exemplary man, and his first words in the Bible told how it is righteous that the Son of God humble himself before another. Christ's first act, an act of humility. And after that act, which contradicts all appearances, God rewards him by sending a dove and saying, "This is my beloved Son, with whom I am well pleased." The way of humility was the way of godliness.

In my little way, I was on this same path. What a joy! What promise in that knowledge! I had a feeling of nearly being lifted from my bed. Of lying there on the cliff, by the dark and largest of oceans, and feeling that I was no longer alone, an alienated man, Byronic, standing on my pinnacle, the solitary sufferer. Rather I felt tugged, as the moon which had already risen tugged the ocean outside my window. You could not see that gravity, those forces of attraction and relation, neither could you see the many forces working on me. But I felt them. I could feel my little kinship with Jesus, with Matthew, and those others who had written down the New Testament. And God was with us—well pleased—that seemed real, too. And wasn't Carter, wherever he was, also in relation to me, his Bible having arrived in visible form as a token of the reality of that relation? It was as if, into me and from me, magnetic, electric forces. I could not find the right metaphor. It felt more like liquid than those, my body melted and the skin over my back and the back of my head tingled with warmth. I thought suddenly of Dante's *Paradiso* and the simile of a soul shaken and illuminated and warmed all at once, like the silver bowl taken from the dark house and set in the light, and the water in it quivers with the shock and gives back to the air the broken and dazzling reflections of the sun.

Such feelings. Such wonderful feelings, encouragement of the most delicious kind to continue, to keep up what I had been doing. And there was also the opposite thing, a tendency to pull myself together, to shake off the dream and all that richness. How much, after all, did it violate reason, that I, Stuart Miller, could feel at one with Jesus Christ, and Dante Alighieri, and the moon and the water, and some nineteen year old, vanished from the present scene, to go to prison for his hippie carelessness with federal laws and regulations. What relation was there? What could there be? "Don't get carried away" was the most frequent advice my parents had given me as a child.

Two days passed. With great delight, I read further in the Bible. Then, almost as if it were a goad to me, the old depression returned the second night. So I got up early the next morning to fulfill another resolve I had made back in New York: to humble myself by doing the feared and detested "body work." I walked over to the lodge and went down to the deck by the swimming pool, where a few people had already gathered waiting to do Tai Chi Chuan.

Tai Chi is an ancient Chinese discipline—a series of slow ballet-like movements that are supposed to be a kind of medi-

tation in action. At Esalen it was done every morning by whoever wanted to come and imitate the leader. This morning the
leader was Martha Portman, who had become proficient at it
over the last few months. Tall and graceful, she was already
beginning the slow walk with hands folded over the belly that
preceded the exercises themselves. We had not spoken, scarcely
even seen each other, since that night in October when she had
been so furious with me. I pushed away the feelings about her
that rushed into me—fear, sorrow, then remembered anger—
and attended to following her.

Confronting Martha, our past, and my present feelings about
her was impossibly far beyond my capabilities. I was suffering
enough on another score.

I was supremely visible. The deck beneath me, the sea and
the sky my backdrop, lawns and rock all around. All I was
aware of were the eyes. Eyes that I could imagine looking at
me with the most patronizing criticism. Occasionally I would
glance up at the lodge windows, my arms chopping clumsily
through the round movements, and I could see the eyes looking
at me; and I could imagine them being as my eyes had been:
comparing. All fall and winter I had watched from breakfast,
letting a piece of omelet dissolve lazily in my mouth, similar
groups of seminarians blunder their way through the Tai Chi
movements. The leader's body would flow, liquid and graceful.
The ladies and gents from Los Angeles, their middle-aged
paunches held by sweat shirts, their legs skinny, scaly, would
try. Then, as one rounded arm became entangled with another,
they would giggle, their laughter breaking the peace. And the
leader, unflappable, knees flexed with quiet power, would
simply continue, avoiding those awkward collisions.

"Go home, go home," I had murmured to myself watching.
"Go hide yourselves, gauche of the earth. Don't even try."

And now, here I was, bearing down with might and main,
tense in every limb, to follow the sweeping slow motions of

Martha Portman. No one had even explained to me what I was supposed to experience or learn. Like a child I was asked only to follow. I wouldn't even know if I was doing well.

But, once more, I forced myself. I forced myself to stay out there and endure the eyes. I tried to keep *my* eyes from straying to their eyes and to concentrate instead on just the rhythmic motion. This was what I had avoided—exposing myself and my awkwardness. It was right to try the new thing, part of reaching out, but I wasn't enjoying it much. I imagined the scorn that Martha would be feeling at my clumsiness. I strained to follow her movements anyway, driving out distracting thoughts, trying only to let myself be led.

Though millions of Chinese do Tai Chi every morning, in order to relax and to center themselves, I finished with exhaustion at the strain and relief. But as I walked to the side of the deck to pick up the jacket I had left there, another feeling came into me. A feeling of satisfaction that briefly enlivened my whole body.

I put my jacket on and looked out at the sea. I knew that Martha was gathering up her things preparing to leave. I wanted to talk to her. Though I felt much too awkward and off balance to discuss the past, to ask for forgiveness, or to simply apologize, I wanted to make some gesture of contact.

I turned around and hurried to where she was climbing the last of the stone steps that go from the front lawn to the rear deck of the lodge. She paused and I looked up at her. I smiled.

"You do those movements so beautifully, Martha: it's marvelous watching."

"Thank you," she said, but she looked a little uncomfortable.

I didn't let her leave. I wanted to try again and all I could think to do was to ask some dumb question: "I just don't think I'll ever be able to get it so well. How did you learn to do it?"

"Oh," she said, stopping where she was turning away, "it's just like everything else, practice, laughing at yourself, and some more practice. You'll get it, too. Besides, the movements aren't really important; the breathing and keeping your attention on the movements are the real things."

"How come?" I asked, partly to keep her engaged but also because I wanted to let myself learn, to let myself be her student. And I asked more questions, which she seemed glad, even eager now, to answer, and we must have gone on for half an hour, me asking questions and she telling me, increasingly warm and friendly, and we spoke and I listened and I saw not aloofness any more but concern in her, and not anger but sweetness, not the yelling fury but beauty, and I found myself quivering again. My life is full of miracles, I thought. An enemy becomes a friend, an angry Martha becomes gentle. The feeling of blessedness had come over me again. Was it a blessing, something from God, outside me, or simply that Martha had changed and I had changed? Whatever it was, it was working, what I was doing was working. Martha and I smiled goodby.

I went back to my house. I didn't understand all that was happening but letting go my fears and simply trusting myself to others, to God perhaps, seemed to leave me incredibly rewarded. When I read in the Bible later that morning, again I was shaken with those strange and wonderful feelings of transcendence. The passage seemed written just for me:

> "Therefore I tell you, do not be anxious about your life, what you shall eat and what you shall drink, nor about your body, what you shall put on. Is not life more than food, and the body more than clothing? Look at the birds of the air: they neither sow nor reap nor gather into barns, and yet your heavenly Father feeds them. Are you not of more value than they? And which of you by being anxious can add one cubit to his span of life?"

I read on, trusting myself now to the Book of Matthew, searching for understanding. And when I came back to a passage I had read earlier, one which I had known from my literary studies but which had been empty to me, it, too, suddenly shone with meaning: "Think not that I have come to abolish the law and the prophets; I have come not to abolish them but to fulfil them. For truly, I say to you, till heaven and earth pass away, not an iota, not a dot, will pass from the law until all is accomplished. Whoever then relaxes one of the least of these commandments and teaches men so, shall be called least in the kingdom of heaven." Trust and humility and an attitude of goodness were important, but so was the active work of doing. I must cultivate a right attitude and also keep to my resolutions to do things.

It was another miracle, God reaching out to show me a way forward. I found myself smiling with satisfaction at being so frequently blessed, knowing I was doing the right thing and being cosmically rewarded. I realized that I was reading the Bible with selective eyes and personal interpretations, but what was wrong with that? Why couldn't God be working through such an instrument as that? Then I felt a certain small embarrassment at being so attended to and even though I thought God would not begrudge me my little pleasure of self-satisfaction, I also knew I must be careful. I must return to humility and the law.

So I closed the book and hurried to lunch, thinking about what I could do next that was fitting, and after lunch I presented myself at the office to ask if there was another job I could do. Sandra was still amused by me but she told me that Mary Jane didn't need any "cabin girls." I should go see Harry, the Restaurant Manager, because he needed a wine steward.

Harry was in the kitchen. The wine-steward job was a new one. They had ripped out the old bar, part of the movement toward a quieter and more orderly place, and now they needed a waiter to serve the wine and beer. With mock-heroic affectation they had decided to call him the "wine steward." Harry told me he was having trouble finding the right person for the job. The men around were too rough and surly, just like the old bartenders. He needed someone to set a quiet tone in the dining room. "Come back at five o'clock, and I'll explain the job to you. Maybe you'll work out."

At five o'clock I came. Shy and nervous and stupid as when I had started those summer jobs in college. My mind began to blank when Harry went through the litany of liqueurs that could be served as apéritifs, and what Cinzano cost, and that we had white and red, and the same with Dubonnet, and that we had three kinds of sherry (Pale, Golden, and something else), and "Old Tawny Port." I would strain to file the information, strain hard to remember it all, and the harder I would strain, the less I remembered, so that I was continually interrupting him, and he had to repeat things, and we went through the candy which the wine steward also sold, eleven types, and he told me that when the cigarettes or wine ran low I could get more from out back, except, of course, the champagne, which was in the kitchen, in the "walk-in," behind me. And on and on and on.

But I caught myself. I felt the old resentments against work rising, and I felt my confusion coming on, and I caught myself and paid attention and calmed myself down.

I put on a little starched jacket and waited, apprehensively. The first customer came. He only wanted a pack of cigarettes. An easy thing. I found the right brand, handed him the matches, took his dollar, made change, and gave it to him. And I made a little extra effort: I smiled and thanked him.

Then the second customer came. Some tall seminarian, in a polo shirt and faded khaki bermuda shorts, knobby knees, and old tennis shoes. "I want something to drink," he said. My head became fuzzy again. I became frightened as when, a few weeks before, I had been unable to look strangers in the eye. This guy was a stranger, and besides all this, he was giving me an order, he was an aggressor. As I saw myself drifting back toward the old paralysis, I tried to think of what to do. And then it hit me—I would become the wine steward. I would become the best wine steward I could be. "We have lots of good things," I say. "Sherries, vermouths, other apéritifs, but I have heard that this 'Old Tawny Port' is particularly good. Why don't you try it?"

The man was obviously surprised because you didn't get treated that solicitously at Esalen in those days. "Now, let's see," I say, searching. "Where is the bottle? Here we are." I reach for a glass, examine it to see that it is properly clean, I hold it to the afternoon light flooding through the windows. I pour, I pull out the round cork-lined tray with a slight flourish. I present him the glass on the tray.

He is tremendously pleased. Tremendously pleased at the service. And I am pleased.

And then the flower of the joyful thing unfolding, as the third and fourth and fifth customer came, and I hustled to find bottles and cigarettes, candy, and matches, and went forth into the darkened dining room and waited on them, and even went onto the deck, far in back, where Herbert and I used to sit, went that far, to find out if people wanted anything to drink before dinner, rather than merely waiting in the nook of the wine steward's station for the seminarians to dare to come forward, as my predecessors had done, surly and angry. And I hustled around the place, in my white jacket with white buttons, carrying drinks and beers and cigarettes, the dining room filling more and more, and more people and more voices, and I still a little shy, and still a little frightened of so many strangers, even a little harassed, for there is much to do, and I am beginning to move very quickly, but I insist on doing the thing right, so everyone who orders a drink is treated very courteously and indulged while he thinks over what he wants, exactly, and suggested to, if he appears to need that when he can't make up his mind, and then I run away, nearly, though not too obviously, for that would, after all, spoil the whole point of the thing, which is to give the man his drink in a pleasant way so that he can relax and have dinner with a smiling stomach, and then I get his drink, smiling at someone else who has come up to the nook—"I'll be right with you"—and dash back to serve the drink, but with a great sense of stillness and courtesy, and then getting paid, and making change, and getting the thing for the other guy who has come up, and then bringing back the change, and sweat starting to come but enjoying myself for, at last, after so many months, I am doing something useful.

I worked a six-hour shift, almost all of it on my feet, and as I got into it, and did the job, I experienced with enormous zest, not only the feeling that I was doing something useful, but also that I was doing something well, and that while I could not, at the present time, do anything very important, too sure of my emptiness for anything important—I could, damn it, I could be the wine steward. And as the evening wore on, I realized that I could be about the best wine steward around. I had found, after all these months, a place at Esalen. I was not a psychologist, or a movement teacher, or an encounter-group leader, or even a very good Resident; and I wasn't a hippie, or a Big Sur artisan, or a Big Sur heavy, or a cultivator of the soil, but I was a good wine steward. And I threw myself into the job with a sense of pride and destiny. It was as if, in some crazy way, God had guided me to the very thing at Esalen, where all my supposed cultivation and sense of style and pleasure in the good life could find a proper use. And there was irony in it for I had been the one who had always insisted on good service in restaurants, expected and demanded it: "You can't get treated right in America," I would explain to people. "In Europe they take care of you but not here." I am Special Stuart, I had thought, I deserved to be treated with care, people should serve me. So it was right now that I who had made such a fuss should, in turn, be a servant. It was a proper penance, the very thing, in fact, and I imagined that if God were watching, he would smile with approval and irony as I poured the wine and scurried to serve it with all the care and grace I could find.

✳ the servant is tried and rewarded ✳

as the days passed I came more and more under the influence of the New Testament, feeling its power more and more, and the gigantic and radiant love that shone from it began, in some small way, to pervade my thoughts and acts. I had read "Blessed are the pure in heart, for they shall see God," and it meant to me the necessity of becoming pure, of giving myself over to that love in the universe which had seemed, so suddenly, to have rushed toward me. And I read: "You have heard that it was said to the men of old, 'You shall not kill; and whoever kills shall be liable to judgment.' But I say to you that every one who is angry with his brother shall be liable to judgment." So, when they came up to me, these strangers at Esalen, afraid of the formidable-seeming staff, I took their order, and then brought it to them with love.

And I learned to uncork the wine bottle with love, and to place the glass and pour the wine with love. And if I were asked to do something extra, or the customer claimed I had brought the wrong thing, I would not argue, or even frown, or even grow chilly, but I would do what he asked. My acts of waiting were spiritual exercises to me.

And it would happen, occasionally, that a stranger would wander in, a guest of some seminarian, who would not know the unwritten laws of the place. He did not know, for example, that the hired help at Esalen were not ordinary hired help, but were usually young middle-class people, many of them with a good deal of education and experience, who worked for very little money in order to stay at Esalen and in Big Sur, and who would not, therefore, let themselves be treated like servants.

He hailed me with a wave of the hand and a shout: "Hey kid, come over here." As if he owned me; as if I were a mere waiter. "That's a good kid. Now what have you got that's good?" A man of about fifty, probably some sort of professional, successful, with a patronizing twinkle in his eye, someone used to command and to show people how used he was to command. "Hey, you're a hippie, aren't you, kid? What's it like to work here? Lots of good-looking girls, huh?"

I could feel the anger rising within me. Who was he, after all, to speak to *me* that way? I'm not even paid for this.

Watching and seeing everything is Deidre. A lady of about thirty-five who has been coming to a lot of workshops, she has a very rich father, and a big neurosis, a lot of chutzpah and strength. Her big brown eyes ironically scan the scene, a smile on her wet red lips; her perfect tits point harshly upward against the softness of a cashmere sweater; with her dark tan in midwinter, perfect nail polish, and lacquered hair, she looks like a very expensive whore, sedate in her female potency. The older man is with her and you can see that she knows he is trying to impress her by putting down the younger waiter. And she knows, which he doesn't, that a couple of months before, she has turned me down flat—treated me like a kid. And she watches me for an answer.

Angry answers spring to my lips, smart remarks for which I was famous here. Deidre waits for me expectantly. I can tell *he* is at the ready.

"But if any one strikes you on the right cheek, turn to him the other also; and if any one would sue you and take your coat, let him have your cloak as well."

I'll give him the cloak too, I thought. "Yes, sir," I said. "We have all kinds of wines and beers. What can I get you?"

"I'll have a beer," he said simply. "Deidre?"

"Me, too."

Everything changed. It had been the right thing to do.

It was amazing that people accepted me this new way. Stuart goes off for a month, is almost forgotten, then returns, still driving his Corvette, but totally transformed, humble in expression, saying little, he works instead of loafing, he does Tai Chi—as if by magic. There were no recriminations, not even expressions of surprise; they simply accepted the new without resistance, or fanfare, or questioning, all of which would have been harmful, because I was just getting started. But Esalen is good that way, they were used to seeing people change and to allowing it. And it was a big help for me not to be made to stand out, for, after all, humility was what I was cultivating. So when Bill Schutz came in each evening, I served him like the others and he treated me pleasantly but with no remarks of wonder, or condescension, or gloating. The only thing he did that was a little special was to order a whole bottle of wine every evening—I think he wanted to make me feel good for making such a large sale.

News of the change in me had penetrated to San Francisco and there the whole tale must have seemed fantastic. So when Mike Murphy popped in one evening as I was serving the wine, he looked at me with wonder and then his radiant smile and he called to me, over the heads of others sitting at the table: "Marvelous, Stuart. Terrific." And I got terribly embarrassed. "And when you pray, you must not be like the hypocrites; for they love to stand and pray in the synagogues and at the street corners, that they may be seen by men. Truly, I say to you, they have their reward." And here was I, apparently exhibiting my virtue. Praise seemed like a temptation, so I mumbled something to Michael, not the thanks that would have been proper, and scurried away.

As time went on I got more and more comfortable with my job and it assumed new aspects. I would arrive about six o'clock at the dining room. The sun would be lowering near the horizon. Shadows gathered from the east, the mountains already dark, night visible beyond them. I would be in a hurry and racing to make my hour, for they were depending on me, the others, the waitresses and the dishwasher and the cook. I nearly ran into the dining room, where the girls, in long skirts and jerseys, brown and serene-looking, lovely, were starting to light the candles in their wrought-iron cylinders. Sometimes I would have to knock on the dining-room door first, for they would turn everyone out so that the tables could be cleared of the remains of afternoon snacks and the plates and place settings laid for the evening meal. It was nice when that happened—I would even enjoy the wait until someone came: because I knew I would be let in. I could go into the heart of the community, when the others were excluded. The door would open, the girl opening it prepared with fierce face to resist the importunities of someone trying to get into the lodge—but it was me, Stuart, the wine steward, the fellow-worker, and I was all right. So she let me in.

I would greet the girl and pass by. She was quick to slide the bolt of the door, shooing off others who were trying to cajole their way in so as to sit indoors with a cup of coffee waiting for dinner, rather than outdoors, with nothing, on the porch. But they would rarely make it. I went to the wine-steward station, behind a screen. It always struck me as incongruously formal and Latin that this little cubbyhole would be called a "station." And I would look over the stock, and note which brands of cigarettes had become depleted, and which brands of candy, and which kinds of wine.

The cook would pop his head out of the kitchen door and greet me, glad to see me, for I meant another pair of hands helping with the work. And the waitresses would say hello as they came by me, which they had to, in order to get into the kitchen. And there would be a delicious sense of self-importance about the thing, which, even in my humility, I couldn't help but share; we all shared it, for we were about to stage the main event of the day in this little community—the evening meal, and all the others had been excluded so that we could get ready, and all the others were held from the food, until we were ready, and then they would come, and we would produce it: "In One Long Act, *The Evening Meal*, featuring roast pork, baked potatoes, and zucchini, with home-made bread (especially delicious) and lots of butter, preceded by delicate green salad, coffee, tea or milk, included; beer and wine extra: produced and directed by Joe the Cook, and with the assistance of Martha and Lynn and Anne, the Waitresses; special assistant, the Wine Steward, Stuart; and all this, in good time, by candlelight, on redwood tables, with a view of the purple and golden sunset, over the mighty Pacific; and as a special added attraction: all of you, pilgrims, funny and sad, tragic and comic, in search of yourselves, or God, or a good time, or a good lay, or a change of life, or the ANSWER, assembled for the millionth time, under this one roof, where sparks will fly and minds will be fucked and, if you are lucky, at least one very dramatic and crazy thing will happen to someone, during the course of a meal."

It was almost like that, the feeling of importance and energy in this little place. The evening meal was the fulcrum of the day. Much would have happened to our sixty seminarians and twenty Residents by now. And the evening—the time for dreams, and nightmares, and love, and sex, and freaky experiences—was coming. And there were no distractions, none of the hypnosis of urban culture: TV shows, and radio, and movies, and restaurants to go to, and places to drive, and night clubs or evening lectures, or anything like that to distract this little company from the business of living and their particular business of learning something important, about themselves or life or both before they had to go back to their cities. So, if you would let yourself, you could pick up on that feeling of energy, and expectation, and drama, and ride it, happy to have something to do with the great production, and happy to be occupied in some simple way so that you need not wonder whom to sit with, or what would they say, or what you would say, or what would eventuate, about the day, or the night, or yourself, or them, or God, or whatever basic thing, important, freaky, religious, psychological, or stuff.

And riding this energy I go through the kitchen, out back where there is a closet, and its door, locked with a combination lock, and I have been entrusted by now with the combination, and by the light of the candle I have lit, I make out the markings on the cylinders, and I turn them: 1848. Believe it or not. And I open the door, take up the candle, and enter and find the cigarettes and the candy and the wine I need, making several trips, out of the closet, along the muddy path, wiping my feet on the piece of rug just inside the kitchen (for it rains during this season) and going through the fluorescent kitchen, stainless-steel tables, and tubs, and appliances, the mixer, the toaster, the huge black stoves, and I replenish my stock, working fast, because we can't keep that front door shut forever, they are knocking at it all the time, eager for the comfort of indoors, and a glass of wine and more cigarettes. And then out again, and back again, until all the racks are filled, I am ready, and the girls have laid the tables, so they are ready, and we open the door and they come in.

Some of the first four or five come up to me and deliver their orders. I serve them, in place, without leaving the station, only asking them to stand aside, for the girls have to get by to go to the kitchen and they still have creamers, and butter plates, and sugar and salt and pepper to bring out, but I ask them gently. And then others filter in and take seats, to get away from the cool of the evening, and I take my little round cork-lined tray and I approach them with diffidence, so as not to interfere, and I ask them if they want an apéritif: "Something before dinner?" with great courtesy, so that I wonder if I am manipulating them, because I want them to order, so Esalen will make money and they will enjoy themselves, but I don't want to be pushy and I ask it in a very nonthreatening, nonintimidating way, so that, if they can't afford the something extra, it won't make them feel that they look cheap in refusing, or poor. And that takes a great deal of art and concentration, on my part, and I delight in how well, with what subtle gestures and nongestures I get my very complex and human messages across. And when they order, I bring the wine or the apéritif bottle over to the table, and without ostentation, except a trifle, so that they can have the pleasure of enjoying the show put on for their exclusive benefit, to make them feel good, and at almost no expense to them. And I place the glass, just so, handy to the tips of their fingers, on the table, and holding the bottle, as I had seen waiters do in fancy places, just a sixteenth of an inch above the glass rim, but not touching, so there will be no unnecessary noise, I slowly pour the red or ruby or amber liquid, thick and sweet, into the glass, and smartly turning the bottle to shake off the last drop, so it doesn't drip. And I am a little concerned, for I want to do it just right for their sake and mine, that, though I know I should turn the bottle at the end of pouring, I don't know whether the drop, that ultimate drop, is supposed, properly, to go back into the bottle or to be shaken into the glass. Then I put the bottle back on my tray, accept the payment, and sometimes, they try, despite what they well know from its being made clear in the Esalen brochure, to tip me for my good services, and what an extra delight it is to tell them, so that they feel all the more well treated, that "it's all taken care of," and they feel that they have received a gift; we smile, and I go back to my station to wait for others to come into the dining room, the candles glittering from the tables and the ceiling.

Then at the word of the mighty cook, it was declared that dinner was ready, the rush back and forth between the dining room and kitchen increased. The girls brought the orders in and the plates out, one of them went around pouring milk and taking orders for coffee; at a certain point, the orders for wine and beer were satisfied for most of the crowd, the girls would be clearing the places of those who had dined early, wiping the tables and hurrying to find new place settings for the others who would take their places. It wasn't part of the job, my job, actually, but I would help out. That was important, somehow, that I would help out, even though I didn't have to. I took on the extra work, because, after all, I owed a debt to my fellow-workers just as I did to my customers. And, of course, I was rewarded once more. For even though it got to be, at these times in the evening, rather hectic for me, hectic keeping up with the occasional orders from different parts of the crowded dining room for beer and wine and cigarettes, and also clearing the tables, pouring milk and water, bringing out new place settings to help the girls, and doing whatever odd jobs—even though it got to be hectic and hard and I would sweat in my white jacket with the white buttons, and it was a strain being universally pleasant and courteous and a good servant, for we were shorthanded, I did it. I was rewarded with that especially warm and largely wordless comradeship and mutual appreciation that comes to workers when the heat is on; even the cook would join the fray in the dining room at this point, for every

hand was needed at the peak hour, bustling with the gray
rubber trays full of dishes, putting plates into the machine,
and the noise of the dishwasher coming from the kitchen, and
Vivaldi, on the scratchy records, sawing away over the hi-fi system, conversation rising as the meal wore on, and more
and more people talking, and we were in it together, holding
the fort, keeping ahead of it, we few, we happy few, the
kitchen staff.

And then, the anticlimax, the gathering of the last dishes, the
filing away of the last glasses, time to think, and time, at last, to
eat. I had, unlike the others, been eating all along. The wine
steward's job was like that, a start-stop job, so there were
pauses; and in those days I was seeing the end of the ravenous
appetite I had developed in adolescence, so it was a special
pleasure, having been admitted to the chosen and nearly tyran-
nical company of the kitchen crew to be able, at my own wish,
though getting, each time, the express permission of the mighty
cook, boss of the kitchen and a much feared figure, to slip away
from my screen and its bottles, and to go just inside the entrance to the kitchen and open the huge white door of the
"walk-in," a small refrigeration room, where, special delight for
me in this place so far removed from any snack bar, I could
satisfy my little boy's appetite on endless quantities of leftovers
which would, otherwise, only be thrown away: cold ham
bones, and celery sticks, cheeses of all sorts, yellow and orange,
pieces of stew with chilled fat congealed around them, olives,
cold ratatouille, bread and butter. And another benefit of the
job was that I could help myself to a reasonable number of
bottles of beer or glasses of wine—what incredible privileges,
what pride of place. So, all during the meal, the dream of a
lifetime, I had at my disposal a seemingly endless supply of
food: the teen-ager's paradise—a refrigerator the size of a
room. And I helped myself, and it all blended, the mysticism,
the ethical reflections, the service, the work, the camaraderie,
and the banqueting, in bites and snorts, between tasks, stand-

ing up, and out of the eye of the people in the dining room.

It was a long time to wait until a quarter of nine for dinner, so that by the time the guests were finished I was hardly hungry. But I always went in for a plate. I would take one from the neat piles, and hold it in front of the cook, in line with the few others on the kitchen crew, and then we would all go outside, into the dining room, stopping to gather silverware and a napkin from the trays near the kitchen entrance, and sit at one table, and eat together. We never said much, for we had been chatting at intervals all along through the evening so there wasn't much left to say. But it was a special moment in the whole performance: there was pride in it, the quintessence of all the pride that we had shared during the evening in being the centers of the stage, the principal managers of the day's biggest communal event, the guardians of the threshold of the kitchen, commanders of life and wine and warmth. And now we had finished serving the others, they are finished eating, many of them had departed, and those who hadn't had to watch us take our break, not like mere hired help, hidden in the kitchen, but almost like lords of the manor, or parents who, the children having been fed and gone off to play, could at last seat themselves together, for a few minutes' peace. And if those we served wanted anything, well, they could see that we were eating, and that they would have to wait. We deserved this respite, and the almost public spectacle of our eating was due us, for we had served and served faithfully, and it was time for us to rest, together. All of this unspoken but somehow understood, and a very private feeling of sharing some special status passing among us as we ate, our elbows nearly touching, close together, at the table, without speaking.

CHAPTER TWENTY-SIX

the height of the vision

i had been back at Esalen for nearly two weeks when Annie returned. I knew she was back before I saw her—someone must have told me, or I may have overheard some conversation about her. The prospect of seeing her was a troublesome one. I had turned her out in my letter to her, and by the time I had come back to Big Sur she had managed to sleep with any number of men, including a hippie who had given her the clap, and the magic anthropoid of my earliest pages. She had also managed to make sure that I would know all of that when I returned. For the most part, I had put her out of my mind. I was very chaste when I first returned, particularly devoted to my resolve to stop treating women as things, and almost being asexual in my attitude toward them.

She was serving breakfast in the dining room when I first saw her. I turned my eyes away, and though I saw her look at me, she pretended not to pay me any attention. I would glance at her from time to time, curious to see if she was looking at me, curious just to see her—she looked thinner, better. I didn't want her to see me looking at her. Above everything, I wanted not to begin again the destructive relationship we had had; it seemed so monstrously inhuman now. Occasionally, she would catch me looking at her and smile to herself. I would feel attracted, challenged, even afraid. I looked away.

One night about ten o'clock, as I was lying in bed reading my Bible and trying to cultivate pure thoughts, not to masturbate, or were I to give in and masturbate, to do it without having fantasies demeaning to women, she arrived, glowing, shy, soft-voiced, a little tentative, and not knowing what tack to take with the new Stuart.

"I'd like to spend one night here, Stuart. We don't have to fuck. Please let me stay. Just one night."

I let her stay and, of course, she moved back in within a couple of days. But it was different. I determined it would be. I told her about my resolves and that I might not be able to love her as much as she wanted, and she should know that, because I did not want to mislead her and she must take responsibility for herself.

She said she would but I wasn't so sure. I tried hard to keep from falling back into the old situation where I would let her suck me into her helplessness and I would feel guilty and then I would retaliate by throwing her out and being cruel. I kept things on a very high level. I tried to treat Annie in a religious manner—as my human sister, albeit my lover. I was simply very very good to her. Never a harsh word, always gentle, always humble, turning the other cheek, and also a trifle distant. We became, this time, not so much lovers as intellectual companions. Late at night, we would lie in bed with the light on, the sound of the ocean breaking on the rocks, and we would discuss the New Testament. She had read it in jail and had, to my amazement, a deep understanding of it. We would discuss the meaning of particular passages. In jail, on the road, poor, with only the strange hippies she would meet each night for comrades, she had learned a lot: "Why do you see the speck that is in your brother's eye, but do not notice the log that is in your own eye?" She knew deeply, I learned with surprise, the strength that comes from giving up all petty pride. We laughed with shared knowledge over that passage. It baffled me that she understood such things because in the past she had been so willful, so self-assertive and grabby.

Because we both waited on tables at the lodge, we came together in this way, also. At night, when the meal was finished and it was time for us to eat, she would go and get me my plate, or, if I had already done that, myself, she would pick up an extra knife and fork for me. We had been working together, and now we were enjoying our rest and our meal together. Before I had left for New York, I had seen her working with the others, another servant, another girl from the hired help, but now it was different.

I did not let Annie occupy my mind, however. I was good to her, I shared my house with her and some of my time, but my mind was elsewhere—bent on implementing my other resolves —exploring the new religious space I had entered, confronting more of Esalen. She was quiet, she did not clamor for every moment, every bit of my energy and attention, as she had in the past. It was as if I had suddenly gained new respect from her. It was nice, at last. A bit austere, but nice; and I felt good that I could see Annie in new lights, not just a guttersnipe or an ignorant hippie, but as my sister, a person of value.

I had been looking forward to the resumption of Esalen workshops. The first one was called "The Anima Experience." I read the write-up in the Esalen brochure with great care.

The English language emphasizes individuality and separateness. The Anima emphasizes other kinds of experiences by suspending the assumption of separateness.

Participants meet in small groups, called "Animas," for
the duration of the experiment. They will explore their
group in the light of new assumptions of relatedness,
symbiosis, and organic growth. There are three rules: (1)
See the group as an organic whole. (2) Be aware. (3) Do
not try to alter what is happening.

The Anima Experience can bring about results which are
deeper than those of conventional encounter groups.

I couldn't make much sense out of this description. There
were words that were close to me now, but I couldn't easily
imagine what such an experiment would actually be like. I was
a little afraid it would turn into some kind of orgy.

We met in the gallery on a Sunday night, three weeks after
my return to Esalen. Bo Cahill, the inventor of this kind of
group, told us that he would not be around much, the groups
were self-directing, and that about all he would do tonight
would be to break us into small groups and repeat the three
rules. There were about thirty people and he suggested we di-
vide ourselves into five groups. I thought his calling the groups
"Animas" was pretentious, even a little ridiculous. Then I put
aside these thoughts.

We chose each other hurriedly. I chose the people who were
nearest to me on the floor of the gallery, where we were sitting.
Except for one person, all the members of my group were Residents or staff members, people whom I had known only slightly
and had not been particularly nice to when I had known them.
I felt awkward, nervous before these strangers, before this
strange situation. I pushed my self-concern aside and tried to
clear my eyes to look at these people. We go around the group
saying our names and then there is silence. I can sense a tension because there are five of us men and only one girl, a pretty

leggy blonde named Emilia who worked as a masseuse. Bo Cahill asks us now to proceed without words, always remembering the three rules. I feel the male energy rising in the group and I watch Nick Moskowitz, tall and craggy and blond, look alternately at Emilia and at Danny, a chubby and elfin-looking person, the only seminarian in the group. Danny is looking silently at Emilia who is sitting between them. Nick Moskowitz, trying to seem playful about it, pushes Danny on the shoulder. Danny rocks, stiffens, and glares at him. I am a little struck with stage fright as I think of what I must do—it may not be the right thing, I don't know my way here but the rule is that we are an organism. All of us are watching these two men and the girl. I rise from the floor and lean forward, extending my arms. I take the hands of Nick and Danny, the tough hairy hands of two men just approaching middle age, and I join them.

Then the two men sit holding each other's hands, Emilia between them, still a little tense, as if reconciliation is what they want but something drives them from it. I don't know what to do now. Martin Capleau gets up and goes outside our little circle; he squats near Danny and Nick, and gently extends his arms to embrace the two of them. Then Ken Barker moves and sits with his back against Danny's. I go over to Nick and we are all together, and we hold each other, and rest with each other, leaning against, holding, touching, the warmth and the energy quiet at first, and then beginning to build between us, as if each of us were generating the warmth and the energy, and each of us adding to it, and each of us also amplifying it as it flows back and forth along arms and backs and through hands, and legs and feet touching, and slowly we began to move together, into more and more of a huddle, scuffing the floor, as we awkwardly change positions, shifting an ankle out from under a folded leg, moving up or down, until we are in a circle, seated on our knees, arms outstretched across shoulders, our heads hung forward into the center, gently touching. And the swaying starts tentatively, from nowhere, and builds, as if the waves that we could faintly hear outside were rocking us, the swaying rhythm of childhood, something very old, not entirely unknown, natural but surprising to recapture; left, then right we sway, a slight modulating motion beginning in and out, the little group rippling, letting the rhythm come and take us. Nothing simply sexual in it, we are, absurdly, suddenly, one— just that easily, for a few moments.

I was very moved. I looked up to find the others and myself all smiling broader and broader smiles. And then those two faded, and there was silence and stillness again. We held hands ·in the circle, sitting, one on his knees, another on his haunches. And then that passed, and the hands dropped, and the whole thing had a kind of peace, like a sort of ballet, and an excitement, too, for I didn't know what would happen next, but I was already confident of the process. And we sat, with our heads forward, separate, thinking, waiting for the next thing to happen, a sudden thickness about the atmosphere, as if the energy had gone down, a heaviness.

We sat separate from each other. I glance up from time to time to find the others sitting with heads down. Occasionally someone raises his head at the same time and our eyes meet. Martin. It happens again. More heaviness. And again, it happens. He grins, his face lights up, I see his eyes flash and his teeth white against his beard; he pushes out his hands, palms forward, and he gestures in an explanatory way. I imitate him; and soon we are clapping; right-left; left-right, right-right, left-left, right-left, left-right; and again, and then again; and we both grin and we begin to breathe harder with the effort, fast and gay and childish smacks; and the others begin too, and we all do it, then we trade partners, and then again.

And after a while we tire, but we are all conscious of the organism by now, no longer because it is one of the ground rules, it has just happened. We wait and someone gets up and it's ring-around-a-rosy this time, and laughing now, and mak-

ing noise, and whooping, and yelling, and other groups, more
silent, looking up at us, and we are proud, for being the noisi-
est, and the most alive, and the closest.

Bo calls us to rest and asks all the groups to continue to be
their Anima, only to talk during the next interval. We are facing each other in a circle again on the floor. For the first time
in many minutes I am aware of my individuality, embarrassed,
not knowing what to say. I feel myself closing off, smaller,
somehow, shrunken into my own little place in the floor. Nick
tells Danny: "You know, I want to be friends with you."

Danny replies, in a slightly schoolmasterly way, "We are
more than friends, we are part of the same organism."

"You know what I mean."

"Yes, I know what you mean." He nods.

They shake hands, and they hold hands for a moment.

There is silence. I am starting to get scared. At last, I push
myself forward. I look very sad. "I don't know what to say."
Silence again. A thoughtful mood. Nick says: "You don't have
to know what to say: you don't even have to say anything." I
have to think for a moment until I get it. It makes me feel
better. I accept his good will, his simple advice, and warmth.

And it went on and on like that for the rest of the evening.
Sometimes we used words, and sometimes we didn't; and
sometimes we sat and sometimes we stood; and every so often
someone might cry in another group—I could hear it. And once
in a while I heard a shuffle and a shout and Bo's voice remind-
ing: "Remember, you are one organism, and you have to recon-
cile contraries in other ways than confrontation." And then the
room would get quiet and a bit dreamy, as people would reach
out to one another.

We held each other and chatted, and we told each other
solemn things about how we were feeling: I told Nick I was
afraid of him, and Emilia that I was attracted to her, and
Danny that he looked like a gremlin. And we all smiled. And
then the others did the same thing.

At last, Bo told us to say good night and all the groups grew silent again. We sat in our circle, the six of us; and then we held hands again. It was amazing, for I couldn't tell how it started, someone did something and in a half-dozen seconds, all our hands were joined; and I held Emilia's cool white hand in mine and Danny's black and hairy hand, strong. I looked around, and people had their eyes shut, so I shut mine. And it was warm and strong, around the circle, as we sat. And then I heard something, it sounded like someone getting up, and then I felt a tug from above, from Danny's side, and without opening my eyes I got up, and then we were moving, we dropped hands, I could hear the shuffle of shoes against the floor, and I could feel my body getting bumped by masses, warm and flannel against my nose, and the brush of wool against the back of my hand, and suddenly the moving around stopped and it felt like we were huddled together, in some kind of mass, and I felt very warm, pressed in on every side, gently. And then it happened again, that swaying, starting from nowhere, as if the motion in our lungs, our chests in breathing, our hearts in pumping, the ripples through the veins had combined, synchronized, so swiftly, and that all those gentle pulsations had found their average, and we moved together for a long time.

At last, we opened our eyes, and looked at each other, a big collective hug, and as if by agreement we just silently nodded good night.

When I went outside, the night was cool but I walked home radiant. Amazing, so much to think about. That rocking. The tides. New relations to myself. New relations to people. Most amazing of all, I found I loved that little group of mine; that little Anima. I still felt part of it. Something very "cozy," that was the word. A new feeling. I couldn't wait to get down the dark path and over across the lawn to tell Annie. We would have a good talk.

And we did. She rejoiced in the good time I was having. I read a little in the Bible and then turned out the light. We didn't make love that night—somehow it didn't feel like the right thing to do. I wanted to keep that special feeling I had gotten from the group and I couldn't do that and make love to Annie. She wanted to but she seemed to understand. I kissed her good night.

The following day I was up early, eager to get to my group, delighted with this adventure. As I walked up the path from my little house, I looked around and tried to pay attention to the nature around me. I wanted to start the day with trying to get outside myself but the objects had no interest. A rock. A flower. A tree. All dead. I wanted to pay attention but of the rock all I could see was gray and black and mass, and of the flower, yellow and white. I tried dissecting, mentally: green stem, stalk, leaves, then the blossom. It didn't help. I began to get just the slightest bit anxious about losing momentum. As if I would fall back away, out of grace unless I continued to push forward to fulfill my resolves and extend myself.

But I was already at the lodge and opening the door.

I suddenly feel rather frightened again by the hippies, the mountain men in their fierce costumes. Then I remember I have a special place to sit, my little group is having breakfast. And the good mornings we exchange are genuine, peculiarly private, and filled with a sense of last night's pleasure, crazy, enclosed feelings of devotion and delight, as if the rest of things happening in the world were not important. What we had, had its own compelling and encircling reality. I am silent during most of the meal, thinking about the events of the night before, amazed at how differently I see these people from the way I used to see them. I have known most of them before. Martin Capleau, the one who rescued us on the journey to Tassajara, a high-voiced twerp I had thought him with his brown beard, looking like D. H. Lawrence but sounding like Tiny Tim. He is eating his eggs now and telling jokes nervously.

It wasn't so much that he was different from the Martin I had known before. Many of the details were the same: the voice, his nervousness, the sense of uncertainty he radiated. He still didn't measure high on the standards of manliness. His conversation was not very involving. But as I sat across from him and ate my own eggs, all this suddenly seemed unimportant. We had met the preceding night, on other ground. On that ground we shared our human embarrassment, our mutual tentativeness, the touch of our bodies and the warmth of our skins. The Anima had shut us off from a lot of the world and these communalities had sprung into sight.

I sat and stared at him: he was still all the things that had made me dismiss him, but he was also profoundly like me. How many more similarities than differences? It became a little scary to think about the reality of common-sense social existence, where people are better or worse, more or less chic, more or less productive, more or less entertaining, more or less intelligent, more or less impressive—all of that, slipping away: clothes, and manners and tones of voice, and bank accounts and achievements, and beauties and deformities, all slipping from us. There is not much difference. Then how is one to choose? How is one to choose whom to be with, what to strive for?

When we go to have our morning session, our group alone, a twilight sense of things is on me. It is not a sad thing, really, not in the ordinary sense. It does not feel bad as I sit in that room and look at those faces. They are all chattering, seeming gay and casual. Nick Moskowitz tall, blond, a manly-looking man, something of a hustler I had thought him. An ex-engineer, he had become a Resident Fellow and from the second month had spent his time running groups to make extra money. He was already a prisoner of his new career. All true. But I look at the face, the lines creasing into flesh, forgetting the gay gestures, the attitude of a man who had things under control.

What pain there must have been. What suffering had made Nick so wooden, his voice always so similar? How much had it taken to choke off the life?

I look at another: Emilia, the girl, a beautiful blonde, with the form of a nymph, lyric, slender but full. Emilia with huge blue eyes, the slightest bulge of wideness that marked her with the look of madness. Emilia whom I had known as a waitress, flirting to get what she wanted, playing dumb, and innocent, depending, sucking on people, helpless in her manner but so obviously potent in her sexual attractiveness. Emilia has no problems, I had thought. She has got it covered—a man would always get her out. The first time I met her I resolved not to be trapped in her melancholy or hysteria.

But now I look again. How complex she is. Elusive, really. And what in the world has driven her so to that? What has she suffered; for you can not fool me any more, I know; I know how people suffer and how they try to cover it up; how they conceal it from everyone; even from themselves.

And what had the others suffered? Danny, a psychiatrist from Boston, with his elfin look but paunchy and baggy of face. And Ken Barker, another Resident and a serious young man, tall and lean, and above all young. Who were these people? Did they share in some way what I had—all that pain and wrong-headedness? They must have. We were brothers. And I had to see it, look hard. But if I didn't look, I would end up being the fool I had been.

I thought as I surveyed these faces, especially Martin's who looked to have suffered the most of all, how dead we all were. For all of these people, all of us, were like me, and didn't I know, couldn't I hear in the reaches of my intellect and imagination a richness, a richness rumbling there, like the noise of a million gold coins being shuffled and ruffled through, images, and metaphors, memories and complexities, my existence, the colors of the dawn on Sunday in New York when I was a child, and the memories of the warmth of the crib when I peed in it during the night, and the feel of my father's hand on my girlish leg after, at age ten, I raced, in short pants across the grass to catch the ball and brought it back to him, and my mother's lipstick, the exact red-violet color, the blue Victor labels on the records of Dumbo the Elephant which my sister would not let me listen to, and the leaden-colored phonograph needles that you bought by the handful because they would only last for a few records—my memory held all such things, a whole world of things. And it held, besides, in it, the lines of epic poets and their heroes, Aeneas, Achilles, and Beowulf; and the worlds of more attenuated fictions, the rustle of a dress in a James drawing room, and the snow under the runners of Edith Wharton's sleigh, dimly remembered—all of that was there. And a thousand landscapes, beautiful, Rome, Calabria, Oberlin with its boxy houses like those of a thousand Midwestern towns, and the jewel-like lights of Pittsburgh, just come on in the evening twilight as I raced in a friend's rickety old plane to find some landing field beyond the Susquehanna, before all the light fails utterly; even the monstrous retorts and the squat cylinders of great chemical fields beside the Jersey Turnpike; all of this. And a thousand voices, thousands of thousands perhaps have gone into me, understood, remembered, not quite caught, vibrating together somewhere in the brain, jangly and smooth and soft: Annie yelling at me, and the elegant tones of my first Latin teacher, a civilized man, and the ecstatic sounds of a girl as she took my virginity and my own sounds joined to hers, a million horns of a million taxi cabs in New York, and the chugging of the Erie Railroad as the dirty and long cars took me to summer camp.

So many thoughts, so many thoughts on reading books, all the minds, great and small: and the thoughts I was thinking now, how small a fraction of them was I even aware of, as I sat there, could I even grasp, try to form into sentences, sentences into paragraphs, paragraphs into theses. I could hear the shuffling of the gold endlessly, or was it lead that I heard, or was it both? No matter what, how much was going on this very second, almost all dimly apprehended; feelings that came in a blink of an eye and gathered associations to them: Martin resented, Martin despised, Martin as Christ, Martin as crypto-faggot, the train slides along at supersonic speed down that one single rail, disappearing in a millionth of a second and I am dimly aware of a thousand such trains of thought and emotion proceeding dimly: and around me, as I think and remember and imagine, I see a hummingbird alone on the red flower outside the window of our room, green stalk in the golden light, and sea and mountain beyond and I hear snatches of conversation from the others, the pick of fingers at lint on the orange carpet, a cough. All this and more I am aware of, and aware mostly of how much more there is that I am only dimly aware of, so much even in me, a not very intelligent, not very courageous, not very handsome, not very strong, not very witty, not very learned, not very sensitive, not very anything, young man, in America, in California, in Big Sur, in a wooden room, part of a silly group; even in me there is all of this, and so there must be in Martin and in each one of the others.

And how little of this can be made external, I think. How little language allows us to convey, even the best language. What a wonder if for the least of us the contents of his humanity, his awareness, could be projected onto a screen, as in a planetarium, each of us a human universe, endlessly rich and complicated. And the tragedy of this is with me. The tragedy of all that life lost, uncaptured, uncomforted, unappreciated. So that, at first glance, a Martin or a Nick or a Stuart would seem like mere examples of social types, persons to be bagged like strawberries at the supermarket, dismissed in a few impressions—nobodies. And I think of the even greater tragedy that I have come to feel, know in my bones, that each of us could be a genius, I know it, each of us is as God, but that somehow, something, nature, or society, or God or something denies that to us, denies the full flowering to us, and that even to the great geniuses has been denied the great flowering—which man has lived out even the slightest of his own possibilities? Who has written the poem that contains the wideness of a single human? And I feel, sitting across the room from Martin and the others that each of us somewhere knows this. This is the secret we share. Tragic truth. All of us must know the richness in us and therefore in others and all of us must sense in our deepest frustrations the power of life in its full flowering, cut off, available to no man. The tragedy being not that we die, but that no one has taught us how to live, to come into realized touch with all those riches, whether of gold or lead, within us, and to externalize that and share it and build upon it with our fellows; for without such knowledge, each of us is finally cut off, only a part of him, a small stinking social part, the tip of the existential iceberg, cold and white and rocky, can be known, above the water line. And tears come to my eyes at the thought that like crippled Gods we blunder through life, mistake follows mistake, and where we should walk in the purple of kings, we affect whatever pathetic dress it may be, the Chesterfield overcoat, or the leather pants of the hippie, or the workingman's dungarees and the faded flannel shirt, the cashmere sweater and the pearls, the smock of the man who shines shoes, or the morning coat, or even the golden armor of the Queen's guards, or the crown of the Queen, what matter, with that lipstick and the hair done that way, those foolish curls? What does it matter to be a monarch when each should wear the clouds of heaven for his cloak and the sun for his diadem?

A heavy silence has settled upon us, as we sit, looking at each other, mindful of our existence as an organism, Cahill's rule, it seems that the same philosophic mood is on the others. We stare. We look around. In the quiet of the morning, a few mote-filled sun rays entering through the windows, warm and dark and light, but we see each other's eyes, and I remember the eyes then, Martin's eyes, looking into them and noticing for the first time in six months of looking at his eyes but not really looking, their width, and their grace, almond-shaped, with the long lashes, and something strong about their size, and pupils large in abundant white. And our eyes stick with each other, and we look, holding each other in mutual gaze—this silly-looking boy and I, and then a split second in which that glance is heavy with recognition, as if in that strange and magical place, on that particular day, we could allow ourselves to look at each other with the full set of knowledges that I have alluded to, that we could look and see, literally see, in and through the eye, into the eye and down its tunnels to the brain and to the spirit, and into the body coursing with its subtle messages, see all the richness that I was feeling and apprehending, however dimly, in myself, and see it in him, and he looking back, sensing the richness in himself, and being aware of the utter hopelessness of ever realizing that richness, making it real, giving it any but the faintest voice, and our eyes almost burning together with the gentle electricity of all those meanings, almost colliding, like magnets, round and polished, out there, in the middle of the room between us, bong they go, and bong again. "Bong" is the sound, for we have to smile. A wide smile full of Martin's teeth framed by brown-black beard and mustache; it creeps outward from the center where his lips were pursed, toward the corners, teeth slowly exposed and the eyes now less full of depth and given more to twinkling, the twinkling of brilliance, the brilliance of wit, a valuable quality in the real world, even if only a reflection, only a tinselly reflection now in the eyes become separated pair from pair, no longer that full penetration, lush, of gaze into gaze down into the body, beyond into the body of all things, God, the world, the stars ringing their circles.

We smile. And then, God help us, a chuckle. We are both too frightened, or embarrassed, or not weighty enough to sustain such a glance, such an experience, such full and moving knowledge. What are we, after all, such men as we, to do with such profundities? How does one respond to them? What action is there to take? I join the smile, the smile and chuckle that dispel the profundity of gaze and experience, as if I would melt, my body and mind and being all dissolve, warm liquid running down into the earth, melting into union, if I were to sustain that gaze and that knowledge.

But I am not bitter, not dwelling on cowardly retreat, rather dwelling in my newness to the whole thing on those depths and as the morning goes on, our talking and playing and hugging, the feeling sweeping over me, larger and larger as the morning goes on of a human closeness, something between the coziness of the first night and the endless depths of the encounter with the glances; a sense that this group, so alien at first, so inadequate in its individuals, tawdry and fat and phony and posing and ambitious and theatrical and pathetic, us, is my family— my family as my own family had never, still hasn't quite now, become.

We begin to talk; to talk about feelings and to share ourselves with our words. And a new level of reality, not as deep as the one we have come from but having more connections with the so-called real world, emerges into view. Emilia says the atmosphere has grown too heavy and she wants to escape it. She wants to play. And the others, I, are taken aback, abrupt, she has broken in too quickly and violated the silence with her "problem" so that we are not quite sure where we are, not wanting to be dragged from the sweet mood after the communion in the silence. The light seems to chasten, to grow whiter and cool as if we had stepped from a warm room with a fire in the hearth, outdoors, into a cloudy day. And then I and the others, are ready to go along with her, to give her what she needs on this level, for we are, after all, an organism, and in a second or two, when we have been startled back into the world of things, someone asks what she would like to do, what she wants to do. "I want to play," she says.

And despite my feeling that she is avoiding, avoiding the

deeper feelings, and avoiding even her own feelings of discomfort, I am ready and we are ready, as a family should be, to go to her aid, to give her, simply, what she wants or needs.

"What would you like to play at?" I ask.

"Let us," she says, "go and play a trick on the other group." She is her own person now. The twinkle of a little girl in her eye. So we move toward the door. Sharing, willing to let ourselves share, her mood, her twinkle, for she needs it, and we are all one. And suddenly our ages topple off, topple downward, from the twenties into the teens. And we emerge from the room but Ken asks, the solemn young man, now looking much younger, he almost seems to be wearing short pants, skinny legs, his hair too long, like a mischievous little boy, "What should we play on them?" And someone, Nick, the big kid now, the craggy-faced man looking like a demonic teen-ager, leader of the gang, a freshman in high school, "Let's go drop our pants at them." And I first react with shock, for this is even further, a light year away, from the communion we had felt only a few minutes before, and I think that it is Nick's thing, his embarrassment at deeper experience, and his fumbling to get into some activity, to work off the enormous energy that we acquired, and he suggests, the surface Nick, awkward and vulgar as all of us can be in our embarrassment, something that does him no justice or honor, but he needs it, this is what he needs now, and if he needs it, well, we are one, and I will go. And, lingering doubt put firmly aside, we go to it, in front of the window of the meeting room and it is funny for a few seconds to watch the startled faces of the others as we scatter off, laughing like wicked children, Emilia leading, down to Dennis's property where I live, careening down the steep road, holding our arms out as children do when in playing games they pretend to fly and be airplanes.

And there is more play that morning, endless play, cops and robbers, and cowboys and Indians, and curiously enough as we near lunch hour, more grown-up things, the staging of whole operas, singing parts from every opera we know. Shouts and jumps, the porch is suddenly a balcony, a rock becomes the shores of India, and finally rolling in the grass, laughing, the fabric of the opera dissolved at last, it is time for lunch and we troop up the hill toward the lodge.

The day has clouded over now and it is good to get back indoors and to pour coffee, black, from the urn near the wine-steward station. We sit down and the talk turns to what has happened. We try to figure out how we grew so intimate so quickly, how we had such a good time so fast with strangers, a rambling conversation that quickly turned into a discussion of the meaning of life. Nick, with his customary ability to deny pleasure, poor Nick, says: "You know, I wonder how real all that was. What did we really accomplish? I felt good and so did the rest of us, but did we really get anywhere; won't we feel the same tomorrow?" Ken starts to answer: we all turn to listen because he seldom talks, partly out of shyness and partly out of scruple to say only serious things: "It was real enough; it was what Fritz talks about—living in the now, that's the important thing: you are 'computing,' Nick, trying to figure things out and getting away from your own experience. You are pro-graming for tomorrow." Nick thinks about this for a moment: "Yeah, I guess that's right, Ken. I know what Fritz says. But I really want to know how you explain it. I had some strange feelings—new things." Ken doesn't understand.

I can feel myself tingling a bit. I'll share with them some-thing of what I have been feeling and thinking over the last few weeks. I am a little anxious about saying it: I feel like I have a lot to say, that in some small way I am inspired, a prophet of God who knows some of the answer to Nick's ques-tions. But I wonder if he will dare to understand. "People want to be good," I say. "I was the bad guy here for a while, did all the things I had wanted to do but had been afraid to do be-cause of social convention or fear of being punished. And finally I realized that what I really wanted to be is good—to love my neighbor as myself, to live for others, to treat people rightly, to share my goods and myself, to be gentle, and all the rest of it. Because that is what is real and satisfying. And the way I look at it, what we were doing this morning was just being together, letting ourselves merge with one another, being good to one another, and just getting in touch with our goodness and sadness and the absolute necessity of simply being good. Loving."

As I say all this, particularly that last word, I experience a feeling of being pleasantly startled, for it is as though some of the speech is coming from some other place, from somebody else. I hear myself saying "Loving," but it is as if the word came from beyond me, behind me, to be exact, from lips not mine but located just at the back of my head, on a level with my lips. Not exactly a hallucination, but an actual body feeling that it is not me who says such things.

There is a silence after I speak. I haven't the vaguest idea of what the others are thinking but I fancy that they are moved by what I have said. I am glad. Glad that I have spoken the word of God so well. It feels good to have served; to have given back to Him the tiniest part of the deep joy I have gotten. I know that the others cannot help but feel God working through me, and I rejoice in that, in the victory of the Lord.

And then, the silence is over. And each of them has something to say: Emilia says that she is tired of all the talk: it never solves anything. The important thing is to play and have fun. And Ken says something about Hegel. And Nick shakes his head and says he still doesn't understand. Then Danny says: "Look at it this way. A good group, a family, needs a social chairman (nodding at Emilia) and a philosopher (nodding at Ken) and a priest (nodding at me)."

I am flustered by the response. "Ken didn't even hear," I say to myself. "He's so full of German philosophy that he couldn't even hear what I said. And Nick heard, but he doesn't understand, he's too frightened. I like Danny's calling me a priest, that makes me feel good, but he's just being a super-nice guy. I get the feeling that he knows, too, but he's just being politic, making everyone equal with everyone else." I begin to get confused. I am angry at these people in a small way. Irritated.

They were all busily talking now, Martin had jumped in, too. The thought occurred to me that maybe I didn't really know anything important after all. What I knew didn't seem to mean much to any of them.

And then I caught myself. I should have known better than to think of myself as anything more than God's humble servant, to fancy myself as understanding *anything* more than my brothers here. How stupid. Humility is the main lesson that I have learned. Humility is what I know. Why cannot I remember it?

part five

✼✼

CHAPTER TWENTY-SEVEN

✠ trying harder ✠

we had two more joyful days in the group and then it was over. Almost immediately I began to worry in earnest about losing my feeling of rightness and closeness to God. I began to feel that I might be drifting away from what I had learned. It was things like the slip during the discussion with Ken and Nick and Danny. Little things. Like when, after being in the Anima all day, and being wine steward at night until eleven, someone asked me to take his place doing the job of cleaning up the lodge, a job that lasts until dawn. I was fearful when I became aware of my own unuttered resistance: "Let *him* do it, I'm tired." I did the job, though, and I found myself whistling as the sun came up. I had won the battle and I was rewarded again with happiness. But I also remembered the resistance.

A couple of days later I told Annie I was going to take a ride up north. "Who're you going to see?" she asked, clearly disappointed that I was going away. "Well, it's kind of a journey of 'restitution.' There are a lot of people up there who I kind of feel I owe things to."

"Like some girls, maybe?"

"Well, there is one that I ought to see."

"Take me with you."

"Annie, it's kind of a private thing."

"Take me with you." Her voice rises nearly to a scream: "You're going to fuck her, whoever she is, that's your 'restitution.'"

I catch the anger that is starting in me at her possessiveness, at her demeaning my motives, her wanting to control me. I know better than that—she only makes those accusations because she isn't herself, too emotional, and can't see things clearly. I will give her love rather than anger. I draw her to me and tell her softly that she really knows I am honest and that I am going for a good reason. "I want to go with you anyway, but I guess it's all right," she says with a grimace. I am pleased with the way I have acted with Annie as I get into the car.

The first person I would visit was Becky Pettle. Forest had asked me to drop in on her, and I wanted her to see how I had changed—that scene in the winter when she had condemned me had hurt. I had called her from Big Sur before leaving. She said that she was fine and she didn't sound like she wanted company, but I told her I thought I would come anyway. I *should* visit my friend's wife if he asked me to. I got to Berkeley in the afternoon and went straight to the cafe on the north side where we were supposed to meet at four o'clock. I waited until four twenty-five and then she walked in, wearing a very short skirt and looking terrific. I knew it the moment I saw her—she was having an affair. After she had sat down, ordered a *cappuccino,* and asked about my health, she told me that she was thinking of divorcing Forest. This other graduate student was so marvelous and Forest was so domineering, angry with her all the time, shouting, blustering, not tender.

At first I was upset by what she said. They had been married a long time, couldn't they work it out. "We've tried it. I flew to New York, Forest cried, but he's still Forest—no softness, he won't show his softness." She was adamant.

I found myself agreeing with her—yes, Forest was that way all right, he had been generous to me but maybe he needed a lesson in humility, I thought, he was still driving his fast car. It was nice to agree with Becky, nice to feel that she would no longer think I was treating her like a thing rather than a person.

I felt very virtuous as I got back in the car and went over to Arthur's and Daisy's. Then I wondered if I weren't betraying Forest a little by siding with Becky. I felt I was, and yet it was for his own good. I thought I was doing the right thing but I also felt I was being hard-hearted toward Forest.

I was glad to arrive at Arthur's and Daisy's and to put an end to this questioning of myself. They remarked at once how I seemed changed and that delighted me.

I turned my new self toward them. I listened to Daisy for the first time, understanding some of her idealisms—she had always been involved in one or another worthy cause. I asked her about her paintings for the first time, and I let Arthur drive my car because he liked that. I helped with the dishes and all that felt good—Christian duty.

But in the end I was glad to get out of there. It was a tremendous strain being with Daisy, she was so incredibly overbearing and opinionated. I tried not to let myself think about that. What was happening to me that I could let myself relapse into considering my comfort more important than giving to others? Humility. Always humility.

I drove to Jo Ann's house, the girl that Annie had gotten so angry about. I was going to see her because I had told her so when I last saw her in December: "Jo Ann, I'll be seeing you." It had been a convenient way at the time to say good-by to another in the list of lovers; another manipulated girl, seventeen, with corn silk hair, already on the road, I had used her like the others, I thought. So when she had written me two weeks before to ask what I was doing, my conscience was stricken, as if she represented all those other girls. I must go see her, beg her forgiveness, and gently say good-by.

She was staying at her parents' house now and she was very glad to see me. I gave her a friendly kiss on the cheek and invited her for a ride in the country. I looked at the huge, sublime trees passing by. I wanted to confess but as I thought about it, I didn't have that much to confess. I hadn't really wronged her but I knew that I would make progress by sticking to my rules and rooting out even the littlest sin. I was about to try and explain this to her when I glanced over and saw that she had let her skirt come way up on her thigh. She was looking at me with wide blue eyes and the slightest grin: she wanted to fuck me!

It threw me completely. I focused my eyes straight ahead and drove on, my mind racing like mad trying to think of what to do.

I talked about the road.

I talked about the countryside and her new plans to go back to school.

When the road turned away from under the tall trees and the sunlight splashed into her lap, I could see tiny blond hairs shimmer on her tanned thigh.

I was tempted. No! I had come here on a holy purpose. She was trying to tempt me. If I were to go to bed with her it would be only pure sex. I must fend her off and be very nice to her at the same time.

I talked about the road, again.

At last we went back to the house. I could see she still wanted me, she brushed her breasts against my arm as she went past me in the kitchen. I forced myself to stay, I owed it to her to be nice to her, pleasant. We ate dinner and I ignored her little flirtations. I would be good and Christian to her. Finally I asked her if there was a bookshop near by. We drove there and I bought her a copy of the Bible. The least I could do I thought was teach her what I had learned. She seemed a little startled. I gave her a kiss good-by on the cheek. As I drove away, back to Esalen, I was relieved but I couldn't help but feel there was something wrong about not having really leveled with her, something wrong about letting her send out those sexy messages and pretending to ignore them: even though I was doing it for her sake, so as not to hurt her, so as not to seem to put myself above her. That would have been wrong to see the log in my brother's eye and not my own. But silence had been unfair.

The whole trip had an odd quality—I was aware of feeling not quite all there with the people I had visited. I was eager to get back to Esalen. I had a feeling things would be simpler there.

Annie was waiting for me. She ran toward me slouching into her old arm-swinging amble that seemed and was intended to seem a mockery of human locomotion—Annie, the funny girl, tomboy, the mocker of her humanity, her girlhood, and incidentally, your humanity, too. Forward she comes; I put on a smile though I am afraid of what I think is happening. I smile my welcome, my compassionate welcome to her, beseeching her, with this gesture, to be gentle, to be my gentle new Annie, colleague in religious reflection. And then she is two or three feet away from me, her arms pumping in imitation of some mechanical doll, up and forward and down and back, rocking her way toward me from heel to instep to toe, a smile on her face, also, but not the gentle return of mine, rather the best human mimicry of a marionette's wooden grin. And then, her arms are around my neck. And then, her legs are around my waist, hitting me with a force that nearly knocks me over, grabbing with thighs of a Russian track star the sides where they press the ribs, and her voice, like the voice of a carnival barker screaming: "Hi, ya, Stu, Baby: how's the old city?" I stagger for a few moments, not protesting what I know is her assault on her better self and her assault on me, trying to remember to turn the other cheek, holding myself in. She finally gets off and this time, as she looks up at me, the wooden smile of anger and insult is changed, melted into a smile that beseeches, an asking smile, intentionally cute, that makes her affectionate, asks for my love, because it is, isn't it, a little girl we have here, a helpless little girl, who loves me and is dependent on my mood. And I give her a peck, not without feeling that something that used to happen is happening.

But even this, I decide, as I put my arm around her and we walk into the lodge for a cup of coffee, I can take, now that I am back from the city and have a clear sense of who I am. I have only to remember my own vulnerability and loneliness and that will remind me of how I am foolish if I judge my neighbor, and how I must love my neighbor; and if I do that, then will not God help me and protect me and keep me from all harm?

And I can already feel it happening, as I refuse to become angered by Annie's antics, but treat her instead as someone for whom I only care; I feel it happening already. So that when she says she has been angry, and that she wants to know—the basic source of her anger—if I have fucked anybody, well, by this point things are O.K.; for I can reassure her that I have not fucked anybody, I can ask her to remember once again, how we had talked about the trip and how important it was for me to go, and why, and though she is still pissed at the whole thing, and I can see her stuffing her annoyance away, we are not fighting, we are not mistreating one another: because J have not risen to the bait. Peace.

But fifteen minutes later, in the lodge, she does the unthinkable, the incredible—what she is so good at doing—namely grabbing the hand of a young man, some new member of the staff who has, in passing, eyed her tits, nipples peeping through the white crocheted blouse which I hated for her to wear, and she knew it, so naturally, she was wearing it on the day I came home, and she calls up to him, sitting in her seat, that mean-merry twinkle in her eye, and yells, her voice assuming an artificial harshness for the purpose, "Come on, Bebee; why just look? Get a good feel." And she jerks up the right side of her blouse exposing a tit of *Playmate* variety, hard and definitely formed, regulation size with a good nipple, it might have been turned on a lathe; and she grabs his bewildered hand and mashes it against her invulnerable Amazonian flesh; not without a glance, first at me, twinkling eye, and then at him, flirting eye, and then at me, a little more revenge for my having gone to the city without her, against her wishes, and then another glance at him, lecherous smile on her face, and suddenly, her sense that what needed to be done has been done, she looks at the youth who, despite his beard, and his leather belt, and worn leather pants, and cowboy boots, shows his fluster, and she says, dismissing him and throwing off the hand she has invited: "That's enough, buster; you've had yours. Come on, Stuart, let's go to the baths."

And before the startled hippie can decide what to do, she has already run to the office, the door of the lodge banging behind her, to get the towels for the baths. And the hippie shuffles off, vanquished, toward the kitchen.

By the time she comes back, she is calm once more, and sweet. And I offer no comment, I say nothing. All those emotions that I have felt, fear, helplessness as she managed the scene, and anger at her manipulations of the boy and of me, embarrassment at her even making such a scene, I endure in silence. I will put away these emotions—they are unworthy of me and useless to Annie. Better far to be, in my Christian gentleness, my soft voice, my total acceptance of her, an example to Annie of holiness and walking with God. There is nothing else, in any case, that I can do, for this course, I know, is the right one. We go to the baths, and lie in the warm water, and I try to enjoy the silence.

CHAPTER TWENTY-EIGHT

✠ miracles of sorts and comedy returns ✠

though annie during the following days began to get difficult from time to time, I more than recovered from the disorientation of my trip to Berkeley. I was able to keep my temper with her and to see her in a spiritual way. So I came again into daily touch with goodness. I continued to work as wine steward, and with that work came every night not only the satisfaction of feeling part of the staff but also inspired moments. Thinking of myself almost exclusively as a Christian servant seemed to help. I would imagine myself each night like a friar coming from the fields at the end of the day and carrying the wine to his brothers. So each day was full of promise for I knew that at the end of it I would do something that was real and good.

And occasionally there were meetings of the Residents. Not

everyone would come. Robert Portman was busy working at the management of Esalen; and Martha was frequently a waitress and would not make it because she was very proud to be a waitress and to be part of the place. And Ken had already ceased to believe in encounter and was resigning from the Program to work on the grounds. Jim Stiner, the new manager, gradually made it to fewer and fewer meetings. And others were away in the city or doing one thing or another. But there were a dozen or so of us that would show up and I enjoyed these meetings a lot.

I didn't have much to offer. Someone would usually come in with a problem he was having and ask the group to help him. And there were all kinds of techniques that people would use, that they had learned from Bill or Fritz or others during the time I had dropped out. Linda Capleau would enter and say that she had been dreaming about her dead sister lately and she thought there was "something there to work on." So someone, Bill or Joseph or Nick or Betty, would say something like: "Put your sister in that chair and talk to her." And Linda would say she missed her sister, recalling how much fun they had had. And someone would suggest Linda tell the sister how angry she was she had died. "Go into the feeling," Ned said, and Linda, to my surprise, got angrier and angrier, and finally she would be transformed into a screaming virago, pounding a pillow that had been brought to represent the sister, shouting her anger, and then anger would give way to tears, tears of loss, and finally, someone would suggest that Linda had never really mourned for the sister or buried her in the past. And so we all were urged to get up and to play mourners, and Linda crying again, covered the pillow with rugs and shirts and whatever else was around, burying the sister at least, putting some termination to the past, looking calm, drained, slightly sad.

I sat there, trying not to reject or criticize as I had in the past, not to evaluate prematurely, but disciplining myself to learn, to try to understand—after all, I had come to know very well that, as Robert Portman once put it, there was much I didn't see.

I liked those meetings, they moved me. I felt, despite my incomprehension, that there was something marvelously loving here, and that this was the way people ought to be: willing to spend lots of time with one another's problems, helping one another to grow. When Linda screamed at her sister, I had recoiled; I was frightened for the sister and I felt sorry for Linda. And when Linda cried out to her sister, tears flooding from her eyes, the need she felt for her, I found myself crying. How different from those months of fall and winter when I had looked upon similar sufferings and remained cold. Now, I found compassion flowing out of me, to Linda, to her sister, and then to every pair of sisters. I apprehended the world, during most of those days as full of meaning, and I would pass, not as a matter of thought, but as a matter of perception and feeling, beyond what consensus might have construed to be the literal event to a sense of deeper things, deepest meanings, and the presence of God.

Sometimes, though I knew my perceptions very deep, I would be surprised when not everyone would see them. Ned came into the group one day and said he was angry at Joseph. Two young men, strong, smart and tall. Joseph smiled almost pleasantly at Ned's challenge. "I've been waiting for this. It's about time. Want to wrestle?" Ned nods coldly and they begin removing their shirts. Ned is the experienced wrestler and Joseph is relishing his own courage in accepting such a formidable challenge.

I am surprised. How foolish for them to fight. Why is Joseph, who is so intelligent in an ordinary way and also gifted in mystic ways, rushing to fight? These two young men are brothers, just as I am a brother, children of God, parts of one another, or of the same thing. That is the sense of the warning: "Every one who is angry with his brother shall be liable to judgment." The sense I feel in waiting on tables, or in reading the Bible or in crying for Linda of something deep down that unites us all, despite all the bluster and the self-importance and the supposed victories in contests. And I know that Joseph understands some of this, for I have talked with him. He has understood for years. I raise my voice softly: "Joseph, don't fight him. He's your brother." And it surprises me the way Joseph replies, without turning to look at me, his eyes looking for an opening in Ned's guard: "Oh please, Stuart. Stop it!" As if I were some acid-demented hippie.

I don't let myself condemn Joseph, because I know to be humble and not to judge my brother even though I am not satisfied that he is right. They fight a furious match which Ned eventually wins and at the end both seem pleased, beaming at each other though I see a pettiness in it all, a smallness when compared to the truth of their deeper brotherhood.

At times, it comes back to me during those days—the firmness of Joseph's rejecting what I had to say from my deepest intuition and awareness; it began to occur to me that maybe even though I spent much of every day in heaven, and even though I understood the Bible, and even though there were miracles to tell me that I was doing something profoundly right, that there were also some things I was missing.

The day after the incident with Joseph and Ned I walked down the road to Catherine's house. She lived a couple of miles from Esalen in a large place she had rented. In many ways she had resumed there the life from which she had come—the suburban matron of advanced views and interests. She had her large calico cat for company and her books borrowed from the Carmel Public Library, odd copies of *Sunset* magazine and the *New Republic* lay around the roomy, comfortable kitchen. She had divorced her movie director husband a year before coming to the Residential Program. I was going to see her because she hadn't been at Esalen for several days and I had heard in the Residential meeting that she was very depressed.

She invited me in when I knocked and gave me a cup of coffee. I enjoyed the unusual luxury in Big Sur of a living room, with proper furniture, and a grand piano, a fireplace, and large windows, a sweet serenity about that comfortable house. It is cool, the day is cloudy, and Catherine is wearing baggy warm clothing, shapeless wool pants, tennis sneakers, and an old gray sweatshirt. She is very sad.

"What's wrong, Catherine?"

"Oh, nothing much."

"Come on, Catherine, tell me."

She sighs and looks down at the floor with her pale and vague blue eyes.

"It's getting to me, Stuart. I mean, what's the point of living here? The Program is almost over, we don't even meet much any more."

I urge her to continue. I can see that she is very upset. She starts to cry.

I sit with her for a few minutes. Then she stops, she is basically a sturdy lady, not given to crying like that. She dries her eyes and makes herself brighten. I just wait with my coffee cup, allowing myself to feel her hurt and simply be with her. Then she tells me about her boredom with screwing kids, her feeling of being older than the other people in the Program, having gone through their problems. And the various workshops didn't seem to help any more either. She feels stuck and lonely.

"You know what helped me a lot, Catherine? Just turning around—deciding to try and forget myself and begin living for others. I couldn't do it in a big way, only little things, like smiling or being the wine steward."

"I didn't know what was making you change so, Stuart, but I've done what you are doing, before I even came here. I want to live for *me*, now."

"Well, I don't know what's the right thing for you, Catherine, but maybe you could try it again. Then it could become an attitude, you know what I mean? I find love all around me now, deep down, at the bottom of everything."

I am a little embarrassed at saying all of this aloud, so plainly and at such length.

"Stuart, you're amazing me. Where did you learn to talk like that? I haven't heard that kind of thing, except from ministers, since I was an adolescent."

"It's just what I've been feeling."

At least she is smiling now. "Tell me more," she says. She looks at me in an amused but searching way.

"Well, just the feeling I get when I put things in right perspective."

"No, come on, tell me more."

I can't be sure now whether her smile is one of amusement at me or some real pleasure that she is picking up from what I am saying. Probably both, I think, so I continue.

"Well, when I see things in the right way, I realize that life is a gift. That I owe almost everything. My voice, my words, my food—all come from others. The world is there for me. All given.

"So, instead of wasting my time like I used to, trying to feel better, I try to spend my time giving back. And I do, it's just like a love affair. I feel taken care of."

Her smile is a grin now. "Say more."

"No, I don't want to. You'll start laughing."

"No, I won't. You're really making me feel better."

But I don't say any more. It would sound too freaky to say it aloud over our coffee cups. I am glad that she feels better. Delighted. We smile at each other and though I can see she is a little amused at the changes in me, she feels them and they help her. Her face becomes solemn for a moment and she says: "You know, Stuart, you really are different." I hug her. We finish our coffee and then I leave. I am thrilled with the sense that, more than what I have said, the power streaming through me has helped Catherine, just a little. It makes me feel grateful. I can't make the lame walk or the blind see but I can perform this little miracle. As I walk back toward the lodge I cultivate my feeling, dwelling on the thoughts that have given me my power, the thoughts of how much I have been given, all of us, the very road I am walking on, the grass planted on the lawn, the coffee, warm in my stomach, which I have drunk. How much love these express and how necessary it is that I attend to giving back the love which God and the world showers on me.

A few days later, I went to my first Gestalt workshop. And when, the first night, I took my turn sitting in the "hot seat" as everyone had for a few minutes, it was God's love that I felt. It had given me the courage to go to the workshop in the first place. So when Don Fast, the leader, asked me what I was aware of in the group I looked around and said just that: "I am aware of the love I feel, of strangers, and of how they must be my brothers, and all of us must be full of goodness." And Don, the Gestalt therapist, more religious than Fritz, smiles at me, a little like Catherine, as if to say that he thinks that what I am saying is amusing but that there is beauty in it.

I don't ask what he finds amusing. I know it is important for me to stay in touch with my sweet feelings and if someone finds them funny I can see beneath to the truth of love.

The next morning, when people seem bent on exposing their worst sides, each of them coming to the chair to fight with a parent, or deal with a sexual problem, or work on some other hang-up, I can feel pity for them and I can see beneath the ugliness, no matter how apparent, to the God-like spirit in them. A meek-looking psychologist, wearing rimless glasses, thin and balding, gets into the chair and after a few minutes announces that what he really wants to do is to kill everyone in the group. He has constant fantasies of murder. He grabs a pillow and twists it, nearly shrieking: "Anna, the bitch, my wife, I'll kill her." So incredibly sad it seems to me that I cry for the pain that must be driving the man, for his wife, and for his misery. At Don's instruction he goes around the group. Don says: "Tell each one of them how you will kill him."

The man has thought it all out: "You with rat poison." He moves on. "And you with a stiletto." Again he moves to the next.

"And I would strangle you."

"And the guillotine for you."

The group laughs at first then fear starts as people are caught in the spell of his anger and malice. When he stops in front of me, I look him in the eyes, putting away my fear and automatic repulsion, silently asking him, pouring my concern into him, if he will see me. He looks at me, also silent. And looks. And says: "I wouldn't kill you."

Another piece of magic, like loving an enemy. He feels my love and in a tiny way it helps him.

I did not live in such psychic space always, though I was trying with my reading and my resolutions to be with God all the time. Rather, it was a space that I would be allowed to move into—sometimes often in a single day. My body would feel it, a slow musical hum over my back and in my arms and behind my eyes as if a tuning fork had been struck in me. Moments full of life, energy uniting me, the sweet and barely audible hum that was enough—simply enough; where worries about the future and the memories of the past, thoughts flying toward this and that, all gone. It was simply enough to experience that state; that was heaven. When I truly loved another, that psychologist turned murderer, for example, the love would come bounding back toward me. The business of my own survival seemed petty with all this love around.

But, ten days after my visit to Berkeley, these feelings began to fall away from me again. I pursued my original program knowing it would help me eventually to get back to what I had begun to think of as God's presence. I would keep surrendering myself to Esalen, trusting others, trying new things. And even though I had no comprehension of why people bothered with handicrafts and such things, there were two workshops being given and I decided to take them. *Especially* because I had no talent as a craftsman or an artist and especially because I had earlier scorned the staff's enthusiasm for the local artisans' work. It had seemed to me, for the most part, incredibly mediocre compared to what I had seen in museums.

The first workshop was in "Sumie Painting and Calligraphy." I had no notion what that was, but I signed up and I paid my twelve dollars for a "Sumie Set"—and "ink stone," various bowls and long brushes, a little spoon, rice paper, and some other stuff I couldn't identify.

Trouble began immediately because Annie, seeing the art supplies, said: "I want to go, too. Please take me."

But I didn't want to take her. I felt she would be trouble. She was already starting to undermine my program. She had nagged me about going to workshops like the Gestalt one. "Just for fucked-up people," she said. "They're just coming to get loosened up so that they can do what I've already done. The Residents are the same. Why don't you just stay home with me, Stuart?"

The Sumie workshop was one she wanted to go to. She wouldn't hear of psychological workshops that probed into people, but she painted and drew a little and she wanted to be with me. I resisted. I was anxious that we not spend too much time together. I felt that if she were upon me too much I would betray myself, get irritated at her and not treat her in the loving way I should treat everyone. I had learned that she had a lot of good qualities, I was even persuaded that she cared for me now, even if she really hadn't at first. But she irritated me. I couldn't say these things, of course. I told her that I would rather go alone, but when she insisted, I let her come. It galled me when I had to pay twelve dollars for her "Sumie Set." It galled me that she was moving aggressively again into so much control. It irritated me that I would let myself be irritated by her. I shoved the feelings down. They were unworthy of me.

We went. Annie wasn't the trouble. In fact, she was quite happy working away with her brushes and rice paper—she had taken art classes before.

But for me everything was new. The instructor, an aged Japanese, appeared dressed in a kimono or whatever you call it that they wear. After showing us what a brush was (he held it up: "Brush") and what paper was ("Paper") and how to place our water dish in the upper left-hand corner of our tables, and how to rub our ink stick into the wet stone to make ink, his instruction seemed to end. He would paint something—we began with a bamboo stalk—showing us just how the stroke was done: "Here is way stloke is done." Then he would do the stroke. I would look at my blank paper with no notion of how to begin.

The others seemed to comprehend perfectly. They were already bent over their rice paper, an assortment of middle-aged ladies and hippie girls from the staff, a couple of men, about fifteen in all, working away like mad and happily producing reasonable imitations of the graceful bamboo stalk the "Master" had painted.

My first attempts were splotches. Too much ink, too much water, too little ink. I sweated on. I strained to keep up. It was important for my spiritual progress, I felt, to submit myself to such a foreign discipline. By the time I had made elementary inroads on the bamboo stalk, the others were half a day ahead of me, drawing multicolored birds with water colors in basic Sumie style. Annie, of course, was one of them.

From time to time, the Sumie Master, who was himself gaily

painting little demonstration pieces for us to imitate, would interrupt to exhibit the next step in refining one's skill. I groaned at the interruption because each such little lesson left me further and further behind in trying to master the previous ones. The master would grin at us first and then speak: "Prease stop." He told us to take out our ink stick and to rub it with water on the stone to make liquid ink while he spoke. "Now, quiet and meditate but rub stone." "Brack ink," he said. "Brack ink," over and over, shorthand for his earlier lesson to the effect that the secret of the whole Sumie effort was "Brack ink."

My body ached with the strain I had made to remember it all, to keep my left hand holding down the paper, so that the right could use the brush; to rub the ink stone at intervals so that I would always have a supply of brack ink, to keep the little nickel-finished weight on top of the paper so it didn't move, and all the rest. Simple instructions to the others, apparently, but not to me. I had thought that I had become humble but I had to confess to myself that under this weight my spirit bucked—it was just too discouraging, too humiliating to be so inept. Of course, I tried to comfort myself with such thoughts as: "the others have done more of this kind of thing" or "working with my hands is just not one of my aptitudes." But I found myself going into the lodge at lunchtime and groaning about how miserable I was.

By the end of the day, when others were neatly putting away all the little bits and pieces of the elaborate Sumie Set, I was just mastering my first bamboo stalk. And for some reason, I found Joseph's words of a week before in my ears, his slightly scornful, "Oh please, Stuart. Stop it!"

CHAPTER TWENTY-NINE

my stomach

even though God had not visited me as a Sumie artist, I persevered. I did an enormous number of good deeds, compulsively stopping for hitchhikers whenever I drove into Big Sur, doing extra jobs besides wine stewarding, even picking up papers on the grounds. I studied the New Testament, Émile Durkheim's *The Elementary Forms of the Religious Life,* other religious books, and thought endlessly about such matters. And still my religious sense of things was fading from me.

I went to another craft workshop—this one with the Guild of Hands. They were artisans who made their living by working at Esalen and every few months they gave a workshop. It said in the brochure that participation in the various crafts, whether baking bread, batiking, or pottery-making, was somehow good for your soul.

We met the first night, the members of the Guild, four or five seminarians, and a few Residents to plan the week. That consisted of deciding to visit the workshops of various craftsmen the next day and get a glimpse of what they did and the basic processes involved. It was not a promising beginning.

After the morning's tour I decided to work only with Harry, the Restaurant Manager who had given me the job as wine steward. I went to his shop, along with Dale Gardner, to learn how to enamel. Dale was a fifty-year-old Jesuit in the Residential Program. I had not quite liked him in the fall. I had thought his religion foolish and he seemed churchy and naïvely "good." The fact that he was an intellectual who had published several books of theology had only made me competitive.

Harry's workshop was in a cottage which lay across the lawn from Dennis's house, near where I lived. I had never had the courage to call on Harry. But at last I was there and I realized he was the gentlest and most patient of men. He carefully showed me and Dale the basic processes and we went to work without saying anything to each other. Each of us a little uncomfortable because we had hardly spoken in months.

But we bowed over the worktable, sprinkling colored mineral dusts with the most exacting care onto flat copper shapes: circles, fish, a cross. We cleaned these first in an acid solution, then, with tweezers, painstakingly transferred one of them to a tiny tripod where we rested it on the delicate points of a triangle of pines. We sprinkled the colored stuff onto the surface in some design, and, slowly, so we wouldn't jar a grain, we moved the copper into the oven for baking. We would wait a few minutes and take the thing out. As it cooled something delightful happened: the copper and the dust became a lustrous and jewelry-like thing.

Of course, it was ridiculous. Arts and crafts at summer camp. Our spiritual sojourn at Esalen, our great journey of self-improvement ending here. We joked about it, Dale and I, it was very funny. I even decided that I would send the first thing I made, a green and gold enameled pin, to my mother. But the astonishing thing was that we were having such a good time. It was simply enormous fun for us—two old intellectuals and sufferers—to spend our time bent over a worktable, carefully and single-mindedly doing something very small. No mystical experience here, no profound revelation about ourselves, nor any deep communion between us, and yet it seemed very important.

We talked about the relief of not trying to unlock the secrets of life, putting aside for the moment Dale's ambitions to save the world, his endless journeys arranging aid programs for the Mexican poor, putting aside my worries even about saving my soul or doing good, my taking myself seriously. We sank into the pleasure of time really taken off. The tiny and simple work at hand, confident already, because it was so simple, that we knew how to do it, and confident that what we did would be something really rather pretty.

And it became very exciting to ask Harry how to mount the pin mechanism on the back. Yes, I nod, very seriously taking in the least of his instructions. Because I want the gold and green pin to be just right. The sound of my humming in the shop disturbed Dale and he told me to shut up, he was concentrating.

I made the pin, and then a pair of cufflinks, and I enameled an emerald and green cross. Harry gave me a length of leather string so that I could wear it.

Dale and I became friends over the workbench, competing for using the same tools. We went to Nepenthe late one afternoon, I treated him to drinks and we had a long discussion about Christian theology. That meant a lot to me because I had really not talked about some of the things I had discovered or read in the Bible to anyone who could talk back. He told me he found my view of the New Testament a bit specialized—humility wasn't the only thing preached there. That point bothered me but we never really got into the matter. He was intensely interested in some of the things I had to say and it made me feel good to have a theological discussion with an expert and know he respected me.

And even though it didn't last, the workshop opened my eyes at last, so when I walked along the road between Harry's house and the lodge, going to lunch, I paid a new kind of attention to the things I saw. Rocks, trees, a patch of grass. And also the intricate iron work, or the way a pane of glass was mounted in a window, or the joints of a wooden table.

The following week, my new intimacy with Dale was over with the suddenness of Esalen workshops: one moment he was my constant companion and the next each of us was gone a separate way. I went back to my wine-stewarding but found I no longer wanted to do it. I was simply going through the motions now of being a servant. As the next couple of days passed I began to get a sense, at once sharp and vague, that I was hankering after something. I didn't know how to put it to myself, it wasn't clear. It was kind of a restlessness. It felt like desire, wanting to move on. It felt like energy, but not the energy of my religious states—this energy came from below. I knew it had been building for a couple of weeks, whatever it was, a complex feeling. God had continued to withdraw from me. Not entirely, but more and more distant.

I went to another Gestalt workshop, and sat in my chair watching the others work on their problems. I looked on with compassion as they explored their tortures and their pain and tried to make themselves whole. I tried to radiate my concern and love for them. The second afternoon, Don, the group leader, asked us all to do the basic Gestalt exercise at the same time, shutting our eyes and registering in ourselves whatever we were aware of from moment to moment. As I closed my eyes, my compassionate smile faded from my face, I relaxed and let my attention travel downward through my body, allow-

ing myself to focus only on myself for the first time in many
weeks. And when I got to my stomach I just had to admit to
myself that there was a pain there—something not particularly
holy, an anxiousness, an energy. Something was going on down
there.

I opened my eyes at the end of the exercise and tried to
ignore it, but every few hours I found myself becoming vividly
aware of it. I became fearful of it, and that only made the
feeling more acute. I would try to shake it off, forget about it,
review my circumstances, all the pleasure I had, all the good
things I had. I would look out at the sun and say things to
myself like "The sun is smiling." But still the feeling persisted.

It was the last day of the workshop and I was watching
someone working on a problem when I became intensely aware
of the feeling in my stomach. This time I do not try to force it
away. I will try the Gestalt approach: as they say, I will "go
into the feeling." I realize that this is a dangerous thing to do,
letting go, not sticking straight to the Bible and good thoughts.
But I take this time the Gestalt assumption that the pain is part
of me and that it has its message. I ask my stomach: "What's
hurting me? What's inside of you?"

"A lot of things," the stomach said, "so many things."

"Be more specific, stomach."

"Annie is in me."

It wasn't the answer I might have wanted, but I knew it was
right. And this moment was the beginning of the end. I had to
admit it to myself. I was truly irritated at Annie, at the resumption of her manipulations of me, at how she allowed herself to
manipulate by carefully keeping herself unaware that she was
doing it. The pain in my stomach had a thousand messages,
some of them about Annie, but one was that I lied to myself
when I turned the other cheek to her. And another that I was
lying to her as well. I keep her away, I don't share myself, don't
even give her my simple anger. It didn't feel good to treat her
this way.

Could this not be a temptation, a final test of my will toward
goodness and saintliness? And if I yield to it, will I not fall
completely from Grace?

Think of all you have to lose, Stuart. All the joys. And even
deeper ones beyond. Think of what you have had so far, already, in a month, with no teachers, no help really. God's gift
of Carter's Bible and with it intimations of connectedness with
all things. The wine-stewarding and the sense of purpose it
gave you, of value as a servant. And the Anima experience,
flashes of the richness of all our lives. You know what you have
had. Perhaps real saintliness, sainthood even, can be yours if
you just keep going, sink into discipline and go all the way,
downward and heavy like an anchor into the water.

✳ finishing and starting ✳

the feelings in my stomach continued. I would be waiting on people in the lodge, wanting to give to my brothers with a full heart, wanting to experience again the old holiness, and I would feel distracted in the very effort of trying. Herman Jones, a Big Sur heavy, came in one night and started drinking heavily in the side room where the bar had used to be. He was screaming and occasionally I would hear a glass crash to the floor. I went in, finally, and walked up to him. He was a big, fierce-looking man with a thick beard and a scar above one eye. "Herman, can you keep it down, you're disturbing other people."

"Tough shit," he said, and picked up a beer bottle by the neck as if to tell me what would happen if I continued to bother him. I looked him in the eye, not afraid, seeing him for what he was, an angry man out of control, I was sympathetic with him, even. He grumbled, put down the bottle, and I thought he lowered his voice after that. I was pleased with the way I had acted, but I realized that I could find no love in myself for him. Before I would have radiated warmth toward him and he would have felt it. I thought that I could still do that now, if I tried, but it was almost as if I didn't want to. Something was nagging at me, distracting me, and the most vivid awareness I could get of it would be that pain again, in my stomach.

That night, lying in bed and looking at Annie while she read her book, I thought of the Christian compassion I had taught myself to feel toward her on other nights. I picked up the Bible and read in it—the good lessons were still there, they comforted me, messages of forbearance, of forgiveness. After a while I put the book down and closed my eyes. Annie turned out the light and I kissed her good night on the cheek. Then I lay back. And behind my closed eyes, something churned, and I could feel tears, of sadness or anger, I couldn't be quite sure, forming behind my lids.

I must let them out, I thought. Let out whatever is there behind my eyelids, in my stomach, whatever is working in my body. Poison, I thought to myself. Poison that is troubling me. I must let it out into the world.

And then I turned over. Letting out all that crap is a stupid thing to do. Foolish. Violence to myself is there. Violence to Annie is there. What about her feelings? What about the risk— my sanctity, my humility, acquired with such pain, such trouble. I don't even know what I want to say to her, exactly. How can I say anything?

But I must do something. There must be some way. I need help. There are things I am feeling that I don't even understand. They frighten me.

And as the dialogue went on, hour after hour, hours becoming days, and I wondered what to do, the thought flashed upon me of the Residents' encounter group and the warm help that they had learned to give each other. Perhaps they could help me.

The more I thought about it, the righter it seemed. I would ask Annie to come with me to an encounter group. They would help us, protect both of us.

She scorns the whole idea. I have told her nothing about the things I am beginning to feel and that I feel I need to say. I couldn't trust myself. "What's going to happen there that's not going to happen here?" she asks. "Why do you want us to go, anyway?" she asks.

I have not the words to explain it to her.

"I just feel it will be good for us," I say.

She resists. I can see her fear at the prospect. She realizes some of her games will be exposed. I feel her apprehension that she will be hurt. And going as far as I have already gone is fearful enough to me, my daring to demand even this much from someone else, that alone seems to me pretty violent, but I do it, I insist. And finally, wearily, angrily, she consents.

As the two days before the next group meeting passed away, the pain in my stomach would not be ignored. Sometimes I thought I could find a way to stifle it. My mind ranged forward in different directions. I could leave Annie, I told myself, and Esalen. I could enter some sort of monastery—there even was one close to hand, in Big Sur, an order where the monks kept their vow of silence and only prayed to God. I could enter such a stark but holy life. I could go that way. And I knew how much there was for me along that way. I still had the Bible, it still made sense to me. I could pray to God and remember my visions. To some extent, I could even call up the feelings of inspiration. It was there, there for me to take if I wanted it, but I would have to leave Esalen and the people I was just starting to know. I would have to go off by myself, or only with others like me, away from things, in the woods, behind walls and there is a sadness in that, too.

In the morning, when the encounter group is to meet, I am still debating when I wake up. It is late, nearly ten o'clock. There is no hope that we can get breakfast at this hour. I stumble into my clothes, not from sleepiness, from fear. Annie is making a lot of noise, she slams drawers trying to find her blue tights: "Where the fuck are my blue tights?" she yells, at no one in particular.

We begin walking toward the Maslow Room where the meeting is to be. The air is cool around us, overcast, and there had been a heavy rain the night before; the pebbles in the moist earth squeak against the rubber soles of my hiking boots. I have been wearing them a while, though they still feel unfamiliar. I am looking down, concentrating on making my way, and I see the red mud that Annie's boots throw up as she walks.

Outside the Maslow Room there is the usual pile of boots and shoes. People take them off so as not to soil the carpet. I bend down to unlace mine. And then I open the door and let Annie pass in front of me.

They were all there, except for those who had dropped out and for Bill who was away. We took our place in the circle and sat down about two feet away from each other. Robert Portman was the leader. A silence fell over the goup, that nervous silence of waiting that I had gotten used to expecting at the beginning of each encounter session. Some people looked at the floor. Joseph was gazing around, a slight smile on his face, looking at each person in turn. Robert was doing the same. Finally, Linda began looking at Ned. She stared at him for a long time. I didn't want her to go first.

I blurted out, "I want to have some help with Annie."

"What do you want?" Robert asked, looking closely at me.

"I want to tell her how angry she makes me," I said, barely audible.

"Go ahead."

"I can't."

"You won't," he said. And I had to admit he was right. I wouldn't let my mind think those bad thoughts. We sat in silence again. I looked at Annie who looked at the far wall. Then Robert told me to get up, and he told Annie to get up, and he told us to face each other and to start pushing against each other, hands outstretched. I stretched out my hands and Annie wreathed her fingers tightly into mine. "Go," Robert said.

I couldn't do it. I couldn't push her. It was wrong I told myself. And we just stood there, with outstretched arms. And we waited. And Annie looked at me with her dark hard eyes, a wicked childish smile on her face. And she hunched down, gathering all her strength, and drove me back into the wall.

A couple of people who had scampered out of the way were grinning at the scene. Everyone loved Annie's "vitality." I said nothing. Robert waved us to the center of the room again. Again we joined hands. And again she pushed me to the wall, and this time I could hear a few guffaws, Annie giggled at the sport.

"Come on, Stuart," Joseph yelled, "are you going to do something here or not? If not, get the hell out of the center, other people have things on their minds."

I went to the center of the circle, and motioned Annie to sit down. I was fighting my feelings. Her pushing me around had made me furious. My back stung from where it had crashed into the wall. And then, I went ahead and started to tell her what I felt. The tension in my body melted away. But as I spoke, I registered with a chill the downwards steps of the descent: anger—"Annie, I hate your pushing on me, constantly, telling me what to do, trying to control me"; scorn—"Annie, I despise your face, its blocky quality, you look like a potato" (and the others shake their heads for Annie is fairly pretty to them and I watch her begin to cry at my saying these things); another step, yelling—"Annie, I hate your tears, you manipulate me with your tears"; and another step, my anger mounting, my past resentments, my frustrations with her, with myself—"Annie, Annie, I hate the way you're getting the group to side against me." There was vanity and pride in that one.

The room had become quiet. I lowered my head and my heart sank as I remembered the words I had dared to speak and my mind, for the first time in so long, began to feel numb. I was terrified at what might happen, God leaving me, Annie leaving me, the group leaving me.

Dazed, I finally looked up. Annie was still crying. One of her furious cryings, sobs from her stomach rippling up her chest. Her lips burst open with a wail and she rushed out of the room.

I looked down at the carpet, then around at the others, afraid to meet their eyes. My body filled with fear and I shrunk inward, wounded by Annie's crying and afraid that the group would despise me for hurting her. They would see me again as a bastard, I was sure. My body turned off, became wooden, and I hung there, looking down. But then, after a long while, when I dared to look round again, I saw on the silent faces, of Robert, and Martha, and Joseph, and the others, not contempt but pity, sympathy. Robert moved toward me. He put an arm on my shoulder and began rubbing it gently, caressing it, his taller body bent over mine as we sat there, giving me comfort. After a few minutes, he brushed his blond hair out of his eyes. Slowly, the feelings in my body came back to me, and I could feel the ache behind my eyes where I had been holding myself together. And then I cried, with everyone watching me. The tears were slow ones, a thaw, until Robert took me in his arms and I wept freely, making a small wet stain on the shoulder of his flannel shirt. And after a while I became aware again of his arms around me and mine around his back, the tension in the muscles holding one another. We loosened our hold at the same moment, his eyes were shining and he smiled at me. I looked round at those other familiar faces. They smiled, too. I returned it, deeply grateful. And then I remembered Annie who had rushed out wailing ten minutes before. I became fearful for her, she was so emotional and rash, she might hurt herself. Robert's hand fell off my shoulder. It was as though Robert could read my mind: "Don't worry, Stuart, Annie will be all right; it's not your last fight with her," and he grinned at me.

I wanted to thank him, but I couldn't find the words; I was worried about Annie. "I'd better go find her," I told them, and a few nodded at me. I struggled up, off the orange carpet, wiping my eyes on the sleeve of my shirt. I walked across the carpet to the wooden door while they watched me, and I felt a little embarrassed so the best I could do, by way of thanks, was to glance backward over my shoulder as I hesitated at the door. They had been good to me, I realized, as I crossed the threshold.

Outside, the air was cooler on my face, the remains of my tears felt cold. I took a deep breath and let it out in a rush, nearly a sigh. I was moved by the group's understanding, I was anxious about Annie, I was apprehensive about what would happen next—so many feelings, so much energy that I didn't know what to do, how to feel, except I realized that I was quietly excited. I tried to contain the excitement. I sat down on the cold path outside the room and fumbled around to find my shoes in the pile. I put on my hiking boots and began to lace them up. Down below me, from the porch of the Maslow Room I could see the lodge, two hundred yards away. I saw Annie's hurrying figure, her straw shoulder bag firmly pressed down beside her waist by the hook of her thumb and forefinger, her steps quick and decisive, she was disappearing through the front door of the lodge. I could tell by the way she was moving that she had regained some of her composure; anger would follow now; she would be furious at being so hurt and at showing it so openly.

I felt for her and I felt frightened of her. I knotted the bow at the top of my second boot, tightly. It would be better for both of us if I were to wait to talk with her until she quieted down. That felt like a good decision. That gave me room to think now. I looked back through the window of the room at the group; they were silent, some lying on their backs and staring at the ceiling, others talking softly in little groups.

I decided to take a walk and to try to get my bearings. I got up and began making my way toward the wide asphalt driveway to the left of the Maslow Room. It connected Esalen with the coast highway and it was very steep. I began to walk up along the driveway toward the coast route. I wanted to get off the property for a few minutes. The driveway was over four hundred yards long and negotiating it on foot left me no energy with which to think. I leaned into it, my steps demanding concentration and I could feel the muscles in my legs, the strain in my arches as I slowly climbed, putting one foot before the other, my head hanging forward. By the time I reached the road I was out of breath.

I stopped to rest, leaning against the white guard rail that protected motorists from plunging off the road. The road towered over everything and I looked down at Esalen with its motley wooden buildings and green lawns and a patch of bare earth that people had just begun to work into a new vegetable garden. The swimming pool was blown by the wind and then a sharp drop to the flecked shore line and the huge blue-black ocean beyond.

I caught my breath and then I started to walk. I began walking slowly, looking southward along the coast, seeing the headlands and the bays alternating for thirty miles into the distance until the mist concealed them.

It had come so suddenly, I realized, my decision to throw everything over. An inspiration—not even, only a pain in my stomach—then an *idée fixe* about confronting Annie, just a couple of days of inner debate, and wham-o.

My eye caught a dark-green cypress rising out of a cluster of gray rocks. There were birds in it, hopping in the branches.

I had not even thought it through. Just like that, an impulse, and I was ready to throw it all away.

A smile came to my face as I thought about what I had done. All those months of suffering and struggle; and then those weeks of sanctity; and I had risked it. What a chance it was, what a gamble, not thinking it through.

My smile grew larger. That was that. I had done it. I knew. It was the right decision. No plan involved in this one. Leaving plans behind, this time.

Then, as I continued to walk and to think, it really seemed too crazy. Maybe I was throwing away my one chance for fulfillment. Giving up my holiness could be giving up the one chance I had. I might even revert completely to the old Stuart, the abuser of people, cold-hearted, pretentious.

I would have to take that chance.

There was a giddiness to my feeling, an animal energy and zest starting to come up through me. I would have to take the chance. Stuart the Rogue might return, maybe Stuart the Saint, too, but my best guess was that they were both finished; I was heading toward something else.

I became very excited now. Thrilled with my daring, excited by the new things to come, the new chances. I had never been this way before, daring to act without a plan,without expectation, follow the flow of things for the next while.

I walked on for over a mile, my decision becoming more and more firm. Then I turned round and began walking back toward the Hot Springs. As I turned a quiet shudder started at my heart and passed through me, lifting me again to God and letting me touch again his purity. Purity of existence I had had, purity which dissolved doubt, no inner conflicts, certain knowledge that I was good. I was turning my back on that purity in this crazy way. I could have still gone to the monastery and been sure of retaining it. The Big Sur monastery was only forty miles south of Esalen, along this very road. I had decided though to go to Annie, and to the group. And I guessed I was going back to struggle and temper and emotion. There would be more screams and tears. I might be going back to pleasures, too, new pleasures. That I didn't know for sure.

In any event, I was going. The air was brisk around me, the wind having picked up, and I felt full of energy and desire. It took me nearly ten minutes to make it back to the top of the Esalen driveway. By then the sun had come out overhead. It was lunchtime. I paused, looked out at the ocean, and began my descent. I felt a faint smile on my face still. Annie would be waiting for me in the lodge, I thought. We would have much to say, much to go through. I hoped she would come back to the group with me, maybe they could help us.

Just before I got half-way down the long hill, I closed my eyes and whispered a wish. I was glad to be going down and full of a sense of promise, but I silently prayed that what I was doing would lead me again, in whatever indirect way, to the Grace which I had had.